THE
NONGRADED PRIMARY
SCHOOL

A Case Study

THE
NONGRADED
PRIMARY
SCHOOL

A Case Study

Lillian Glogau
Murray Fessel

PARKER PUBLISHING COMPANY, Inc.
West Nyack, N. Y.

Fifth Printing.., ..June, 1969

This book is dedicated to
the teachers of
the Old Bethpage School
in gratitude

FOREWORD

One of the most important dimensions of the current educational reform movement, which some go so far as to call a *revolution,* is repudiation of certain rigid structures and policies associated with the graded school. The use of grade-level-expectancy standards in describing and appraising each child's performance, the use of an ordinal vocabulary ("First Grade," "Second Grade," "Third Grade," and so on) to identify distinct segments of the school program, the assumption that each of these segments should start for each child in September and end in June, and the reward-punishment system associated with "promotion" and "non promotion" ——— these and other characteristics of the rigid graded school have been scorned by increasing numbers within the teaching profession, and there has been in recent years a mounting interest in the alternative known as nongradedness.

Francis Keppel has described nongradedness as probably the fastest-moving innovation on the elementary school scene today. The officers of several national educational organizations report that the topic of nongradedness is very high on the list of topics in which their members are interested. In a national poll of parents in 1966 over two-thirds of the respondents expressed approval of nongraded schools. Virtually every article or book dealing with educational innovation, whether aimed at the general public or at educators, makes direct or indirect reference to nongradedness and the inherently flexible, hygienic, and presumably efficient practices with which that term is associated.

To this burgeoning literature is now added a detailed and revealing account of one school's experience with nongraded organization. Appropriately labelled as a case study, this book tells with commendable frankness the story of Old Bethpage School in the 1964-1965 school year, during which the important transition was made to a form of nongradedness. The authors, in their roles as principal and assistant principal, are at once the narrators of the story, and two of its chief characters. As the reader will shortly discover, the authors have not been unwilling to report both their problems and their successes, to explain the various decisions that were made, and (especially in the final two chapters) to acknowledge that much work and rethinking lies ahead. Their story, as a result, is a valuable addition to a literature which has thus far been relatively long on theory and short on practical examples.

I am hopeful that people will argue about this book, and (in the constructive spirit of Chapter 14, in particular) seek to find better answers to the problems Mr. Fessel and Mrs. Glogau have noted. I for one hope to see in Old Bethpage a more energetic development of cooperative teaching, an expansion of the concept of inter-age grouping to allow for more total-class (or total team) heterogeneity, and continued progress in the development of better curricular guides. I would hope for the relaxation of such vestigial structures as *Fourth Grade* (italics mine!) in the schools that receive Old Bethpage's children, and for the evolution of a truly superior records-keeping and progress-report technology. However, for the moment these are distant targets, and this case book reminds us that it takes quite a while to build telescopes and artillery.

ROBERT H. ANDERSON
Professor of Education
Harvard University
Cambridge, Massachusetts

PREFACE

No matter what the level of vigor of discussion is found in the literature concerning the theoretic bases for nongrading, unless the profession as a whole is confronted at the same level of importunacy as is Eliza Doolittle's suitor when in utter disdain she cries to him, "don't talk of love . . . show me, show me, show me now," the action will remain in the verbal realm only. Happily, this will not be the case. In the ensuing pages we have a precise, thorough, discriminating, and fully coherent particularization of a successful nongraded program. It is a case study approach. It leaves nothing out. Even though there is yet to come a definitive model of a nongraded school, this present work serves as an excellent handbook which cannot help but apply to any nongraded program. The material herein has application for nongraded programs, be they partial reading levels programs or programs that are aspirationally oriented toward the complete individualization of instruction for all children at all levels.

This is a book that deals with the realities. Each of the goals that were sought after are fully discussed. The relevant aspects of the resultant action are carefully reported to the reader.

The minutes of the various many meetings are revelatory. Real issues arise, real problems emerge, real solutions are attempted; some are successful, others less so. The concept underpinning nongraded education is never once in danger.

The recounting here is that of professionals putting into action the theoretic aspects of a wholesome idea about the way youngsters should be educated. Nongraded education generally forces the teacher to recognize the individual differences that abound in children in any classroom, and it gives them an organization in which they can do something about those differences.

In this book we see how the teacher moves from recognition to action. We see how the administrators move from recognition to action. We see how the parents of the school move to a recognition of a different way of educating their children. Most importantly, we are shown the arduously slow, sometimes very difficult process of transition from what is customary to what is a very exciting educational program. This book may well represent what might be termed "the-necessary-step-book" of the present nongraded movement in America. It is a book that shows how it can be done and its insights are readily adaptable to many other school situations.

But it is not only a book of techniques. The evolvement of the plan is based on firm philosophical and psychological considerations. The reader will undoubtedly agree that in spite of all of the difficulties and hard work that go into making educacation an effective entity for children, to be able to emerge with a program which successfully brings with it better growth makes it all the more worthwhile.

Not only is the program that this book reports on one that is rewarding for the children involved, the teachers, administrators and the parents of the children in the school, but also the book itself is a rewarding experience to read. Hopefully it will spur action to create similar opportunities for educating the youth of other communities and truly bring us closer to the fulfillment of our total commitment to the learner.

MAURIE HILLSON, PROFESSOR OF EDUCATION
GRADUATE SCHOOL OF EDUCATION
RUTGERS—THE STATE UNIVERSITY OF NEW JERSEY

INTRODUCTION

Often the most exciting and the most difficult experiences in schools are never recorded. No one ever seems to have the time. Because there are two of us, we vowed that we would take the time to record our case study. We did this because we believe it will be helpful to other educators embarking on programs of change to see how the drama unfolds in reality.

Programs of change involve much careful thought and planning and many a creative writer has shown us the way. But implementation, that bugaboo of the educational world, requires a multitude of other skills. Until such time as computors program change for us, we as educators will have to continue to assume the full responsibility as change agents.

Our book, in a word, describes for you as accurately and honestly as possible a wonderful change experience—the first year in the introduction of a nongraded organizational plan into our primary school. It was a year of adventure and danger but an excursion well worth taking.

Our experience has interest, we believe, for four different groups. First, administrators planning to embark on the installation of a nongraded program in their schools should find our hints and clues invaluable. Certainly, our mistakes should serve as fair warning. Second, adminstrators and teachers in schools organized in any of a hundred ways, may find our continued use of Primary Meetings a supervisory technique well worth examination. Third, teachers in training, should gain worthwhile insights into techniques of teacher planning: for individuals and groups, curricular implementation, and selection of materials and activities, taken from the actual teachers' descriptions recorded throughout the book. Finally, we feel parents who have heard of the spread of nongrading in American schools, may find in this book an explanation of this phenomenon meaningful and understandable to them. To our readers, thank you for joining us on our nongraded excursion. To our fellow travelers, do let us hear from you.

LILLIAN GLOGAU
MURRAY FESSEL

CONTENTS

ILLUSTRATIONS

THE
NONGRADED PRIMARY
SCHOOL

A Case Study

1

THE TWO PURPOSES OF THIS BOOK

Why is it that there always seems to be such a difference between theory and practice? Why is it every time we try something new it turns out to be slightly different from the way we planned it? We asked ourselves these questions before we introduced the nongraded organization plan into the Old Bethpage School at Plainview, Long Island and determined that we were going to see for ourselves whether, just this once, things might be different.

We were equipped with certain information before we started. We had a rather specific idea of the nongraded plan which we had derived from our exhaustive study of the literature and our intensive visitation program. We knew rather well, the way nongrading was supposed to work and what it was supposed to do. Incidentally, it seems no two innovators whom we visited agreed on the methods and procedures of implementing a nongraded program. Of course, we turned out to be no different.

It was at this point that we decided to embark on a new approach to innovation, for us that is. First we put down on paper the major goals and objectives on nongraded organization as exemplified by the authorities in the field. Second, we put down on paper our own goals and objectives of the nongraded plan as we saw them for the first year. Third, we planned and put the program into operation for the first year. Fourth, *we recorded every act, decision, meeting, and conference that took place during the school year.* Fifth, at the end of the school year we analyzed our written records by comparing them with our pre-recorded goals and objectives for the school year. The questions we asked ourselves were quite simple. How did each objective measure up in practice? How major were the difficulties which we encountered and how could we help to alleviate them in the future? What goals and objectives should we set up for the coming year?

Once we were able to make such specific comparisons of outcomes as against objectives, we, as administrators, felt much more secure in the knowledge that nongraded organization was for us; and we were indeed on the track of something worthwhile in nongrading.

The purpose of this book is twofold. Our first purpose is to show you why we feel that nongrading is a successful organizational pattern for elementary schools. You the reader will be able to make these same comparisons, and draw your own conclusions. If you decide that nongrading is a meaningful goal for your school, our second purpose for this book will be particularly relevant for you, since you will be able to read the actual day by day, week by week, month by month account of what actually took place during the school year with children, teachers, administrators, and parents. This is how it really happened. Step by step you can follow our school as it went through its anguishes and successes, as it met problems, as it found solutions, as it created new problems. It's all here for you. We feel that many of you might be more comfortable if you could read for yourselves about how this creature called the nongraded program really works. In all instances whenever we quote, unless otherwise indicated, it is a direct quotation from minutes or conferences which we held. There has been no attempt to eliminate anything. We have tried to faithfully record the total year's experience because this is the only way we feel that we can be of help to others who wish to nongrade their schools.

Background of Plainview-Old Bethpage

The Old Bethpage School is located in Plainview, Long Island. Plainview is a suburban community of some 33,000 people which is a little above average mid-income level of the nation with a balanced mixture of Roman Catholic and Jewish families, a smattering of other denominations being in the minority; dwellings are mostly detached one family homes ranging in value from $10,000 to $40,000, though there are relatively few in the latter class. The average home owner earns $9,000 per year. There are nine elementary schools in Plainview-Old Bethpage, two junior high schools, one senior high school in operation and a second being completed this year. There are also two or three active parochial schools in the area. Forty-five per cent of the population are under twenty-one years of age. Most important is the fact that the town has consistently been supportive of education, and in large part supportive of educational innovation. The Superintendent of Schools, Dr. Robert F. Savitt, has been responsible in large part for creating a climate conducive to educational innovation.

The parents in a recent survey represent a twenty per cent college background. To say that they are interested in education for their children would be understating the case. The vast proportion of them see college as the only future for their children. Although these families represent some differences in ethnic background, they really do, represent in practice almost a homogeneous group with similar goals, tastes, aspirations, and hopes. The Old Bethpage Parent-Teacher Association is extremely well supported and represents a good portion of the energy output of these families, as do all school and school-related matters in the community. These parents of professional and semi-professional backgrounds (sixty-four per cent in white collar jobs) believe in education and getting the best for their children and they are

quite willing to devote many hours of their lives to accomplish-
ing these goals.

A number of years ago, Plainview-Old Bethpage was a typical
mushrooming suburban "bedroom" community. Most of the
fathers commuted to New York City, some thirty-five miles
away for their livelihood. In recent years this has changed somewhat. About 64% of the fathers do not commute to New York
City any longer, but are employed some place closer to home, the
other 36% still commute to the metropolitan area for their work.

The children in the Old Bethpage School reflect their parents.
They are good youngsters, sweet, cooperative, albeit a bit overprotected. Their average I.Q. is somewhat higher than the
national average being somewhere between 113 and 115 mean
average. In general their attitude toward school is excellent and
we have relatively few discipline problems.

Plainview-Old Bethpage has had an excellent reputation in
educational circles these past five years. The teachers are above
average in education, background, interest, and devotion to their
profession. They are, as a group, quite sophisticated to the total
world around them and are on a par socio-economically with
the parents of the children they teach, though most often it is
the two weekly paychecks of both teacher and spouse which
make this possible. They are and always have been receptive to
change which is meaningful and fruitful. Most importantly they
have been quite willing to give the extra time and energy necessary for innovation.

The Old Bethpage School has an enrollment anywhere from
750 pupils to 900 pupils per school year. Some 440 were involved
in the seventeen nongraded classes. The rest of the school population is represented by some 200 kindergarten youngsters and
some 200 fourth grade youngsters. These last figures represent
the 1964-1965 school year only, since rezoning patterns have
made for marked changes in our school enrollment from year to
year. As you can suppose we use every inch of available space
for classrooms and offices. We are extremely well-equipped with
materials, audio-visual equipment, supplies, and textbooks, and

operate a 6,300 volume library with a full time librarian in resi-
dence. In addition to one teacher per approximately 25 children
we have a full time vocal music specialist, art specialist, secretary,
nurse-teacher, physical education teacher, assistant principal and
principal (these last two being the co-authors of this book). Part
time employees include an additional physical education teacher,
half time clerk, a school psychologist for two days a week, a
speech therapist for two and one-half days a week, a reading
consultant for two days a week, and an instrumental music
teacher for one day a week.

Objectives of the Nongraded

The leaders in the field of the nongraded organization are
Goodlad and Anderson.[1] The objectives of the nongraded listed
here are interpretations of Goodlad and Anderson's work and as
reported in a speech given by Anderson [2] last year.

1. The program must be arranged so successive experiences
are essentially pertinent to the child at each point of his development.

2. Success is guaranteed to the child if he is diligent, for he is
not asked to do that which is impossible for him to achieve.

3. When the child is successful, he is intrinsically rewarded.
This success will, in turn, produce a favorable self-image and
enhance self-confidence.

A project on nongraded schools conducted by the New York
State Education Department [3] established seven criteria which
must be met by the nongraded school.

1. There must be an adaptable curriculum operationally defined.

---

[1] John I. Goodlad and Robert H. Anderson, *The Nongraded Elementary
School* (New York: Harcourt, Brace and World, Inc., 1963).

[2] Robert H. Anderson, Speech made at South Huntington, January 7,
1965 (tape).

[3] Anderson, Speech.

2. There must be a system for inventorying and diagnosing of pupils' skills and deficiencies.

3. There must be many arrangements for individualizing instruction.

4. There must be neither forced nor obstructive instruction.

5. There must be a reporting system which is consistent with the program. There must be no promotion as children advance daily.

6. There must be an absence of grade labels.

7. There must be significant modification of curricula—at least in the areas of reading and mathematics.

Objectives of the Nongraded Program-Old Bethpage School

Our goals for the first year of the program were established as follows:

Overall Goal

To provide an organizational framework that permits a flexible learning situation for all children in the primary program [4]

Specific Goals

1. To facilitate the grouping of all youngsters by providing a broader class base use (Chapter 2).

2. To provide levels in which the children in any one class have a narrower range of reading abilities (Chapter 3).

3. To place and move children in learning situations where satisfaction and self-development come through continual progress and success (Chapter 4).

4. To eliminate the pressures of grade level barriers and predetermined time and subject matter schedules with identical demands for all pupils (Chapter 5).

---

[4] Footnote—"Overall Goal and Specific Goals" (2-8) were derived from Edward W. Smith, Stanley W. Krouse, Mark M. Atkinson (eds.), *The Educator's Encyclopedia* (Englewood Cliffs, N.J.: Prentice-Hall, Inc., 1961), p. 142.

5. To provide goals and levels of work instead of time allowances to assure a developmental educational program of sequential experiences for all children (Chapter 6).

6. To provide increased opportunities for staff members to fulfill the individual instructional needs of their children (Chapter 7).

7. To provide an organizational program for slow learners without the dangers characteristic of continuous failure (Chapter 8).

8. To provide levels of enrichment for the rapid learners (Chapter 9).

9. To remove the trauma associated with acceleration and retention (Chapter 10).

10. To explore more fully the range of teaching techniques and implementation of curricula within the class (Chapter 11).

11. To encourage the use of differentiated instructional materials and experiences (Chapter 12).

12. To help parents adjust to the ideals and philosophy of individualized goals for children inherent in the nongraded program (Chapter 13).

Introduction of the Nongraded Program

Since this book represents documentation from September 1964 through June 1965, we thought it might be important to acquaint you briefly with the steps taken the spring before to introduce the nongraded plan to both parents and teachers. Seventeen classes with children ranging in age from five and one-half to nine years of age were to compose the nongraded primary school, the other fourteen classes in our school representing kindergarten and fourth grade youngsters.

The teachers and we participated in a study program which involved reading all articles and books in print on the nongraded plan, plus a planned program of visitation to the nongraded schools geographically feasible. We met and talked and together

decided many of the aspects of the program which we were
going to incorporate into our school. The teachers were quite
enthusiastic about nongrading though there was some natural
apprehension about interage grouping. We held an evening
meeting with the parents and explained our new program in
detail. In addition a carefully planned brochure on the nongraded in our school was distributed to all the parents of the
school. (See Appendix, p. 222).

Our district provided us with excellent curricular material
which lent itself admirably to the nongraded concept. Curricula
in reading, mathematics, social studies, science, and language
arts were completed or in the revision stage. These curricula reflected quite well the criteria established at the Woods Hole
Conference in 1959 reported by Bruner.[5] The curricula are sequential, structured, and organized around broad conceptual
bases. In addition, in the preceding school year we had already
switched to the use of the GCMP mathematics materials as these
seemed to permit best implementation of our own district mathe-
mathics curriculum.

In summary then, it can be said we had, to the best of our
abilities in the time allowed us, prepared the parents, the teachers, and ourselves for nongrading and were also in possession of
excellent curricula for use in the nongraded. This is how during
the preceding spring, we approached our major objective, the
provision of an organizational framework that permits a flexible
situation for all children in the primary program.

Format of the Book

From September and on throughout the school year we kept
accurate recorded minutes and notes of all meetings and conferences. These minutes form the basis of most of the material
for the rest of the book. The greatest portion of the actual occur-

---

[5] Jerome Bruner, *The Process of Education.* (Cambridge, Mass.: Harvard
University Press, 1962).

rences at the Old Bethpage School are revealed through the records of the weekly meetings which were held with teachers, called Primary Meetings.[6] We divided our seventeen primary teachers into three groups, the teachers in each group having classes with similar grouping patterns and therefore similar problems. We had open-ended one hour meetings with these groups every week. The agenda items came from the teachers, the school psychologist, the speech correctionist, the reading consultant, the special teachers, the administrators, or anyone directly connected with the primary school. The purpose of these meetings was expressly the improvement of instruction. They constituted the supervisory technique to which we were most indebted. We know of no other procedure which has reaped the harvest these meetings have for all of us.

First, and most important, these meetings were the arena for surgery. It was here that we dissected, chewed, cut up, and tried out every idea and thought each of us had about our new program. Second, they were the arena for therapy. We were all under pressure, and it was at these meetings that we let our hair down and confessed our fears and our triumphs, our anxieties and our accomplishments. It was here that we held each other's hands. Third, it was at these meetings that we got a real look at the total picture of our program, its weaknesses and its strengths. We determined where we needed further work and where we were successfully on the way. Fourth, these meetings provided time to examine individual children and what we were really doing for them. Fifth, the meetings opened new avenues for us to explore.

A few examples selected at random from our minutes may give a taste of the topics discussed: the thinking process, creative music, flow sheets for recording each child's achievement in curricular areas, criteria for levels of achievement, the unit approach to the teaching of social studies. It is especially interesting to note that some of the agenda items at our weekly meetings were ex-

---

[6] Lillian Glogau, "Make Me a Nongraded," *The National Elementary Principal*, XLIV (May 1965), 51.

panded to become the subjects of full fledged workshops or study programs designed to explore the specific problems as we met them. Our meetings with the primary teachers reflected the heartbeat of our school. The pulse of the school could be detected by readings of the minutes of each group's weekly meetings. We considered these meetings the core of our new program.

Slowly we are making a nongraded. We have a long, long way to go, but are quite pleased with our beginnings. We have been learning a great deal. We feel very positive learning is taking place. The odd thing about our total experience this year is that most of the changes of which we are proudest are not apparent to the eye. If you were to visit our building, you would find no fireworks shooting from the roof and no oriental gongs chiming in the hall. The changes are subtle. They represent refinements in teaching techniques and learning situations which only the very trained observer could note during a classroom visitation. Yet there have been changes, and they are continuing every day in every way.

The essential truth of what has happened, as we see it, is quite simple and can be easily stated. The basic structure of the nongraded program forces the classroom teacher to note the differences among children in a way graded structure does not. She sees each child as an individual with special needs, problems, hopes, and learning rates. When the teacher recognizes and accepts these differences, she begins to make changes in her curriculum, her patterns of interacting with pupils, her teaching techniques, and her instructional materials in order to accommodate these differences. The process is slow, tortuous, and wearying but unbelievably rewarding.[7]

We cordially invite you into our world. This is how it all really happened. Our book is organized around our specific goals and how they worked out in reality. There is a chapter devoted to each objective. All examples and specific references stem from our accurate records of meetings and conferences as they were held during the school year. The book closes with two chapters

---

[7] Ibid.

describing the problems we encountered carefully documented and a description of our efforts at eliminating them at that time or our plans for the future. We feel that this case study approach will be useful to other educators. We hope you will find our experiences helpful and practical because this is our intent in writing this book.

2

THE PLACEMENT OF CHILDREN

Objective: To facilitate the grouping of all youngsters by providing a broader class base use.

One of the most obvious advantages of the nongraded seems to be the ability to better place children in classes for purposes of instruction. We call this process grouping. Let us show you how this worked in practice for us. The figures below represent enrollment for our primary school under a graded structure:

144 pupils	first grade
153 pupils	second grade
145 pupils	third grade

Our goal for classes was to keep class enrollment at twenty-five or below for the first grade. In a graded structure we would have required six first grade classes. In the second and third grade classes we kept enrollment at close to twenty-six pupils per class. Simple arithmetic shows you that we would have required six second grade classes and six third grade classes, thus making a total of eighteen classes required for the 442 children in these three grades.

In the nongraded structure we were able to account for all 442 children in seventeen classes with an average of twenty-six children per class. Once we eliminated the actual grade barrier we were free to group all the youngsters in the primary school throughout all our classes. This gave us an opportunity to spread the children throughout all the classes without worrying about the enrollment count in each grade.

Of course, the most significant factor about this facilitated mass grouping was the advantage it gave us in grouping children to their best educational advantage. Those children who seemed able to function best together regardless of their former grade label or age were grouped together for academic or social reasons. The following chapter will describe in detail how we used this facilitated grouping for instructional sub-grouping in reading. The rest of this chapter will try to show the advantages we found in grouping in the nongraded for social or emotional reasons.

In our school we had carefully identified (as noted by classroom teachers and records) twenty-three children seven years of age and eight children eight years of age who represented either social, emotional, or physical problems and who therefore required special placement. By special placement we meant some class with some teacher best suited to handle the problem the pupil had. There was always a problem in placing youngsters of this type since they do require extra solicitous care on the part of the teacher and subsequently the right teacher must be matched with the right child. But, in addition there was another relevant factor. One couldn't give too many of these children to the same teacher since this would be an unfair burden on her energies and the rest of the children in the class. Now if we had twenty-three seven year olds who were special placement problems and we were still graded, no amount of conjuring could alter the fact that all twenty-three children must be placed in *six classes (above)*. On the other hand the eight children eight years of age who required special placement would have been placed in six third grade classes. Thus in the second grade classes approximately four special placement children per class would have been the only possible equitable solution; while in the third grade four teachers would have had one special placement problem assigned to her and two teachers would have had two such children.

In the nongraded situation we were able to handle the situation more efficaciously by placing these children in the following manner: five teachers received two special placement children while seven teachers received three children with problems. We do not mean to imply that three children with special problems is an ideal situation, but we do know that as long as there will be children there will be children with problems. And as long as there are children with problems, we in the schools must handle them. Therefore, any system which we could find which would help these children was a good one for us.

You may easily ask were you helping any of these children or teachers when you gave her three problem children instead of four in her class. The answer is a resounding yes. Children with problems require delicate care and handling and an inordinate amount of additional time. The more we reduced the teacher's burden the more time she was able to devote to *the other children* in her class who didn't need as much of her time or energy but still needed her. Perhaps if we give you some examples of specific children and the kinds of diverse problems we encountered this year you will have a clearer picture of the teacher's responsibilities.

Ernest

We had one little boy, Ernest, who came to us at the beginning of the school year from Arabia. His parents were both highly intelligent professional people and Ernest was their only child. Ernest was brought to us the first day in tears. You can certainly imagine his fears. He had arrived only the day before by plane in a new country unable to speak the language and was being placed at six years of age the very next day in a strange new school away from his parents. He was a most pathetic child and it was a physical effort to even get him down to his classroom. We chose with great care the teacher with whom we placed this little boy and felt that two factors combined to make her the correct choice for this youngster. One, her own extraordinarily sensitive and receptive nature and two, the fact that there was a very small group of children already in her class who were having difficulties with learning to read. Mrs. E. was developing for these children a very special reading program which we thought Ernest might just possibly adjust to in time. None of us were capable of speaking Arabic which didn't help the situation much either. Below we quote directly from the minutes of a Primary Meeting held on March 2, 1965 as Mrs. E. reports:

> Ernest, as you know, came to us some four months ago from Arabia speaking only his native tongue. He is doing very well with oral English and has made a good social adjustment with his class, though there is some evidence of difficulty with children outside his class. He is a bright child, but is having difficulty, as is to be expected, with written English. I feel that Ernest is now about ready for the beginning of formal reading. I am concerned lest Ernest develop a defeatist attitude since he is functioning below the level of the other children in reading.[1]

By the end of the first school year we were happy to note that Ernest was reading and on a level satisfactory enough so that he could be moved ahead with his group.

Let us now follow the progress of another youngster who required special placement where the prognosis is not so favorable nor the future so promising as in Ernest's case.

Edward

Edward came to us about a month after school opened. We very carefully tested him in reading and found that he functioned quite well on Level 8 and so placed him in a class with Mrs. M. Mrs. M. had a reading group on his level and a group of able pupils with whom we felt Edward would do well.

Oct. 6, Mrs. M. reports:

> Edward just came to me this week. He seems to be on level academically, but I am concerned about his physical, or possible emotional symptoms. I hope that when we receive his records

---

[1] Minutes of Meetings, Reports Filed, and Anecdotal Records are source of all quotations unless otherwise stated.

from his former school we'll have some more information about him.

Oct. 20, Mrs. M. reports:

My new child, Edward, still continues to show signs of some types of disturbance. I hope the medical and achievement records from his former school will indicate to us some reason for his outbreaks and outcries in class. (The records, when we received them, showed absolutely no evidence of anything being wrong with this child either academically or medically. His former teachers seemed to regard him as an average child with no special problems of any sort.) I am going to start keeping an anecdotal record of his behavior so that we can have a clearer picture of him totally. In my talks with Edward's parents I have not been able to find out anything different or special about Edward. As far as they are concerned he seems to be an average child.

Nov. 3, Mrs. M. reports:

There is no change for the better in Edward's behavior. The pattern of immaturity and acting out continues. Miss C., our school psychologist, has observed Edward in and out of class and has now seen the parents. Certain facts came out at their conference. Edward's older sister is also an isolate socially as is Edward. They do not mingle much with other children. Edward, himself, finds it difficult to cope with children and is also extremely sensitive. I think the other children in class make fun of Edward (when I am not looking or when they are out of class) and this doesn't help the situation either. Perhaps, until we can determine exactly what type of help Edward needs we can place him in another class where there may be less attempt by the other children to tease and make fun of him.

On November 19, the school psychologist, the boys' teacher, and the two school administrators had a conference. It was determined at that time that there was no doubt that Edward was suffering some disturbance, and that the root of his behavioral problems was some psychological or physiological problem. The psychologist felt that, regardless of the past records of this child and the parents' protestations, Edward's problem had existed for a long time and would bear some type of treatment. It was her considered opinion, however, that the parents, at this time, would not be receptive to this kind of suggestion. She felt that the parents had lived far too long deluding themselves into thinking of Edward as an average boy. It was going to take a good deal of patience and time before she could suggest to them the need for professional help for Edward. She felt that by the end of the school year the parents would have begun to accept the fact that Edward did have problems and at that time she would make specific suggestions to them as to the type and kinds of examinations and professionals to whom Edward might best be referred. In the meantime, Edward's class was changed. There was some hope that the new class housed somewhat more mature children (although not older necessarily) who might be counted upon to react less humorously to Edward's behavior and therefore reduce the amount of conflict that all were undergoing.

Nov. 24, Mr. N., the new teacher, reports:

> Edward has already had one flair up in his new class situation which I handled quite well and quickly. The children responded well. I shall continue keeping an anecdotal record of Edward's behavior just as Mrs. M. did, though I recognize that eventually these parents will have to be told that Edward must have outside professional help. I know that Miss C. suggested this approach and I am fully in accord if we wish to have the cooperation of these parents.

Dec. 1, Mr. N. reports:

> Edward is still showing signs of disturbance and there still are occasional outbursts. He still reacts to the teasing by the other youngsters.

And so the situation remained relatively the same and no amount of special handling or attention was able to do what only others, better equipped than we were, could do. Finally, in the month of April, the psychologist was able to diplomatically approach both parents at a conference. They accepted the situation for what it really was and agreed to begin procuring professional help for Edward. It will be a long, slow pull, and in the meantime, Edward will still be in school (and, of course, should be) and will still require special placement and special attention and care.

Another child particularly interesting to take note of is one where the teacher evidenced much concern about retaining the child in her class. We had been extremely cautious about Claire's placement since she was a youngster with whom we had past experience and felt we knew the type and kind of teacher who would best suit her needs. Mrs. L. was selected as Claire's teacher although Mrs. L.'s highest reading group was one level below the level of achievement Claire was capable of in reading. In a graded structure Claire could not have been placed in this class. In the nongraded, however, there were some nine other children in this class who were Claire's age. The decision was made to place Claire in this class because we felt Mrs. L. was best suited to handle her problems.

Oct. 17, Mrs. L. reports:

> Claire has many emotional problems. She is under treatment privately and she needs much tender loving care. Claire has a high I.Q., is inquisitive, and grasps concepts quickly if she is not affected emotionally. She gets along well with children of all ages and levels in class, though there are, of course, occasional outbursts and over reactions. She is very enthusiastic. She is a well developed child physically (confirmed by school physician). She works above level in all academic areas and is more advanced than the other pupils academically. I feel that Claire would do much better in a group where there would be other children to challenge her.

Oct. 27, Mrs. L. reports:

> Claire contributes to the total class picture and is performing her work by herself. These are two areas where she did not function in the past I have been told.

Oct. 27, Mrs. F. reports:

> I accidentally ran into Claire's mother and she told me that both
> she and Claire's father are very pleased with Claire's placement,
> although they know she can function on a higher level. They
> feel that she has made a very good adjustment in Mrs. L.'s class
> (Mrs. F. was Claire's former teacher).

Mrs. L. continued to report during the course of the school
year on the progress of this outgoing, exuberant child who had
been out of control in the past and almost totally nonfunctioning
academically. She felt some guilt at the beginning of the school
term (above) because she wasn't challenging Claire sufficiently
in the academic areas. We assured her that we all felt (and this
included our own psychologist) that Claire's academic functioning was not nearly as important at this time as was her emotional
and social adjustment. Claire was no longer performing and acting out as much as in the past which was quite an improvement
for her and, of course, she was doing her class work which represented still further improvement in her behavior. For these
reasons it was agreed that Claire would remain in the class with
Mrs. L.

Ernest, Edward, and Claire are but three of our thirty-one
pupils who required special placement. All thirty-one of them
presented some type of behavior which required special skill on
the part of the teacher. However, when we speak of children who
required special placement; children with academic, social, emotional, psychological, or physical problems, we are not referring
to the extreme cases. In our district excellent programs have
been developed for the severely disturbed youngster (emotionally and mentally). These children are in special classes with
trained teachers. Other handicapped children are transported to
neighboring school districts where special programs are offered
commensurate with their abilities. The pupils we refer to as
requiring special placement have problems, but not of such a
severe nature that they cannot attend regular classes. Thus, they

are in the schools and require individual attention from the teacher.

There is still another virtue of nongraded grouping, we found, which requires pointing up. It is the simple fact that it was easier to place a youngster with the best teacher for his kind of problem when we had seventeen teachers to select from than when we had only six (as in the graded situation with the same enroll-ments). Educators recognize, as do all of us who deal in human relations, that certain personalities are better suited to handling certain types of children. The teacher who is a whiz with alert, bright youngsters easily comes to mind; the male teacher who handles the school bully with as much ease as we handle a cigarette is another example; still another is the gentle female teacher who seems to have such a way with the shy, retiring youngster. Think then of the extreme advantage we had when we first met Ernest. Instead of looking for the characteristics we had determined as necessary in a teacher for Ernest (patience, sensitivity, tolerance, understanding, and sympathy for the slow learning rate a foreign child would first exhibit) among six pos-sible teachers, we were able to broaden these possibilities and search out the best teacher for Ernest from among seventeen teachers. The odds, therefore, for better placement of our chil-dren with problems became increasingly better as we increased the number of teachers from whom we could select.

We hope that by giving you some representative examples of the types and kinds of problem youngsters we had in our school (selected from the total of thirty-one such identified pupils), that we might emphasize the need we felt for distrib-uting these children equitably and in as small a number as pos-sible to as many teachers as possible. One can easily see how much time and effort Edward, Ernest, Claire or any of the other twenty-eight required from their teachers. It is for this reason also that we felt that the grouping, which was possible through nongrading when the class base was broadened, was such a positive aspect of nongrading.

In summary, nongraded grouping had four specific advantages

for us, we were able to consolidate our classes from eighteen to seventeen; we were able to distribute all the children throughout seventeen classes without reliance on grade label or age; we were able to place children with problems with the best possible teacher available for them; we were able to distribute our children with problems more equitably among all our classes and teachers.

3

THE GROUPING OF CHILDREN

Objective: to provide levels in which the children in any one class have a narrower range of reading abilities.

We had developed for use in the grouping of all the children a very specific plan for our first year of operation. Naturally we understood that we would have to modify our grouping criteria and procedures as we became more and more acquainted with the nongraded in practice. This was true of other aspects of the nongraded too. Many of our plans and arrangements were conceived of as first steps. We recognized full well that time would show us the necessity for making further refinements and improvements. But for a start we had some rather specific goals in mind when it came to grouping. Grouping was to accomplish certain ends for us: first, it was to provide the best possible placement for each pupil; second, it was to provide a narrower range of reading abilities within each class.

We believed that class placement and groups within the classes constituted an important aspect of the learning atmosphere for each child. We have always felt that certain arrangements of children under one roof can often result in better learning environments for children. However, we also had begun to feel after years of experience that a narrower range of the reading levels within one class also made for more efficacious teaching and learning situations. We do wish to emphasize one pertinent fact. We do not now or at any time champion the cause of homogeneous grouping. Our classes are grouped heterogeneously but there is a narrower range of reading levels within one class than we had heretofore countenanced. It would be easier to illustrate this point than to try to describe.

In the school year 1963-1964 the distribution of children completing second grade looked like this:

Reading Levels

Level 9	52 children
Level 8	64 children
Level 7	13 children
Level 6	14 children
Level 5	9 children
Level 4	1 child
Level 3	3 children
	156 children

These children were then grouped in the following manner:

GRADED GROUPING CHART

Reading Level	Class A	Class B	Class C	Class D	Class E	Class F
Nine	9	11	11	7	7	7
Eight	11	9	10	12	12	10
Seven	–	–	–	9	4	–
Six	–	–	4	–	–	10
Five	–	4	–	–	5	–
Four	1	–	–	–	–	–
Three	3	–	–	–	–	–

Fig. 3-1.

We know that the reader understands that this is just the skeletal frame. We are not endeavoring at this time to point out the many other childhood factors (psychological, social, etc.) which dictated these particular class compositions. We are just trying to explain the class compositions as they were made on the basis of the criterion of reading achievement level.

Now if we look at the nongraded class composition we will be able to point out the changes we made. In the 1964-1965 school year our children, according to achievement in reading, fell as follows:

Reading Levels

Level 2 .... 35 children
Level 3 .... 54 children
Level 4 ....119 children
Level 5 .... 51 children
Level 6 .... 32 children
Level 7 .... 42 children
Level 8 .... 25 children
Level 9 .... 47 children
Level 10 .... 10 children
Level 11 .... 9 children
Level 12 .... 17 children
                     ——————————
                     441 children

Examination of the two grouping examples (Figures 3-1 and 3-2) bear out the fact that we were careful in the nongraded wherever possible to decrease the range of reading levels in each class. This was in marked contrast to the 1963-1964 year when the ranges were much larger and there were gaps between levels in almost all the classes. In the nongraded, except for the P and Q classes, there are no gaps between instructional levels in reading at all. In the P and Q classes there was just no other way that these pupils could be grouped without skipping the one level you can note on the chart. Classes M and O seem to represent classes with larger ranges also; however, the three youngsters so indicated represent marked deviation from an instructional and emotional point of view and would have required individual programs and attention in any class in which they were placed. They were, therefore, placed with the teachers best suited to their individual needs (preceding chapter).

These children were then grouped in the following manner:

Nongraded Grouping Chart

Reading Level	A	B	C	D	E	F	G	H	I	J	K	L	M	N	O	P	Q
Two	5	5	5	5	5	5	5+ (1)										
Three	9	7	7	8	8	5+ (1)	6	(2+) [1]									
Four	11	12	12	12	12	(11)	(12)	(8+) [3]	(12+) [1]	11	(1)		[1]				
Five								(13)	(7)	(8)	(12)	9		[2]			
Six								(7)	(8)	(7)	[10]						
Seven											6	(9)	(7+) [3]	[11]	[6]		
Eight													(4+) [3]	[9]	[9]		
Nine													(5)	(9)	[12]	[10]	[11]
Ten															[10]		
Eleven																	(2+) [7]
Twelve																[8]	(1+) [8]

Code

Not Circled - Six Year Olds
Circled - Seven Year Olds
Squared - Eight Year Olds

Fig. 3-2.

As you can see there were a number of criteria established for the first year which the nongraded chart shows quite clearly. Each class was to house children whose age span did not exceed two chronological years. Each class was to house three contiguous reading groups; each reading group capable of being instructed at approximately the same achievement level. To aid us in the grouping of children, we used a Profile Card (Figures 3-3 and

Profile Card - Nongraded Primary Placement

```
┌─────────────────────────────────────────────────────────────┐
│                                          1964 - 1965          │
│                                          Old Bethpage School  │
│    _____                          │
│            Child's name                 ┌──────────────────┐ │
│    _____        _____         │ IRI LEVEL        │ │
│        Yrs.              Mo.             │                  │ │
│                Age                       │      _____       │ │
│  Check where appropriate and comment (back). └──────────────┘ │
│                                                              │
│  EMOTIONAL          _____             LEARNING RATE        │
│                                                              │
│  HEALTH             _____             SLOW       _____   │
│                                                              │
│  SPEECH             _____             AVERAGE    _____   │
│                                                              │
│          SOCIAL                         ABOVE AVER. _____  │
│                                                              │
│  MATURE  _____  IMMATURE _____      _____  │
│                                            Sending Teacher   │
│  ISOLATE            _____                                  │
│                                         _____  │
│  LEADER             _____               Receiving Teacher  │
│                                                              │
└─────────────────────────────────────────────────────────────┘
```

Fig. 3-3.

Profile Card - Kindergarten into First Year Primary

```
┌─────────────────────────────────────────────────────────────┐
│                                       1964 - 1965            │
│                                       Old Bethpage School    │
│    _____                          │
│            Child's name             METROPOLITAN READINESS SCORES │
│    _____        _____     SUBTEST #6 COPYING  _____ │
│        Yrs.             Mos.                     READING      │
│                Age                  LETTER RATINGS, READINESS _____ │
│  Check where appropriate                                     │
│    and comment (back).              %ILE - TOTAL READINESS _____ │
│  EMOTIONAL          _____                                  │
│                                                              │
│  HEALTH             _____                         Please   │
│                                                  leave blank.│
│  SPEECH             _____         LEVEL (1-4)              │
│                                     ┌──────┐     ┌──────┐    │
│          SOCIAL                     └──────┘     └──────┘    │
│                                                              │
│  MATURE  _____  IMMATURE _____  _____      │
│                                        Sending Teacher       │
│  ISOLATE            _____                                  │
│                                     _____      │
│  LEADER             _____           Receiving Teacher      │
│                                                              │
└─────────────────────────────────────────────────────────────┘
```

Fig. 3-4.

3-4) for each child entering the primary school. It was a fairly comprehensive card indicating special characteristics which we take note of in any pupil's placement: special problems (already outlined in the preceding chapter), leadership characteristics, learning rate, and social maturity. Each card also indicated the reading and mathematic instructional level of the child as determined by individually administered Informal Reading Inventories and Mathematics Progress Tests. These Informal Reading Inventories, developed in large part by the Reading Department of the district and especially adapted for our school by our reading consultant, have been found to be especially effective in determining the exact instructional reading level at which a pupil is operating. For the pupils who were entering the primary school, we used our own interpretation of the percentile scores children received on certain sub scores of the Metropolitan Readiness Tests. Over the years we have found certain portions of this standardized test to be an effective tool in predicting the reading facility of the children before they begin our reading program. The Informal Reading Inventory scores and the Metropolitan scores were used as a guide for determining the actual instructional level in reading for each child and this level was then indicated on the pupil's Profile Card. Armed with this information about each child, we then drew up a Master Paper Plan based on the cumulative totals which were then available to us (i.e., thirty-five children on level two, etc. *above*).

The next step was the actual grouping of the children according to our criteria: three contiguous reading groups in each class, distribution of leadership qualities, distribution of special problem children. We held many small meetings with classroom teachers, special teachers, the school nurse-teacher, speech therapist, reading consultant, and school psychologist, reviewing and analyzing our class placements. In all cases, the child's former teacher helped to decide his group placement in the nongraded. We once estimated that it took us six full weeks of solid work to complete our total grouping for the nongraded. Of course, theoretically, this is a procedure which need not be repeated each school year; once the nongraded is operational most of the children move along quite naturally and there is no annual promotion or reorganization. It is only new entrants and kindergarten children who require this special care at the end of each school year. The next chapter will illustrate more clearly how movements of pupils who required class changes for one reason or another were accomplished through an ongoing process during the school year.

Shortly after the beginning of the school year we discussed at length with each teacher her reading groups and how they were working. This checkup was something which we did consistently throughout the school year to insure that children were proceeding in reading as predicted. Problems, of course, were uncovered and we will see adequate examples of this and the special programs developed for children with reading problems later in the book. For the moment we should like to indicate how the first report sounded:

October 19—Minutes of Primary Meeting

> We reviewed the instructional reading levels and groups in each class to see how they compared with our original breakdown. Mrs. W., the reading consultant, had collected the data from each teacher.

> Miss S. reported that all her groups were functioning well on the predicted levels.

> Mrs. S. moved one youngster, Ira I., who was frustrating at his assigned level. Her top reading group, working in a level ten reader, seems to be having difficulty with comprehension. They can handle the skills well, and they can read orally with proficiency. She is developing a special program of comprehension skills for these youngsters (using extra materials—*Practice Readers*,[1] *Reading for Meaning*,[2] etc.) to provide these pupils with additional lessons in increasing comprehension. Some of the other

---

[1] Clarence Stone, Grover, and Evalyn B. Kinkead et al., *Practice Readers* (New York: Webster Division, McGraw-Hill Book Company, 1962).

[2] Guiler and Coleman, *Reading for Meaning* (Philadelphia, Pa.: J.B. Lippincott Company, 1962).

teachers thought that, perhaps, the basal reader itself, *High Roads*[3] might be too difficult for these youngsters. Mrs. S. and Mrs. W., the reading consultant felt, however, that this was a bright group of youngsters and actually the material should not be beyond their comprehension level. Increased experiences in comprehension certainly seemed called for as does a slower approach to the basal reader itself.

Miss O., who has three reading groups, plus one youngster being handled as an isolate, has decided to split her top reading group of thirteen since she finds thirteen too large a number to deal with. Miss O. is skilled in a multi approach to instruction and will have no problem with handling an additional instructional group. We all agreed that thirteen might be too large a number to deal with if you hoped to do any individualization.

Mrs. K. reported that her three groups are functioning on the predicted levels.

Mrs. T. has one reading group functioning on a level other than that which we recommended, giving her two reading groups on the same level, although she is using a different basal text for each group. Mrs. W. will spend some time checking out this group.

(Once this group of youngsters had been exposed to an intensive two week phonics review program recommended by the reading consultant, they were quite able to move on to the original level predicted for them.)

Thus one group of primary teachers reported. Being individuals, they all made their own adjustments with their own children, and we wanted them to; but on the whole the assigned reading levels proved to be quite stable as you can see. More importantly, we feel this narrower range of reading levels permitted teachers to devote more time to individual problems and special programs in reading and other curricular areas. This had not been as possible when the range of reading achievement levels in any one class had been greater. Not one of our teachers has ever disagreed with us on this point.

---

[3] Paul McKee, Annie McCowen, M. Lucile Harrison, Elizabeth Lehr, *High Roads* (Boston, Mass.: Houghton Mifflin Company, 1957).

We established and put into operation a grouping procedure based on certain specific criteria which we deemed important to education as we saw it. It was our considered judgment that our class groups lent themselves well to good classroom instruction and to individualized instruction. This is well documented in Chapter 7 which goes into the details of our approaches to individualized instruction. Perhaps, the most significant factor to emphasize in this chapter on grouping is that the type of grouping arrangement which we preferred was more easily attainable once we began to consider the possibilities of interage grouping. As soon as we eliminated the age and grade factors, we found we could group our pupils in classes which were much better suited to their learning needs than in the past when we were bound by artificial and meaningless restrictions of grade or age.

4

THE MOVEMENT OF CHILDREN

Objective: to place and move children in learning situations where satisfaction and self-development come through continual progress and success.

As has already been stated, it has always been our feeling that the learning situation could be improved through better grouping of children in classes. A previous chapter illustrates how carefully we evaluated children with social, emotional, physical, or psychological problems. We placed these thirty-one pupils carefully with the proper teacher and in the best possible classroom situation to suit their needs. Thirty-one youngsters from a total of 442 youngsters still left us with 411 children to be placed in classes. Although these children did not have any outstanding problems which required special placement, we felt that there still might be placement for these children which was better suited to them academically than just random placement. It is for this reason that we had developed a very carefully documented grouping plan which took into account certain intellectual factors such as the maturity of the child, the rate at which he learned, and the level of his achievement in reading. The preceding chapter explored these factors in detail and described our precise grouping mechanics.

What happened, however, after we had carefully grouped all these children according to all our aforementioned social, emotional, physical, psychological, and intellectual criteria and found, after the new year started, that some of our children did not fit the nicely prescribed molds we had created for them? The answer became obvious. We had to move these children and move them to classroom situations better suited to them and the way they learned. And move them we did—all during the school year.

It is especially interesting to watch how all of this actually unfolded in the Old Bethpage School during the course of our first year of nongrading. Remember the only factor which we had all recognized in advance of the school year was that certain children were going to have to be moved.

September 28—Minutes of Primary Meeting

Criteria for Shifting Pupils from One Class to Another

It may be necessary as time proceeds to make some shifts of children from one class to another. This, of course, is part and parcel of the nongraded concept. We are beginning to determine accurate and precise data for making these shifts.

1. The first factor on which we are all agreed is that condition number one warranting a change from class to class has to be the fact that the youngster is an instructional isolate in the class (i.e., that there is no group in reading in the class in which this child can function).

2. Wherever possible a determination of the mathematics level will be made and placement will recognize the fulfillment of this academic need also. However, we have often found that the fulfillment of both the reading and the mathematics levels becomes impossible and in these cases reading will take precedence.

3. All factors relating to the youngster's emotional, social, mental, and physical development will be taken into account.

4. A specific sheet is being developed which will detail all the items above before a youngster is considered for a shift.

5. The precise people who may be involved in the decision have not been determined. To date, the following personnel have been mentioned and it is possible that they will all be involved in the formalized procedure—classroom teacher, receiving teacher, administrators, psychologist, speech therapist, school nurse-teacher, and reading consultant, wherever relevant.

6. Procedures for parental conferences and notification have not yet been discussed.

And so the school year had just started and both teachers and administrators became aware immediately of the necessity to create some type of formal steps for the shifting of pupils who were not placed correctly. It is important to note that many of the important decisions relevant to our nongraded were made with the full cooperation of all the teachers in the Primary School. Certainly shifting criteria were a good example of the way we cooperatively made many of our major decisions during the course of the actual school year. Since we had arranged very carefully that every teacher was to be seen at a meeting for at least one hour per week with her primary group and the administrators, this involvement in decision making became a relatively simple matter to administer.

September 29—Minutes of another Primary Group Meeting during the same week:

> Youngsters who become potential candidates for shifting from one primary class to another were the first item discussed. Specific criteria were reviewed: instructional isolate, no appropriate reading level in class, emotional, mental, and social preparedness, judgment of teacher, psychologist, administrators, etc.

Oct. 5—Minutes of Primary Meeting

> A profile sheet has been developed which a teacher will be asked to complete whenever she wishes the group to consider a youngster for shifting. This will be filled out in triplicate (one for child's folder, etc.). The form is basically anecdotal in type.

The actual form (Figure 4-1) was formulated by Mrs. W., the reading consultant and Mrs. G., the assistant principal, from the specific suggestions made by the teachers. Space for short anecdotal comments was included with the request that the teacher comment on: emotional aspects of the child, mental aspects of the child, social aspects of the child, and physical aspects of the child. The form also asked that the teacher indicate her reasons for requesting a shift for the youngster and her suggestions for future placement. The second sheet had appropriate space for comments by other personnel who might be involved, though not

OLD BETHPAGE SCHOOL

MOVEMENT RECORD

Date ——————————————

(Please complete 3 copies.)

NAME OF CHILD: ————————————————

NAME OF TEACHER: ——————————————

READING LEVEL IN CLASS: ————————————

COMMENT ON:

    EMOTIONAL ASPECTS OF CHILD: ———————

————————————————————————————

————————————————————————————

    MENTAL ASPECTS OF CHILD: ——————————

————————————————————————————

————————————————————————————

    SOCIAL ASPECTS OF CHILD: ———————————

————————————————————————————

————————————————————————————

    PHYSICAL ASPECTS OF CHILD: ————————————

————————————————————————————

SUMMARY: REASON FOR RECOMMENDED MOVEMENT:

————————————————————————————

————————————————————————————

————————————————————————————

SUGGESTED PLACEMENT: ———————————————

————————————————————————————

PARENT NOTIFICATION—DATE: _____

PARENT REACTION: _____

_____

_____

CONFERENCE WITH CHILD—DATE: _____

CHILD'S REACTION: _____

_____

_____

APPROVED BY: (WHERE NECESSARY)

READING CONSULTANT: _____

SCHOOL PSYCHOLOGIST: _____

SCHOOL NURSE—TEACHER: _____

SPEECH CORRECTIONIST: _____

ADMINISTRATOR: _____

SENDING TEACHER: _____

RECEIVING TEACHER: _____

ACTION:

MOVED—DATE: _____

TO: _____

LEVELS IN NEW CLASS: _____

RECEIVING TEACHER'S REACTIONS—DATE: _____

_____

_____

Fig. 4-1.

necessarily, in the shift of the youngster (psychologist, reading consultant, speech therapist, etc.). Finally, the form included space for recording our final decision and reason, and the new class assignment (if one were made) and the parental reaction to the change.

Oct. 5 (con't.)

> The procedure we will follow will be as follows: The teacher will speak directly to the parents on the phone, making them aware of the reasons for the change. A conference will not be required if there is full parental understanding during the phone conversation. Following this successful contact, the teacher will explain to the youngster carefully the reasons for the change (on a level consistent with the youngster's understanding of his own needs). A postcard will then be mailed directly to the parents, formalizing the change. A copy of this postcard will be issued to the office for all necessary attendance changes (status forms, etc.). A file of cards and profile sheets on all youngsters considered for movement or actually moved will be kept in the principal's office.

Procedures were established and all we asked was that the teacher complete the form before bringing any child's name up for movement consideration at a primary meeting. The group itself, which included the five or six teachers in that primary meeting group, the administrators, and any other personnel relevant to a decision of the movement of a particular child made the decision together. Of course, as in most instances in decision making, the ultimate decision was the principal's responsibility. Two interesting developments occurred during the school year which bear mentioning at this point. In almost all cases there was complete agreement by all the members of the group on the movement or non-movement of a youngster. One case where a teacher's persistent insistence caused us to make a change against our better judgment, was the only case where we did not all agree. (The full story of this movement, Susan, is given below.) Second, the notification of parents by phone, which we predicted was going to cause some difficulty, turned out to be a good method. We made a total of thirty-nine changes during the school year.

Of these, thirty-eight parents, notified by phone only, accepted our decision without any further need for clarification. One parent at the close of the phone call requested a conference which she was granted immediately. At the conference the reasons for the change were explained in much greater detail and she felt quite pleased and agreed to the shift.

As with all procedures, as you work with them, you can always find techniques for their improvement.

Oct. 20—Minutes of Primary Meeting

> An excellent suggestion was made that for those youngsters entering the primary school from kindergarten who might be considered movement candidates, we include on the Pupil Movement Record a space for indicating Metrotolitan scores. Scores on the Metropolitan which we are most interested in are sub test six, sub test seven, and sub test eight, since we feel these scores are indicative of a youngster's future performance in reading and this would be an excellent check for us. For all other youngsters being considered for movement their most recent Informal Reading Inventory scores were to be included.

As the year progressed and youngsters were moved from one class to another certain questions began to be raised, the most pertinent being, "In what way is our system of shifting children possibly harmful?" This was a very broad question with major ramifications which will be explored in depth in our follow-ups of children during the next few years. However, we do mention it here since our evaluation of procedures for movement brought some of these problems to light.

Dec. 1—Minutes of Primary Meeting

> It seems from the discussions held this week with all three primary groups that the general consensus of opinion is that we continue with our pattern of movement as the needs become apparent for any child without establishing specific dates for movement. We think the most pertinent observation was made by Mrs. C. when she said, "If we establish arbitrary dates for the movement of youngsters, (i.e., four times per year), parents who are anxious about academic progress of their children might

well use these dates to their own purpose by continuing to pressure children to perform well by such and such a date in order that they might be moved to a more advanced level." An even more artificial situation that we would be perpetuating would be having parents "kind of, sort of" holding their breath to see if their youngsters "made it." There does not seem too much gained then from the use of arbitrary times for movement and much to be gained from the continual progress of each youngster in our natural, normal approach.

Once again the group made a decision together after much discussion and evaluation. We had established criteria for movement which we found working out well for us and felt that we should continue in this pattern. This decision became even more meaningful as we began to recognize more and more the role the parents were playing in the actual academic progress of some of the children. This too is a vast topic which will be explored in our sections on problems. Suffice it to say for the moment, we had established criteria, tried the procedure for awhile and decided to continue with it. In late spring when movement criteria were once again evaluated, we again reaffirmed our faith in the techniques we had developed and were using successfully.

Let us now turn to specifics. What children did we move and why? There were many reasons for movement, all of them significant and important. A list of reasons would include the following:

1. A youngster became an instructional isolate, that is, in all academic areas he had to work alone since he could either do more advanced work than all the other children or could do less advanced work than all the other children in the group.

2. A youngster became a social isolate and was not relating well to the other members of his class. This could be a result of psychological, emotional, or physical reasons.

3. A youngster did not relate well to the teacher to whom he was assigned. This was nothing more than a personality clash which one must always be alert to if one is at all aware of human relations.

These were our major reasons for changing a child's class placement. It was always our opinion that a child should be placed in the best possible situation for him as an individual. If at any time we felt a youngster could do better with a change of environment, we were perfectly willing to consider and make the change. Many factors could interfere between the late spring (when grouping and class assignments had been made) and early fall (when classes started). Many factors could occur during the course of a school year which would cause a child to be a misfit in the class to which he was assigned. Children mature at different rates and a youngster could evidence a sudden growth spurt during the summer. Children learn at different rates and a pupil could suddenly "catch on" and begin to learn at a more accelerated rate. Children participate in many major experiences outside their school which can alter them appreciably; the death of a parent is a dramatic instance of this type of change. And so no matter how carefully or systematically the children had been grouped in the spring, some changes were necessary during the school year. Let us look at a few examples.

Nathan

Oct. 5—Mrs. Q. Reports:

Although Nathan is functioning on the ninth reading level, and I have a group on this level in my class, he is evidencing serious social and emotional problems because the overall work of this class is putting him under too much pressure. There is actual evidence of his degree of unhappiness from Nathan's continued absence from the room "to go to the bathroom."

This was the first time we heard about Nathan. Mrs. Q. then completed a Movement Record for the child which indicated the following: "Nathan is very quiet and does not contribute to class discussions; he does little work on his own and completes very few assignments, a 'lazy' worker; although he doesn't socialize much, he doesn't appear to be too unhappy." During the follow-

ing week the principal and the reading consultant observed
Nathan in class.

Oct. 15—Minutes of Primary Meeting

The psychologist, reading consultant, administrators, sending
and receiving teachers, all agreed to shift this youngster as of
October 16 to Miss O.'s class where there is a group on an appropriate reading level for him and in general the youngsters in the
class themselves will not cause him the amount of pressure which
he seems to be feeling in Mrs. Q.'s class. We shall watch Nathan
carefully and observe the type of adjustment he makes in his
new class situation. The school psychologist gave Mrs. Q. some
specific suggestions on what to tell Nathan as to the reasons for
change to make the transition easier for him.

And so an otherwise bright little boy began to function poorly
in a situation where we had thought he would do quite well and
we all agreed to try him out in a situation less threatening to him.
On October 15 the parent was notified of the proposed change of
class by Mrs. Q. who reported that the parent reaction to the
change was good, since the parent had already questioned the
wisdom of this placement for Nathan, feeling the child could
not work on the expected levels of the rest of the class.

The sending teacher, Mrs. Q., reported on October 17, when
she told Nathan he was to be moved to a new class, "There were
tears at first, but in a little while he was quite pleased and happy
when he realized who some of the children would be in his new
class."

On October 17 Miss O., the receiving teacher, reported after
Nathan's first day in his new class, "Nathan seems to be reacting
better in this new class situation than Mrs. Q. reported of him
in his old class." On November 10 Miss O. reported: "Nathan is
now outgoing socially and has been trying to complete his work
in class." On November 30 Miss O. reported, "Nathan, who was
an emotional problem in his former class and was transferred to
me about a month ago, now seems to be much less tense and is
adjusting academically and is also beginning to complete

all class assignments." It is certainly easy to conjecture that if Nathan had been permitted to remain in his original class, the tension and pressure he felt would have continued and he would have ended up on a much less successful note than he did by the end of the school year in Miss O.'s class. Nathan was an example of a pupil whom we moved because we felt his emotional problems would be lessened in another class situation and thus his ability and desire to learn would be improved.

Ellie

Ellie was a little girl who came to us from kindergarten already reading. Her kindergarten teacher felt that she should not be placed with any advanced reading group but be allowed to read individually and be a social part of the total group. Let's watch and see what happened.

September 29, Mrs. A. reports:

> Ellie is a very mature little girl. She is reading on level nine without any help from me. My top reading group is on level four. She is a distinct instructional isolate. She works alone completely since there is no one else in class who can hope to attain her level.

On October 8, Mrs. A. completed a Movement Record for Ellie in which she said:

> Ellie is cooperative, apparently free of tensions and well behaved. She has great ability to think through a problem. She is capable of reading on the twelfth instructional level. Her comprehension is excellent and she is very receptive to learning. She is also very well accepted by her peers. She is large, mature, and well coordinated. I feel that every day she is becoming more and more of an instructional isolate.

At this point the assistant principal, the reading consultant, and the school psychologist observed Ellie in class and on October 19 the decision was made by all to move Ellie to Miss K.'s class.

The children in Miss K.'s class were functioning slightly below Ellie academically, but were not so much older than she that a social problem would be created. Miss K. agreed to instruct Ellie individually in reading but have her participate on the same level as the other children in other academic areas. On October 19 Mrs. A. informed Ellie's parents of the change by phone and she stated: "Parent was pleased with the move—felt that Ellie's abilities could be better provided for by placement with this older group." Further, Ellie herself when informed of the change on the same day accepted the decision with great stability and assurance.

Finally, Miss K. reported on November 30: "Ellie's adjustment has been excellent. She is well accepted by the class. Her arithmetic skills are now up-to-date (she had been functioning on a lower mathematics level in her former class). Her manuscript needs further improvement and, of course, her reading is clearly superior." This pattern of excellent adjustment continued throughout the school year and we present the case here as an example of a pupil who was clearly an instructional isolate in her former class and therefore required movement to a more challenging learning situation.

Susan

If you recall we mentioned Susan earlier as an example of a child whom we had moved where the results were not as successful as we had hoped. Let's follow her story.

September 29, Mrs. C. reports:

> Susan wasn't tested for reading in kindergarten because her teacher did not want her made to feel different from the other children in the class. However, she is now a distinct instructional isolate. She is reading on level ten instructionally. My top reading group is on level three. I do recognize, of course, that Susan is emotionally immature and this compounds the problem.

October 9, Mrs. C. completed a movement form for Susan:

> Susan is quite uncooperative, has a bad temper, will yell,
> argue, hit other children. She is very difficult to manage (this
> from a teacher who generally has children in the palm of her
> hand). She is extremely bright and retains things instantly with
> complete understanding. She finds it hard to cooperate and work
> as part of the group. She requires much individual attention. She
> is physically very large and well built.

Thus, on October 9, Mrs. C. concluded that "although Susan
is very bright and reading well above level, she is not ready to
function in a formal learning situation and wants to play constantly. I feel, therefore, that she should remain in my class."
All personnel involved in the study of Susan agreed wholeheartedly with this decision.

On November 25, Mrs. C. completed a second movement form
on Susan:

> Susan is very mature and reliable in some respects. She does
> get angry easily. Will sometimes cause disturbances, but this has
> improved a great deal. She is extremely bright and needs much
> intellectual stimulation. She learns very quickly, and is often
> bored with the work in the class. She evidences many good
> leadership qualities and gets along well with other children. She
> has good physical coordination and is well built. I feel she has
> made a good adjustment and is now functioning well as a member
> of the group. I feel Susan needs a much higher level of work in
> all areas in order to maintain her interest. I'm sure that any
> slight behavior problems that still remain would disappear when
> Susan is in a group in which she can work up to her full capacity.

At this time all of us got intimately involved in the Susan
situation again and spent a good deal of time determining our
course of action. Finally, after repeated insistances from Mrs. C.
further substantiated by some evidence from other primary
teachers who had watched Susan's social growth from September
through November, we agreed that Susan would be moved. This
was one time when the decision was certainly not unanimous.
Most of us in the front office had some serious doubt about the

wisdom of moving this obviously socially immature child. However, the teachers were equally sure that this step would be for
Susan's benefit. So on November 30 Susan was moved to Mrs.
L.'s class where all the children were at least one year older than
Susan. Mrs. L. was selected because she had appropriate reading
groups in her class where Susan could function, but more particularly since every other class which had appropriate reading
levels for Susan contained children who were chronologically
and socially too mature for her. Also Mrs. L. had the kind of
personality we felt Susan would work well with since she was a
child with social problems and needed special attention.

On December 1 Mrs. L. reported that Susan "seems immature
for the group after only one day in class. Has fought with other
children in class. Did not work with class in most activities." Sad
to relate this remained the pattern throughout the rest of the
school year. This little girl with the bright mind was too immature socially to make the adjustment in her new class, and she
certainly had not made a good adjustment in her old class. As it
turned out though since she had evidenced some growth in her
first class, might it not have been wiser to have kept her with
this group? What do they say about hindsight?

We did learn one valuable lesson from this experience: movement decisions, as they had been in all other cases, had to be
unanimous for them to have a chance to succeed. If you remember, a number of us had from the start expressed doubts
about the efficacy of this movement, and unfortunately we
may have been right. The end of the school year brought some
other matters to light, however. Other teachers who saw Susan
on visits and knew her from other school connected activities
thought that she had made some good social adjustments even
though we didn't feel they were adequate. In addition, there was
increased evidence that this child had very special emotional
and social problems which might require help from professionals
outside the school. If this turns out to be the case, then really all
we are saying is that no class situation would really have ap-

preciably helped Susan at this point in her social life. Only time will tell.

Paul

Paul is a youngster who represents still another reason for moving a child. Paul simply found the work in the class to which he was assigned too difficult. His case is short and simple.

November 30, Miss D. completed a movement form:

> Paul is a stable youngster who appears to be an average boy. He has an average I.Q. and achieves on an average or below average level in all academic areas. He is a nice child, well liked by his peers and generally a follower. He is athletic and enjoys sports. Paul is becoming a discipline problem in my class because he is not kept interested in the work. And he is not kept interested because the work seems to be too difficult for him. He needs work on which he can achieve in order to be satisfied and not act up.

The reading consultant looked in on Paul and completely substantiated Miss D.'s findings and it was recommended that Paul be moved to a class which had reading levels and achievement levels in other academic areas consistent with his abilities. We decided to place him with Mrs. F.'s class and both Paul and his parents were informed of the change. There was no problem, though his parents did evidence some concern about Paul's achievement level. We reassured them that Paul was achieving at a level which we found satisfactory for him and they seemed satisfied. On December 7 his new teacher reported, "Paul seems to be adjusting nicely. He seems interested in the work and is completing his assignments. I am sure he will be less of a behavior problem now that he can do the work." Paul's shift continued to be a success and most interestingly where he had been noted as a follower by his former teacher (where the work had been too advanced for him) he was, by the end of the spring, noted as a leader in his new class. Somehow the satisfaction of achieving academically had even changed Paul socially.

As has already been stated, we have thirty-nine such case studies in miniature of children who were moved during the course of the first year of our nongraded with complete documentation and follow-up evaluations on all. We felt personally that only Susan represented some question in our minds. We are still not sure whether her class change was effective, but we are very positive in our evaluations in the other thirty-eight cases. These children adjusted well and benefited from the change of class. We had placed all our children originally in the best possible situation for them and in those cases where we found that for some reason they were no longer in the best classroom situation, we moved them. In that way we satisfied our objective of placing and moving children in learning situations where satisfaction and self development came through continuous progress and success. Dr. Anderson stated it better when he said:

> Success is guaranteed to the child if he is diligent, for he is not asked to do that which is impossible for him to achieve.
>
> When the child is successful, he is intrinsically rewarded. This will in turn produce a favorable self-image and enhance self-confidence.[1]

---

[1] Anderson, Speech.

5

THE DIFFERENCES AMONG CHILDREN

Objective: to eliminate the pressures of grade level barriers and predetermined time and subject matter schedules with identical demands for all pupils.

One of the most telling objectives of the nongraded school is the one we shall be discussing in this chapter. It is such an obvious objective that many of us wonder why we never recognized this great need in the past. All of us were aware that children were different. None of us ever disputed this point. But all we ever really did was to say in essence, yes, children are different; they have different personalities; they learn differently; they mature at different rates; and then we let it go at that. The good teacher always adapted her program for the differences among children within her classroom, but she was always faced with a problem, a serious one too. If Johnny can read on fourth grade level and I give him reading work on fourth grade level, what will his next year's fourth grade teacher give him? The reverse situation presented essentially the same problem to the teacher. If Mary cannot finish her second grade reader this year, how will she be ready to start her third grade reader when she enters the third grade? Oddly enough, both these examples can be multiplied by hundreds in any school. There are many children who refuse to fall into the grade we assign them. For a host of reasons they are capable of doing work on levels quite different from the one to which they are assigned by some arbitrary grade label.

Grade labels make assumptions and we are governed by these assumptions. They assume that all children can learn the same amount of work in the same amount of time. All children in grade two must learn grade two mathematics, reading, language arts, music, art, physical education, library skills, social studies, and science. And they must learn it at the same chronological time and during the same chronological period of time. But children have for years been telling us in many ways that they cannot do this. They are not computers. They are far more complicated mechanisms. They learn at different rates of speed at different chronological periods of time. What is even more complicated is that certain children vary in their learning rates from one curricular area to another. It is quite usual for a pupil to be capable of doing second grade mathematics, but fourth grade reading.

Consider then the position in which we have traditionally placed the teacher. We have told her children are different, but have tied her to a system which has not permitted her really to make adjustments to these differences. Nongrading, as we saw it, was to eliminate this tremendous burden. It was to free the teacher to recognize these differences among children and to so adjust her program that all children could comfortably have these differences accommodated. It was simply a restatement of Anderson's pronouncement that children were not to be asked to do what they couldn't do; and that children when they do what they can do, are self-fulfilled and therefore more satisfied human beings. No small goals these.

All our teachers felt the importance of these credos and we were all sincerely resolved to adapt our program to the needs of all our children. In two other chapters we will explore in depth our curricula adaptations for children who learn at different rates. One chapter will illustrate the programs we designed for certain individual pupils, and still another chapter will explore the special programs designed for groups of youngsters. It is our purpose here to show you how we began to recognize those children who were different. It may seem an elementary point to talk about recognition of differences, but we have found that it was not as elementary as it first sounded. Before any special programs could be designed for a group of children or for one child

Cooking becomes a scientific discovery experience

Small group
reinforcement in reading

Mathematics experiences
on a one-to-one basis

we had to recognize first that this child was different, and understand how he differed and why.

The road to success was not an easy one and we present below some examples of difficulties which we encountered along the way. The most normal and natural experience we had went something like this. A teacher being alert to our objective (the recognition of individual differences among children) would so accurately identify a pupil. She would present this pupil's name to us at a primary meeting (with a fully documented Movement Form) and ask that the pupil be placed in *some other class* which might better provide for him. Now, as we have said, this was a most normal and natural action on the teacher's part. But it was one we had to most carefully guard against. We were quite willing, as we have already demonstrated, to move pupils when we felt that there was a better placement for them but there were times when the teacher and class to whom the pupil was attached was the best place for that child and movement was not the answer. The answer lay in providing an individualized or small group program within the same class itself. These were delicate situations which required much diplomacy and care. Decisions had to be carefully weighed. Most importantly, teachers had to understand the reasons for decisions of this nature and recognize that they were not arbitrary. Let's look at one such case.

George

Oct. 27, Mrs. T. reports:

> George is a well adjusted youngster of superior mental ability. I feel he can function on a higher level than any of the groups in my class. He has no social problems. He plays well with all children and often takes the lead in activities. I feel he should be moved to a class with children who are working on more advanced work.

On the surface this certainly looked like a legitimate request that we could easily accommodate. However, there were certain other factors in the situation which caused us to consider carefully before making this class change. Mrs. T. had four other pupils in her class who were quite close academically to George's achievement levels. He was not a total instructional isolate. The total structure of Mrs. T.'s class was such that she required certain academic and social leaders in her class to make for good group dynamics. If George were removed, a good deal of the viability and spontaneity of this class might be damaged. The significant factor for us in this case, however, was a larger one. It was Mrs. T. herself. Mrs. T. was an outstanding teacher whose preparation, planning, and implementation were a joy to behold. She was precisely one of those teachers on whom we were counting to set an example in accommodation of program for children with differences. The fact that she was one of the first to identify a child who required a special program certainly bore out this fact. We felt the need to handle this recommendation for movement with a denial. Of course, a tremendous amount of tact and patience were evidenced in making this decision known to Mrs. T. and the other teachers in her particular primary group. Our decisions were generally mutually agreed upon and we wanted all of them aware this time of the reasons for asking Mrs. T. to keep George in her class.

November 2, Minutes of Primary Meeting

It was suggested to Mrs. T. that she consider carefully her total class, its structure, and composition. She had an interage group and quite a number of the children would be proceeding from her class to a regular fourth grade the following year. George was one of these children as were the other four above average children (previously referred to). Perhaps there was some tendency on her part, as there is for all of us, to think in terms of her former grade designation and confine her program to this grade. This is the essential core of the problem as revealed in our discussions with all the interage teachers. We must remember that this program is terribly new to all of us and that in time and with patience we will make the necessary adjustments. In the meantime slowly and with careful deliberation we can begin to explore the possibilities of speeding up the program or offering more difficult experiences to all the youngsters who are in her class and ready for more advanced work. Materials themselves can be helpful in this regard (differentiated texts, use of the SRA kit,[1] more advanced research, books, etc.). Please note that both the administrators and Mrs. W. will be happy to explore this area in depth with any and all teachers for whom it is a concern.

George stayed in Mrs. T.'s class. He worked well and diligently and Mrs. T. provided him with an enriched program more adequately suited to his rate and level of achievement. We continued to have private conferences with Mrs. T. throughout the school year, discussing the type and kinds of experiences which might be offered this and other similar youngsters.

In going over all our documents before we started to write this book, we quite naturally studied the records of many of our pupils. We wanted to use examples that were fairly typical as representations of particular points. In this chapter we have been particularly careful to give as examples those children who were not outstanding deviates in any way. Children who were either extremely rapid learners or extremely slow learners are described in a separate chapter wherein we attempt to show you how we made decisions relative to a four-year or a two-year primary program for some of them. This chapter describes children who were different and who required special programs, but who were not different enough to require more or less time in the primary school. In other words, we adjusted our programs for them. We arranged for them to complete long range work loads in more or less time than an "average" child. In a total evaluation of these children, we did not feel that they required either a shortened or lengthened time in the primary school. Pupils who worked rapidly were provided with enriched experiences and advanced experiences. Pupils who worked slowly were provided with more reinforcement and more concrete experiences. In our judgment the children discussed in this chapter would require three years to complete primary school, even though some of them would be

---

[1] Don H. Parker and Genevieve Scannell, *Reading Laboratory* (Chicago, Ill.: Science Research Associates, Inc., 1961).

above level in certain curricular areas and some of them would be below level in certain curricular areas by the time they reached fourth grade. Here is an example of one such youngster:

Steven

Steven is a good example to use because he represented what one could almost refer to as a delayed decision. Since he was in his first year of primary school with us, we had at least one more year before we would be forced to decide whether to keep him in the primary school for a fourth year. Before we would make a decision of this sort, we were going to provide him with the most exacting type of program especially designed for him to see if we could help him with his academic difficulties, and thus have him complete primary school in the requisite amount of time.

November 23, Mrs. F. completed a Movement Form:

> Steven is a somewhat nervous, immature child and shy with his peers. He is a slow learner, operating on the third reading level. He is hearing sounds, but cannot associate them with the letter or the alphabet which he cannot learn. He tends to play with only one other child. His muscular coordination is relatively poor, but is improving as he is provided with more concrete experiences for muscular development. It is difficult for him to keep up with his group, now that the pace is picking up in the class. His I.Q. on a group test is 93, but I do not have much faith in group I.Q. scores for young, immature children. Perhaps there is a class where he will function better.

The decision in November was to keep Steven with Mrs. F. and to provide him with an individualized phonics program as recommended by the reading consultant.

December 15, Mrs. F. reports:

> I have brought Steven up before the group once before. He is an isolate in reading and mathematics. He is in the second pre-primer group. He has an average I.Q. and is socially immature. Perhaps he will, in the long run, require four years to complete

the primary school, but we need not consider this point this year. A lengthy discussion followed relative to youngsters of Steven's type who seem, for no obvious reason, to learn very slowly. They are the youngsters who subsequently become reading remediation problems in graded classes. Questions were asked. Are these youngters instructed at too early an age? Are they being instructed with a phonics approach which simply will not work for them? Are we proceeding too quickly for them? How many youngsters with this type of problem should we group together in one class? Should they be handled alone? Could there be any psychological reasons for their learning difficulties? It was suggested that for Steven, at least, we proceed as follows: a complete physical examination be provided to determine whether there are any organic difficulties causing his learning difficulties; the reading consultant give Steven an eye examination using the Telebinocular to determine whether there are any visual difficulties (coordination, fusion, dominance, etc.) not generally obvious in Snellen Eye Chart testing or for that matter in opthamologist reports; Mrs. F. will administer a Durrell Reading Test,[2] matching upper and lower case letter test, and our own Learning Rate test.

It would be wonderful to report that all this investigation and work resulted in some dramatic faults being uncovered in Steven, but quite the contrary was true. Steven continued to be a child with no serious problems (social, physical, psychological, or emotional) who continued to learn at a slow rate, and who continued to require a special reading program (sight and phonic). Each learning experience provided him needed more reinforcement than was usually necessary and the more concrete the experience the better he learned. He was the traditional slow learner and the name implied just what it said. Teach him more slowly because he learns more slowly. This we shall continue to do and by the middle of next year, we shall see if there is any change; and if there isn't, we can safely predict that it will take this slow learning child four years to complete Primary School. However, our examinations have all revealed that Steven is an

---

[2] Donald D. Durrell, "Identifying Letter Names," in *Improving Reading Instruction* (Yonkers-on-Hudson, N.Y.: World Book Company, 1956).

average child, and if so, the rate at which he is learning is not really understandable to us. The real hope which we all have is that somewhere in the next year Steven will make an adjustment and proceed to learn at a rate we feel more consistent with his abilities, and not require the fourth year in Primary School.

Now the parade started, and it was a grand parade, better than any we had ever seen in the circus or on Fifth Avenue; it was the parade of teachers bringing up the names of children—children who were different. They were beginning to recognize them; they wanted to provide for them. We were all intoxicated by the excitement of the discovery. All children were really different. They all learned differently. We grouped them together in classes or within classes at certain times simply because it was a more convenient way for us to instruct them, but none of them were really the same.

Names were brought forward, forms completed, and discussions held. Over and over again the pattern continued (and hopefully will always) and the teachers began to accept that we were not going to move every child who didn't "fit" their class. Rather, they were going to adjust their program to that child even if it meant individual instruction for many children during a small part of the school day. The teachers identified these children but they did not necessarily accompany this identification with a request for class change. Rather, pupils were being recognized as having differences and they were brought up for discussion so that ideas could be analyzed and suggestions offered for special program adaptations. Ideas and suggestions were freely given. Teachers exchanged experiences. Slowly we were building a new approach to teaching, the essential approach necessary to the nongraded: recognition and provision for the differences among children. We still continued to move certain children (see Chap. 4) but only when individualized programs in their original classes were not as meaningful as new class placement might be.

We illustrate below with random examples taken from our files.

Louis

October 28, Mrs. E. reports:

Louis is very young in his attitude. He must always be given individual directions. He finds it necessary to verbalize constantly. He seems very unsure of himself. He has above average intelligence and is capable of learning, though he has limited experiential knowledge and a poor memory. He does not relate well to the other children but plays alone. Seems to be having some trouble with eye-hand coordination and small muscle development. His Metropolitan Readiness score places him in the 57th percentile.

A little boy was identified. He had problems in reading. He was not proceeding as well as his teacher thought he should. Mrs. E. began to zero in on his particular problems. Since he was socially immature, she tried to provide experiences for him which helped make him sure of himself. His particular difficulties in reading stemmed from poor eye-hand and small muscle coordination. For this child exercises were designed to give him more expertise. By May of the school year, this little one presented his mother with a wonderful Mother's Day gift. At a gala party given in this classroom, Louis served his mother a special lunch and for dessert he read to her from his third pre-primer! A reading problem avoided, who can say? It's nice to think maybe.

Herbert

October 28, Mrs. E. reports:

Herbert is extremely nervous and tense. He is easily brought to hysteria. He is fearful of changes. He is exceptionally bright and observant. Has come to school with a wealthy background of knowledge and experiences. Has total familiarity with numerals and letters of alphabet. Socially, he functions alongside the group. He does not like to sit near other children, though the children will choose him at game time. His perception is very poor. He cannot see a whole. Has poor eye-hand coordination and cannot hold a pencil properly. He is a left-handed child. His Metropolitan Readiness score places him in the 47th percentile.

Here is the same teacher as she discussed another of her children evidencing problems with beginning reading—a child totally different in almost all aspects from Louis, but also having difficulties. Mrs. E. recognized his problems and knew she had to provide for them. She paid particular attention to his left-handedness, seeing in this the possible source of some headaches for this child, particularly if there were some attempts at home to have the child switch to his right hand. Very discreet conferences were held with Herbert's mother and cooperation was sought in eliminating any and all attempts at trying to have Herbert switch to the use of his right hand. The process was slow, but Herbert made progress, most particularly in reading. At the end of the school year, he had not made as good a social adjustment as was hoped, but all are alert to Herbert now and constant provision will be made for his social and academic growth in his next year in primary school.

Irma

December 24, Mrs. J. reports:

Irma is lethargic, gets annoyed easily when she is corrected about anything at all. Exhibits very little patience in any situation or with anyone. She has a low average I.Q. but does not work up to this level of expectation in any academic area. She is reading on primer level, although this is her second year in primary school. She shows little patience for her peers, especially any one of them who does not agree with her about anything. She does not have too many friends. She is normal in all physical aspects. I am seriously concerned about her reading problem and need some guidance and help.

Here was an older child with severe reading problems on the way to becoming a real reading remediation problem. Her teacher singled her out feeling that something had to be done to help this child. The school psychologist and the principal spent some time observing and watching this pupil. They found nothing in particular that could account for this youngster's problems and so the reading consultant was called in.

January 15, Mrs. W., the reading consultant reported:

> Irma frustrates in silent comprehension at a first grade level. She frustrates at the first grade level on word recognition also. She lacks word analysis skills and has no method of word attack. Her instructional level is the primer. (This confirmed all which Irma's classroom teacher had reported.)
>
> Irma needs exercises in final consonant sounds, structural elements and vowel sounds. I shall spend one hour a week personally with Irma to build this new foundation and shall leave specific exercises with Mrs. J. every week so that she can individually continue these experiences with Irma. She is also to be instructed in her group with the *Phonics We Use—Book B*[3] for ending sounds and in *Ted and Polly*[4] for comprehension.

A hand-tailored program was outlined for Irma which was to be individually administered to her by the teacher and by the reading consultant. This child showed growth by the end of the school year. She was reading on first grade level by June. We will see to it that this intensive program particularly and especially designed for Irma's needs is continued next year and who knows how much growth she will evidence at the end of another full year.

These are but minute examples from our records of pupils more closely and clearly identified by teachers. The teachers not only identified these pupils and their differences, but also searched long and hard for ways and means of meeting their problems. Differences were of course, recognized which were not problematical in nature. Children with special talents were one such

---

[3] Mary Meighen, Marjorie Pratt et al., *Phonics We Use* (Chicago, Ill.: Lyons and Carnahan, 1964).

[4] William H. Burton, Grace K. Kemp, Clara Belle Baker, et al., *Ted and Polly*, Developmental Reading Text Workbook (Indianapolis, Ind.: Bobbs-Merrill Company, Inc., 1961).

area of which we were very proud. Special experiences and opportunities were provided for these children also and will be
described in a later chapter.

From the many specific cases brought to our attention during
the school year, certain generalizations were made which, we
feel, demonstrate our increased awareness of the differences
among children and their subsequent behavior. The minutes of
January 17, 1965 most clearly bear this out.

Some Evidence Beginning to Become Observable about Children

1. Younger, immature, shy, or diffident children should not be
   grouped with older youngsters. It is not to their social or
   emotional advantage.
2. Physically mature older youngsters who are achieving well
   should not be grouped with younger children who do not
   achieve well since this is damaging to the ego of the younger
   child.
3. Possibility of suggesting that indications of maturity and immaturity might well be included on Profile Cards for grouping
   next year. The school psychologist and/or others will provide
   a list of criteria which teacher will use to guage the social and
   emotional level of maturity.
4. The well-adjusted, mature youngster is the one who does
   better with the older child in the interage class.
5. Some youngsters are being offered a better opportunity for
   development in the interage situation which they could never
   have been afforded under a graded set up. This is particularly
   true of the physically mature youngsters and the rapid learning youngsters who are placed with older children.

Our senses were keener; we were becoming more and more
perceptive in our observations about children generally and
specifically. Uniqueness was no longer overlooked, and differences gross and minute were being recognized; but even more
importantly, they were being accomplished. To us, all of us, it
seemed that once the grade level barriers were eliminated, we
were all freed to see children more nearly as they really were.
Herbert and Louis were not first graders who had to learn to
read in one year. They were little boys with beginning reading

problems and we had to eliminate their problems in whatever amount of time it took us. Irma was not a little girl in second grade who couldn't read a second grade reader. She was a little girl with a large academic handicap which affected her reading. We had to find out what this handicap was and help overcome it, in order for her to learn to read on any level. And so the examples can be mutiplied. More and more recognition of children for what they were, more and more special and extra programs designed to help. This became for us the most precious aspect of nongrading.

6

LEVELS OF INSTRUCTION

Objective: to provide goals and levels of work instead of time
allowances to assure a developmental educational program of
sequential experiences for all children.

We've talked of eliminating grade level barriers without ex-
plaining sufficiently exactly how this was accomplished. In
previous years we had planned that children be exposed to
certain bodies of knowledge during their years in primary school.
This body of knowledge included facts, concepts, attitudes, and
appreciations in each curricular area. We know that nongrading
our school did not give us carte blanche to eliminate these essentials of learning. We did not say that children were no longer
to be responsible for mastering certain knowledge as a result of
their time in the nongraded. We said instead, as did Anderson,
that children were not to be exposed to forced learning—learning
too difficult for them at a particular stage in their development;
they were not to be exposed to obstructive learning—learning
too elementary for them at a particular stage in their development. It became very clear that children would have to be very
carefully identified at every stage of their development in each
curricular area before we could determine what we were going
to teach them. It is for this reason that so much time and effort
was spent in identifying individual children and their differences
(Chapter 5). Once we identified these children learning experiences had to be selected for them appropriate to their stage
of development.

Before this nongraded criterion had been established, the approach was much simpler. In every grade and in every curricular

area on that grade there was a body of knowledge which it was assumed every child could master. This, of course, was not the case. Children could not master all this knowledge at the exact time that we said they could. In addition, some children were quite capable of learning much more in certain curricular areas than we had permitted them to.

Curricular areas had to be rearranged and restructured. We had to arrange them in levels of ascendancy of difficulty, from the simple to the complex, from the specific to the general. We had to identify the precise level children were capable of functioning at and then we had to match the pupil, his abilities, and the appropriate curricular level. The vastness of this undertaking was understood by all of us. Here is the record of a preliminary discussion held with the faculty.

September 28—Minutes of Primary Meeting

> There was a discussion relating to the actual goals of instruction in every classroom. This is a vast area which will be returned to over and over again during the school year. It was introduced on a more or less philosophical basis at this time. The feeling expressed being that there is increasing evidence to the fact that much which we teach children they already know before they get to us, or they are retaught too many times. There is also a feeling on the part of the administrators that the rote learning of concepts may have replaced the rote learning of facts and this presents a new and different type of instructional problem which will require our attention. These are complicated, involved areas which will require skillful analysis and study by all of us.

To say that we solved many of the curricular problems discussed above in the one year of our nongraded operation would be foolish. We were indeed grateful that all of us even recognized that the problems existed and that it would be many years before we hopefully could begin to scratch the surface of these major problems. But the teachers were aware that such problems existed. In our individual observations of teachers at work with their classes or in our individual appraisals in conferences of their long and short range plans for individuals or groups of children we again and again watched growth in adjustments of program to new instructional goals in classes.

We had always felt that awareness was the first important step in the handling of problems. Here a different group of teachers discussed the same general problem at a meeting the very same week.

September 29—Minutes of Primary Meeting

It is a matter of great concern that all youngsters be exposed to activities and experiences appropriate to their level. Thus, younger children in classes with older children must not, for instance, be exposed to activities beyond their motor capacities. The physical education teacher must be particularly aware of this fact. In the classroom, for example, cursive writing should not be taught to the youngster who though mentally ready and reading at the appropriate level, does not have the requisite motor skills. Also, the reverse, the older child in a class where there are younger children, must be given experiences appropriate to his mental age. If these children are in a reading group which has a mixed age group, they may well require a longer reading period of time than the younger children—their attention span being more mature, etc. The teacher must make these allowances and provide activities for their other younger children. One teacher described some musical activities which she had developed for youngsters of this category while the rest of the group continued with their reading assignment. These are very important factors to be watched by the nongraded teacher and, of course, totally new to all of us, and will need much exploration and trial and error on our part.

One month later, the first specific case of sequential, appropriate levels of instruction was brought to our attention by a group of teachers.

October 20—Minutes of Primary Meeting

We explored the area of penmanship so as to establish certain ground rules for the teachers who have youngsters in their classes who may normally be expected to enter fourth grade next year. It is expected that these youngsters master the skills of cursive writing. Since there are certain youngsters in these classes who will not be expected to enter the fourth grade next year, how do we handle the overall situation? To whom do we teach cursive writing?

Our approach will be the same as that recommended in all areas of study. The youngster going into fourth grade next year will receive formalized instruction in cursive penmanship. Those youngsters who are not ready (poor motor development, etc.) for these experiences will not be so instructed. Those other youngsters in the class, not being directly instructed, who may pick up the techniques of cursive writing through observation and begin to use it correctly will be permitted to continue to use cursive writing wherever comfortable. Any youngster who may pick up incorrect cursive habits from indirect observation will be discouraged from continuing with the use of cursive by the teacher in a discreet manner. Lessons prepared by the teacher for all the children in the class which are dittoed or printed on the chalkboard will be in manuscript. Only those lessons directly relating to the groups learning cursive will be written in cursive form.

We were beginning to differentiate. We were beginning to assign curricular experiences to appropriate levels. In the example above it wasn't long before two of the teachers in individual conferences related that some of their younger children were picking up cursive writing so expertly from their indirect exposure in the classroom that they had decided to include them in the group learning cursive writing formally, although chronologically they might be considered too young for this experience. Of course, here was the gist of the entire matter. Who was to say what child was too young or too old for any experience? These children quite naturally, and without any pressure, demonstrated rather nicely that they were ready for an experience which heretofore they were not permitted to have.

Old shackles and old concepts had to be broken and, as we all knew too well, old habits are hard to break. There was a kind of security in having a grade level designation. Certainly, it was a simpler way to teach. At the beginning of the school year you went to the book room and removed twenty-five second grade readers, social studies and science texts, etc., for your twenty-five children and you were off and running. Now the assignment was much more complex. Your twenty-five children weren't wearing tags and symbols. You couldn't go to the book room for twenty five second grade readers or twenty-five anything. There was a most complicated job you had to accomplish first. You, the teacher, had to assess each child, in each currimular area, and determine his instructional level before you could procure any textbooks for him, or for that matter, before you could plan any instructional program for him. The difference between the first approach and the enormity of the second was so extensive that we are certain the reader needs no further clarification of this point.

What we should like to explore with you first are the methods and means which we used to identify the levels of instruction in each curricular area for each child. We must preface this section of our report with an apology. In our estimation this area of our nongraded plan was, and still is, the weakest, not through any fault of ours, we feel, but rather that this aspect required so much work and study that we did not have the time in our first year of operation to explore it in depth. As we have said, the closing chapters of this book are devoted to problems we encountered and our plans and objectives for future years. It is in those chapters that you will find a more adequate treatment of this area of concern. For the present, let us show you what tools we did use and how.

Reading, the single most important curricular area of the primary school, was handled quite efficiently. We felt that we could not permit ourselves to run a nongraded school without planning for an accurate method of identifying the proper instructional level at which a child was operating. It is of significance to point out here that the major reason that we were able to successfully develop methods and means of identifying a child's instructional level in reading was that we had available to us the services, for two and one-half days a week, of a reading consultant. In other curricular areas we were not so blessed, and all the study and analysis necessary for proper techniques of identification and instruction were accomplished by the faculty alone without the help and guidance of a curricular specialist. Naturally, reading came out ahead of the other curricular areas.

Since reading is the most significant curricular area in a primary school, we counted ourselves quite fortunate.

Reading instructional levels were assigned to children through the use of a number of techniques. First and foremost was the administration (by the teacher) to each child of an Informal Reading Inventory. Simply, this was a technique whereby children read certain passages (arranged from the most simple to the most difficult) both orally and silently. Their silent and oral reading were checked according to specific scales and they were evaluated according to their skill in comprehension, word attack, and oral proficiency. They were assigned a reading level as a result of the scores they achieved on the Informal Reading Inventory and this was the level at which the teacher was to instruct the pupil. This instrument has proven to be remarkably reliable for us in determining the exact and precise level at which a pupil is to be instructed in reading.

The teacher had but to consult the Profile Card for each child in order to determine the recommended reading instructional level for each child. For those children who were entering the primary school from kindergarten, of course, the problem was quite different. Relatively few of these children were actually reading (we had only two such children last year) and some method and means had to be determined for deciding reading instructional levels for these children. Once again, our own former experience provided a good answer for us to this problem. We administered Metropolitan Readiness Tests[1] to all kindergarten children in the very late spring. We had learned that three aspects of the scores on the Metropolitan had relevance for us. We took a mean average of these three sub test scores and assigned a numerical ranking number to each child. Children were then grouped into four quartiles: those with the highest scores being ready to read, those with the high average scores being ready for a short readiness program, those with low average scores being ready for an average readiness program, those with

---

[1] *Metropolitan Readiness Test*—Form R (New York, N.Y.: Harcourt, Brace and World, 1949).

the lowest scores being ready for what we termed "an extended readiness program" (described more fully in Chapter 7). Here too we have found our predictions of instructional levels worked rather well. The total error in prediction was approximately ten children out of two hundred.

The reading levels used throughout the primary school looked like this:

Level One ....Extended Readiness

Level Two ....Reading Readiness, Concrete Experiences

Level Three ....Reading Readiness, Written Experiences

Level Four ....Pre-Primer

Level Five ....Primer

Level Six ....Skills formerly associated with first grade, second half readers

Level Seven ....Skills formerly associated with second grade, first half readers

Level Eight ....Skills formerly associated with second grade, second half readers

Level Nine ....Skills formerly associated with third grade, first half readers

Level Ten ....Skills formerly associated with third grade, second half readers

Level Eleven ....Skills formerly associated with fourth grade, first half readers

Level Twelve ....Skills formerly associated with fourth grade, second half readers and above

If you are wondering why we described our reading levels with graded terminology, let us quickly explain that in our discussions and work we actually referred to only the level designations. We were, however, bound by the graded designations somewhat since the materials (which we used in reading instruction) had the skills and appreciations (which we expected at each level) assigned to grade level texts as we have outlined them above. Textbook manufacturers are still using graded designations and until such time as they discontinue this practice, this becomes the only descriptive manner left at our disposal. In other words, the skills and appreciations which we wished to teach on level eight in the primary school were found in the texts of the major publishers in books labeled Grade Two, second half. Our specific goals and objectives at level eight were clearly defined as they were for all levels in reading (see Reading Level Skills, Appendix, p. 192). This was the result of the work done by our district reading curricular people and published in their guide. The specific goals and levels selected for instructional purposes in our school, however, were a result of the direct efforts of our own reading consultant, Mrs. W. These were very specific skills and experiences a pupil was expected to master before we permitted him to proceed to the next instructional level in reading.

As you can see the reading instruction level was not determined by age or number of years in school. A pupil could be eight years of age, six years of age, or seven years of age and still be functioning on level eight in reading (see Nongraded Grouping Chart, p. 25). An instructional level was assigned to a pupil which was commensurate with his ability, needs, interests, and capabilities; his chronological age did not enter into this assignment; his class placement did not enter into this assignment (though we have previously demonstrated how we did attempt to place sub groups of children functioning at similar instructional levels within one class); and, finally, we did not expect that a pupil proceed from one instructional level to another in any specific period of time.

In mathematics the assessment of instructional levels was also relatively simple for us. The district curricular committee in mathematics had completed some two years previously a rather concise guide to levels of instruction in the eight broad structural areas of mathematics. The year before, we had conducted an extensive search for mathematics materials which were consistent with the sequential, structured mathematics program outlined in our district curriculum. The result of our search had been the selection of the Greater Cleveland Mathematics Program for use in our school. This math program and the materials developed by these people seemed to suit our instructional needs most admirably. Our teachers had been using the GCMP program for one full year before the onset of the nongraded program and were quite conversant with all the materials. Quite simply what we said was that the GCMP program was sequentially developed and we used their level designations for determining the instructional level of each pupil.

Level One—GCMP	Readiness, Concrete Experiences
Level Two—GCMP	Readiness, Number Experiences
Level Three—GCMP	First Grade, first half
Level Four—GCMP	First Grade, second half
Level Five—GCMP	Second Grade, first half
Level Six—GCMP	Second Grade, second half
Level Seven—GCMP	Third Grade, first half
Level Eight—GCMP	Third Grade, second half
Level Nine—GCMP	Fourth Grade, first half
Level Ten—GCMP	Fourth Grade, second half and above

In other words, the GCMP graded representations corresponded to the skills and concepts which we expected to be mastered at the levels shown above. In both the case of reading and mathematics levels, pupils not only had an assigned instructional level, but also at the beginning of the school year they continued at precisely that point within their instructional level at which they left off at the end of June. This point was carefully identified on the pupil's records for the edification of his next year's teacher (if he experienced a change of teacher). This was done in order to insure that continuous, uninterrupted learning took place.

In other instructional areas, language arts, science, and social studies, we have not established instructional levels to date, though this represents part of our planning for the future. We approached the subject differently. To begin with, there were excellent curricula in language arts, science, and social studies in print in our district and, of course, each teacher had a desk copy available. Each subject matter curriculum was developed sequentially and conceptually. There were specific goals and objectives listed for each learning area. More specifically, there were skills and concepts identified for instructional purposes (Appendix, Social Studies Skills, p. 214). Children were expected to have been exposed to experiences provided for them by their teachers which would represent those specific skills and concepts. For instance, all children were to have an awareness of the interdependency of man on a universal level; all children were to be capable of certain proficiency in library research. We accepted the goals and objectives of these curricula as they were. We then assigned to each year of the primary school certain topics for study, expecting that the classroom teacher would provide within these topics of study for the appropriate skills and concepts relevant to the abilities, needs, interests, and capabilities of the children in her class (Appendix, Unit Titles, p. 283). For instance, in the second year of primary school, the social studies topic, "Community Helpers" (Appendix, Unit of Study, p. 273) is listed. There were quite definite concepts (described in the curriculum guide) which could be taught during a unit of study on community helpers—man's interdependence, the need for government and organization, the meaning of urbanization, etc. (Appendix, Multi-Disciplinary Approach, p. 279). There were also quite definitive skills which could be taught throughout this same unit of study, depending upon the readiness of the children—the library as a research center, interviewing for information, looking up information in an encyclopedia, etc. In social studies, there was a total of some five through ten topics of study outlined for

Culminating activity-
Social studies unit on early
American settlements

Illustrating a social
studies project

Early readiness activity

each year of the nongraded program (see Appendix, Scope and Sequence Chart, p. 201). Alternate topics, which could be used to teach the same skills and concepts, were also available in case any pupil had already been exposed to any of the suggested topics. Teachers were expected, on their own, to select the appropriate skills and concepts from the curricular guide which were to be taught in connection with these topics and to arrange them sequentially in units of study (Appendix, Social Studies Skills, p. 214) throughout the progress of the school year. They were also expected to differentiate their instruction for pupils who were on different levels of instruction in the class though all the children were studying the same major topic at the same time (Appendix, Unit of Study, p. 273).

Differentiated instruction within the same topics of study was as close as we came to the actual assignment of instructional levels in these curricular areas. The future will illustrate whether instructional level assignations will prove to be necessary in the nongraded program for these other curricular areas. We are not prepared to make any predictions. As in all our nongraded plans, the pulse of the teachers was the chief barometer we read. To date, the teachers have not had enough time to assess the need for more definitive instructional level identification in these other curricular areas. However, they did certainly evidence awareness of the problem and it came up for discussion in various ways during the course of the year. As witness this discussion.

November 5—Minutes of Primary Meeting

> Discussion centered around facts and concepts, the amount, number, and type of facts which are necessary for a child to understand a concept; how many times the child must be re-exposed to a fact or concept; how we know whether he was exposed to this fact or concept before; how much the teacher should directly teach to children as a total group; how much group work should be encouraged; what basic ground work of knowledge the teacher should provide for the youngster; the development of work study skills through the social studies; the development of

reason and logic through the social studies; how much a child should be encouraged to explore on his own.

Our objective was to provide goals and levels of achievement instead of time allowances to assure a developmental, sequential learning program for all children. We have been partially successful in reading and mathematics (though still somewhat grade bound) and have come part of the way in the other curricular areas. In the other curricular areas, instructional levels have not as yet been developed, nor are we sure that they will ever really be necessary. However, instructional goals and levels of achievement have been established on a yearly basis with individuated and differentiated instruction being stressed to allow for the differences in learning among the children in each class. We have included two additional chapters devoted to curricular adaptations which will more precisely demonstrate how teachers did differentiate their instruction in these other subject matter areas.

7

DIFFERENTIATED INSTRUCTIONAL
PROGRAMS

Objective: to provide increased opportunities for staff members to fulfill the individual instructional needs of their children.

The establishment of instructional levels in curricular areas was the first step in the complex procedure of adjusting teaching programs to the individual needs of children. Once a teacher was aware of the placement of each pupil in each curricular area, her work was just beginning. It was then up to her to evaluate each child, his abilities and interests, and hand tailor a program for him in each curricular area. That is not to say that all children were to be taught individually all the time. We had so grouped our classes that there would be certain similarities of abilities among certain children in each class to facilitate some degree of sub-grouping for instruction. What happened in actuality was something like this. A teacher would instruct three or four reading groups, each group operating on a different achievement level. The number of groups in mathematics would be smaller and in the other curricular areas she would adjust assignments to the level of each individual child. In the course of much of this sub-grouping, re-grouping, identification of levels, and individualized assignments, the teachers became more and more aware of individualized instructional problems within levels which they brought to our attention and for which specialized programs were designed. One such instructional problem you can follow from the minutes as the story unfolds.

The Immature Child

September 22—Minutes of Primary Meeting

This meeting concerned itself with the immaturity of some of the youngsters coming from the kindergarten classes and placed in primary classes. This is the children's first exposure to a full school day. Most of the teachers found, therefore, that they had to make, and are still making, great allowance for this fact. They are increasing the amount of time for rest during the school day. They are also placing greater emphasis in their curriculum on play and play activities and the larger gross motor activities for these children.

October 6—Minutes of Primary Meeting

The group once again returned to the problem of the immaturity of a number of their children and to specific techniques for alleviating some of these problems. Specifically the types of reactions which these teachers were referring to were: the inability to sit still for adequate lengths of time, the inability to concentrate on an activity for an adequate length of time, the inability to follow directions, the inability to listen, the inability to respect the rights of others, the inability to work in groups, the inability to get along with one's peers, the inability to make decisions. Because so many, if not all, of the aforementioned abilities are crucial to learning, the teachers are planning work in these classrooms specifically designed to give the youngsters practice in these necessary learning skills. Of course, all of this perforce necessitates a slower start in the early stages of a reading program. The pacing may well be slower, but the ultimate goals of the reading program will be better met by establishing these learning patterns first. The meeting closed with the suggestion that a meeting be held with the kindergarten teachers. On the agenda will be techniques for working with the immature child and providing special activities for same.

November 17—Minutes of Special Meeting Held with Early Primary Teachers and Kindergarten Teachers

In general it is our over-all opinion that some of the children we are receiving in kindergarten and first year of primary school are becoming progressively more immature, lack the proper manipulative skills, lack training in personal habits (buttoning, etc.), have a poor attention span, seem to be somewhat insecure, do not follow directions well, do not sit still, etc. They seem to be displaying many symptoms indicative of the fact that they are generally less well prepared to start formalized schooling and learning, although essentially they are bright youngsters and verbally precocious.

This problem is increasing somewhat in intensity and we have devised a program which we hope will be helpful to these youngsters and their development. Mrs. H., one of our kindergarten teachers, will conduct a series of four workshops devoted to mothers and the home environment. These workshops will be held on Wednesdays, December 2nd, January 13th, May 5th, and June 2nd at the Old Bethpage School from 1:30 P.M. through 3:00 P.M. (while the children are still in school). The two Fall Workshops will have as participants the invited mothers of our current kindergarten children. The two Spring Workshops will add to their list of participants by inviting, in addition, all the mothers of our following year's kindergartners.

These workshops will have as their over-all goal the more successful preparation of children for beginning school experiences. It will be designed to be helpful to parents by giving them specific ideas and suggestions for handling their youngsters at home before they are ready to enter school. We will call the workshops, "Getting Children Ready for School." Mrs. H. is especially well equipped to handle these workshops because of her own extensive background with very young children, her own devotion and understanding of the very young child, and her community image which is so outstanding. The parents of the Old Bethpage area hold her in extremely high esteem and we can think of no one who could successfully offer this type of program as discreetly and diplomatically as Mrs. H.

The areas which will be covered are getting ready for writing, getting ready for mathematics, getting ready for reading, getting ready for manipulative skills, getting ready for getting along with other children, and getting ready for teacher and class. Mrs. H. will use a variety of methods and techniques to develop her program, one of which will be having the parents perform some of the activities which she will suggest for the children themselves.

The discussion which all of us held was quite lively since the immaturity of some of our youngsters is beginning to be a problem for us and we welcome any effort to improve the situation. Just so long as we have to delay the learning situation in class and continue to provide the pupils with experiences which they should have already been exposed to at home, we shall have increased difficulties. Below is a random list of the thoughts which we bandied around as possible suggestions and guides for Mrs. H. in planning her workshop series:

1. There seems to be pressure from parents to have children perform well in school. This is a college oriented community. Thus, there seems to be emphasis on providing experiences which the parents think will help the children to learn (memorizing the alphabet, etc.) and a neglect of the normal functions which children need to master before they can begin formal learning.

2. There has been observation of the fact that parents find it increasingly difficult to release their children for school without emotional reactions which they foster even if the the child makes the adjustment with ease.

3. Some children seem to be showing a need for actual physical love which is a stage they should be past by the time they are in school (climbing on lap, etc.).

4. There is evidence in some homes of the separation of parents from children to their own areas of house (family room), less sharing of total family activities in this type of set up. Children seem to represent a burden and an intrusion, at times, into parents' programs and needs for themselves. One example of this need is the children's birthday party which is now turning out to be a coffee hour for mothers.

5. In the rush of living and getting everything done today, some parents are doing too much for children (tying laces, putting toys aways, etc.) since it takes less time to perform these activities for children than to permit children to do them themselves. This is a hindrance in efforts to have children learn to do things for themselves and to have children learn to be responsible for themselves.

6. In general, the feeling is that the parents will welcome any

concrete suggestions which will be offered to help them in rearing their young since they themselves are not too sure of what's right and what's good for children, and since there is so much conflicting evidence around today in books and magazines.

7. There is much evidence to support feeling that certain activities (needed by youngsters for their development) which are dirty or dirt producing are being prohibited in the home (digging, painting, clay work, etc.).

8. The youngster who is raised in an over protected environment lives in a sterile situation and cannot really be creative since the atmosphere is stifling to real feeling and emotions.

9. Some children need more spiritual development, training in an appreciation of beauty in things around them (picking flowers, etc.). Our emphasis seems to be on the materialistic with little time for the other senses and their development.

10. Children are not culturally deprived. They have the travel and wide experiences which parents provide; they are sold short on the home experiences, the small experiences which children need to have.

Additional thoughts and suggestions which any of us may have about these workshops will be placed in Mrs. H.'s mail box.

The most important caution which Mrs. H. emphasized herself is the realization of the delicacy with which these workshops must be handled. The parents must not be put on the defensive or made to feel guilty. They must be reassured and helped to find the proper and helpful roads for their children since their intentions are good.

December 15—Minutes of Primary Meeting

A lengthy discussion followed relating to the immature learner. This type of youngster is not to be equated with the extended readiness learner, but is rather a child with average or above average ability who doesn't seem to be ready for formal learning activities. He lacks attention, is constantly fidgeting and restless, lacks self-discipline, cannot work in a group, cannot work alone, doesn't know how to listen. In general, the best approach to this youngster is on the one to one basis, but, of course, this isn't consistently possible in a class situation. Thus we have been discussing ways and means to approach this type of youngster and involve him in a productive learning situation.

Some factors brought out were the need for structure which these children evidence. Mrs. T., in particular, stressed the necessity for establishing firm routines and organizational patterns with these children to give them the security and framework within which to function. She emphasized how hard it is to establish these patterns with the children and how long it takes, but stated that now that her class is firmly in hand and understands the structural pattern in which they must function, better and productive learning is taking place.

Mr. F. talked about the amount of direction and talking to which some of these children are subjected at home. He feels that possibly we just compound the felony with these youngsters by placing them in further teacher-directed activities and in further discussion situations. He feels strongly that there is too much emphasis upon teacher directed activities with these youngsters and too much discussion. What these children need is more doing, manipulating, and participating on a direct level in first hand experiences and activities. The teacher should, therefore, be thinking in terms of many differentiated experiences and activities of interest to these youngsters and giving them a chance to do them.

Mrs. B. mentioned how valuable she is finding creative dance as a "doing" activity for these children. They are given a chance to move their bodies freely and yet within the structure and confines of the music played.

There is also a question of program planning and timing. It is possible that pursuing the basic academic program during the morning and leaving the other activities for the afternoon makes for a poor balance so that in the afternoon the children find it difficult to sit still and concentrate, etc. Perhaps, interspersing some other experiences (other than reading, mathematics, and language arts) in the morning might be helpful for these children.

The story almost told itself. Some five teachers became increasingly aware that some of their children were socially and emotionally immature, too immature to begin formal learning. They were sensitive enough to the situation to recognize that no amount of pressuring of these pupils was going to help the learning situation. These children, all of them above average or average intelligence, needed more pre-school and kindergarten experience before they could begin formal learning. This they proceeded to provide them. However, they became increasingly concerned lest this pattern continue with other children coming to school. They also felt that they wished to understand the kindergarten teachers reactions to their problems and asked for a meeting with them. The meeting was an eye opener. The kindergarten teachers confirmed everything these teachers said. They further clarified the kinds of immature behavior they were encountering with these children in kindergarten. Their experiences showed that they were being forced to offer some children pre-school experiences in kindergarten which made it necessary for the primary teachers to offer kindergarten experiences in the primary school. After a great deal of discussion, all felt that some of the onus rested with the home. Parents were genuinely misguided in their well intentioned efforts with their children. They were generally providing their little ones with the incorrect types of home experiences. Perhaps, they all said, if we can carefully explain to them the real needs of a child, they will be more cooperative at home in fulfilling these real needs. No one felt this was an easy task, and we still do not. However, efforts were going to be made. And the teachers planned a workshop for parents of young children—an experience they plan to continue offering in the years to come. So from all sides, an instructional problem was attacked. The teachers worked out special programs and experiences for these children in school, and the parents were instructed and hopefully began to offer better experiences for the children at home. This story is a good example of special planning for special children. It is also, however, an example of how our meetings with teachers encouraged group solutions of problems and group actions. Throughout most of the discussions held on this topic, the administrators offered encouragement and support; but the problem was brought up by the teachers, discussed by the teachers, and operated by the teachers. We think this is the fact about which we were most pleased.

Another instructional problem was brought to our attention by the primary teachers and also resulted in a special program being planned for certain children.

Extended Readiness Program

October 20—Minutes of Primary Meeting

There are certain youngsters who have begun to be identified as requiring an extended readiness program. These are pupils who have vision difficulties, eye coordination difficulties, short attention span, motor coordination difficulties, etc. They are youngsters who do not require a full second year of kindergarten experiences, but an increased and intensified program of readiness experiences and gross and refined motor activities before starting a formal reading readiness program. There are two such youngsters in Mrs. F.'s class and one in Mrs. G.'s class. At this meeting, Mrs. E. identified four such children in her class, Mrs. A. four in her class, Mrs. C. five in her class, Mrs. B. one in her class. This makes a total of seventeen pupils out of a total of approximately one hundred eighty children at this age level.

What can we do to help these pupils? The first suggestion was that we regroup these children into three classes, giving each child a working group and a teacher the chance to develop a special program for this group, treating them as a separate reading group. All the teachers have been requested to carefully re-evaluate these children and we shall come to a decision at the next meeting on the disposition of this matter. The district kindergarten reading readiness form was recommended for use (see Appendix, Kindergarten Check Sheet for Reading Readiness, p. 203).

If we make the decision to move these children into two classes, Mrs. E. and Mrs. A. have volunteered to welcome these children into their classes. Mrs. B. indicated that she would have room to accommodate any pupils who may be shifted, into her class, since she has lost four children from her register who have moved out of the district.

October 27—Minutes of Primary Meeting

There are a total of seventeen children revealed and confirmed as requiring an extended readiness program. We have decided to move these children into two classes with Mrs. E. and Mrs. A. A few pupils will require movement to other classes to accommodate these children and they are going to Mrs. B. who has room for them and appropriate groups. Mrs. C. will keep and continue to work with her five extended readiness children.

At this time there was much action and planning. There was a great effort made at providing a very special program for these children. The program included many experiences taken from the Montessori method and from a neighboring school district which operated an experimental extended readiness program for just such children. The director of this program, Mrs. Phoebe Lazarus, was invited to speak to our teachers and she demonstrated many of the kinesthetic techniques and methods that they had developed for use with these children, and which we borrowed liberally. In addition, one of our teachers, a very gifted woman indeed, who had a special interest in this type of child developed many of her own highly imaginative materials for use with these children which she constantly shared with the other teachers. The administrators explored in depth the catalogs of the major manufacturers and ordered some two hundred dollars worth of materials, equipment, and games designed to give these children the kinds of concrete kinesthetic experiences they required before they could learn to read.

November 19—Minutes of Primary Meeting

Seventeen of our youngsters have been identified as qualifying for an extended readiness program before formal reading can take place. These pupils have been grouped together in three classes where specific activities and experiences are being provided to satisfy their needs.

We wished to take a careful look at the records of these children to see if there was anything in their past record or performance in kindergarten which would make it possible for us to spot these children and group them together for instructional purposes (next year) in the Primary School. Were there any specific characteristics which we could identify at the end of the school year which would be helpful in identifying these pupils and would help us in grouping for the following years?

These teachers were not content to handle these children and their problems at the moment. They looked for ways and means of providing for other such children in years to come. The theorists have said that most of us make "satisficing decisions," decisions designed to handle the situation at the moment; certainly this was an excellent example of a group who was concerned with tomorrow. Further time and effort was devoted to studying ways and means of identifying these children before they entered the primary school. The results are reported in the minutes:

November 27—Minutes of Primary Meeting

All children in the kindergarten last May were administered (under very careful conditions supervised by Miss C.) a Metropolitan Readiness Test. This test was selected because of its high degree of accuracy in predicting future academic achievement.

A careful analysis was made of these test scores and certain factors became evident. There were recurrent factors evident in the test scores of these seventeen pupils which we could have used to help identify them as children who would have required extended readiness programs.

However, using these criteria we would also have had added to the list, eleven additional children who would have looked like extended readiness candidates. Discussion with the teachers of these eleven pupils revealed that five of these children did require a limited extended readiness program at the beginning of the school year, but are now well along the way academically. The other six children adjusted to the reading program without any extended readiness experiences.

There was some indication that I.Q. tests might be used to help identify the future achievement levels of youngsters in kindergarten. This was disputed: one, because of the variability of test scores on a group basis administered in the kindergarten; two, because the Metropolitan Readiness Test has been shown to be the best instrument to date for this use.

The conclusion was then that we will use the test data from the Metropolitan Readiness Test as the basis for identifying children who require an extended readiness program. We will group these children together in classes which will also contain an average readiness group to enable the teacher to shift those children who may be incorrectly diagnosed into the higher group without any discomfiture on the teacher's or child's part.

Specific and detailed directions for administering, scoring, and interpreting the Metropolitan Test data will be made available to all the kindergarten teachers at primary meetings to insure the best possible identification of children's future academic level of achievement, since this makes for the best possible grouping arrangements for optimum instructional purposes.

Identification and provision was once again made for a group of children requiring a differentiated instructional program. It was our considered opinion that had either the group of above average immature children (a small number of children within reading level two), or average extended readiness children (a small number of children within reading level one) been exposed to the same readiness and beginning reading programs offered to other pupils on their levels, without adequate provision for their specific needs, they would not have completed a very successful first year in the primary school. As it was, we can happily report that except for two children, these group programs bore fine results. The children responded well to the experiences and proceeded to formal reading and are all doing rather nicely. The two children who did not have as successful an experience, are pupils now clearly identified as having emotional and/or psychological problems which seem to be complicating the learning situation even further.

The Range of Reading Levels

The area over which we kept closest watch was reading. We felt reading was the hard core of our program, but more relevantly we had amassed records in the past in reading with which we could make some comparisons. The comparisons which we shall be discussing, let us say from the first, are not valid or reliable from the point of view of research. However, there is a research paradigm for longitudinal studies which can be used to validate our findings once another analysis of scores is made two years from now. At this time, our statistics provide us with clues and insights into what is occurring at the Old Bethpage School and it is for this reason that we present them here. The figures below all report the instructional reading level of children in our school as reported by teachers in June of 1963 and June of 1965. June, 1963, of course, represents our school one year before we began to talk about nongrading. June, 1965 represents our school at the end of the first year of the operating nongraded primary school. The figures are compiled from the records and Profile Cards which we keep on file for each pupil. The figures and level designations for each child are accurate and represent the actual functioning level of each child in reading.

READING INSTRUCTIONAL LEVELS

JUNE 1963 FIRST GRADE—134 children		JUNE 1965 FIRST YEAR PRIMARY— 207 children	
Level 4	8 children	Level 3	1 child
Level 5	33 children	Level 4	36 children
Level 6	93 children	Level 5	50 children
		Level 6	64 children
		Level 7	43 children
		Level 8	4 children
		Level 9	6 children
		Level 10	—
		Level 11	1 child
		Level 12	2 children

JUNE 1963		JUNE 1965	
SECOND GRADE—155 children		SECOND YEAR PRIMARY —129 children	
Level 5	5 children	Level 5	6 children
Level 6	11 children	Level 6	17 children
Level 7	39 children	Level 7	38 children
Level 8	67 children	Level 8	32 children
Level 9	33 children	Level 9	25 children
		Level 10	9 children
		Level 11	2 children

JUNE 1963		JUNE 1965	
THIRD GRADE—156 children		THIRD YEAR PRIMARY— 120 children	
Level 6	4 children	Level 5	1 child
Level 7	4 children	Level 6	2 children
Level 8	4 children	Level 7	5 children
Level 9	28 children	Level 8	8 children
Level 10	64 children	Level 9	24 children
Level 11	31 children	Level 10	18 children
Level 12	21 children	Level 11	21 children
		Level 12	30 children
		Level 13	6 children
		Level 14	5 children

Fig. 7-1.

PERCENTAGE CONVERSIONS

JUNE 1963 — FIRST GRADE

6% of the children were designated as below grade.
94% of the children were designated as on grade.
0% of the children were designated as above grade.

JUNE 1965 — FIRST YEAR PRIMARY

17% of the children were designated as below grade
55% of the children were designated as on grade
27% of the children were designated as above grade

Thus there is an increase of 11% in below grade readers, which incidentally, is a more realistic and consistent figure for our building than the 6% so identified back in 1963. You can assume that what happened was that in 1963 some of the below level readers were not accurately identified. In addition, the change from no children identified as above grade back in 1963 to 27% of the children so identified in 1965 is, of course, wonderful. It is not saying too much to realize that there must have been above level readers in 1963, but we were still not identifying them sufficiently.

JUNE 1963 – SECOND GRADE
10% of the children identified as below grade
68% of the children identified as on grade
21% of the children identified as above grade

JUNE 1965 – SECOND YEAR PRIMARY
18% of the children identified as below grade
54% of the children identified as on grade
27% of the children identified as above grade

Once again, the increase of 8% in below level children and the increase of 6% in above level children more closely approximates the school picture as we have come to recognize it.

JUNE 1963 – THIRD GRADE
8% of the children identified as below grade
59% of the children identified as on grade
33% of the children identified as above grade

JUNE 1965 – THIRD YEAR PRIMARY
13% of the children identified as below grade
35% of the children identified as on grade
51% of the children identified as above grade

Fig. 7-2.

Again dramatically sharp increases indicate a more realistic and accurate identification of children and their functioning levels than was present back in 1963. Below level increased 5%, and above level increased 18%.

A quick perusal of the figures and percentages bears out our contention that the teachers were becoming more and more aware of the differences among children and providing programs adapted to their needs. The range of reading levels extended dramatically by the end of the first year. Teachers were instructing their children on many more differentiated reading levels. There was much closer recognition and more careful identification of these levels and much more adaptation of programs to these differences. Although teachers started with three reading groups in their classes, they were adjusting their programs within these sub groups to individual children so that the children were doing work more consistent with their actual abilities. If our objective was the fulfillment of individual instructional needs of all children, here indeed was proof that in reading, at least, this major objective was beginning to take shape. Other curricular areas showed evidence of changes also, but the reader will have to take our word for this since we do not have past figures with which to make comparisons, though we have begun to compile them for future studies. Chapter 11 of this book will discuss in more detail some of these other curricular adaptations.

8

CHILDREN WHO LEARN SLOWLY

Objective: to provide an organizational program for slow learners without the dangers characteristic of continuous failure.

Certainly every school has its proportion of children who are slow learners. Any administrator will talk to you about efforts which are made in his school to find these children and provide programs for them. In the nongraded we found we were able to identify slow learners at an earlier stage in their school careers. These children stood out more clearly and teachers identified them rather quickly as you have already seen. Early identification was but the first step. Step two concerned itself with finding reasons, wherever possible, for the pupil's slow rate of learning. Step three, the most important step, concerned itself with providing a learning program for the slow learner with full awareness of the reasons for his problems.

A child could learn slowly for a host of reasons. There could be psychological or emotional variables which confounded his learning ability. Children who showed evidence of having their learning abilities impaired for psychological or emotional reasons were scrutinized carefully by all the professionals at our resource. Essentially the school psychologist was in charge of these investigations. Once the source of a child's problem was determined, all the machinery at our disposal was brought to bear in an effort to help alleviate the source of the difficulties. Often the parents were called in and special arrangements were made for helping the youngster and additional professional help from outside the school itself was procured.

No matter how much help we procured from outside, the direct responsibility for each child still rested with us and more directly with the classroom teacher. Our teachers were always aware of this responsibility and many hours were devoted to discussions and plans for children with learning problems of this nature. Listen to one such generalized discussion held by a group of teachers.

April 6—Minutes of Primary Meeting

The slow starter—lengthy discussion followed about children who start late, or mature more slowly, or who are slow learners. Many of these youngsters, it has been found, have a poor self image. If a real situation can be created which will give this type of child a meaningful place in the sun, his self-image improves greatly and it reflects a corollary improvement in academic learning. Two examples were given. Kenneth S., because of his physical agility, has become the star of the physical education show. Mr. L., physical education instructor, has worked long and hard to build this youngster's ego. Subsequently, Kenneth's class work is now improving. Stuart N., who had the lead in his class play, has gained more respect from his classmates and is now improving in his academic work.

The teachers all agreed if you can find some strength that a child possesses and capitalize on this strength we could do much to improve the child's opinion of himself and his academic work in the classroom. Some suggestions were made: roles in class plays, performance in other areas in which a child excels, using the youngster to demonstrate a particular area in which he is expert. It was noted here that for many of the youngsters, the nongraded primary interage class has proved a boon. Since there are older children in a class, the younger children tend to look up to them because of their age and physical maturity for guidance and leadership. These children in graded classes with peers do not have this opportunity for leadership.

Just as there were psychological or emotional reasons for a pupil being a slow learner, there were too, very often, mental reasons. The child was a slow learner simply because it was inherent in his nature to be a slow learner. These children were also the cause of much concern on our part. We determined that we would try our best to do something special for them. Our teachers once again gave us the lead.

December 14—Minutes of Primary Meeting

There was a long, generalized discussion about many of the areas of reading. The remedial reader was brought up, especially as we see him in secondary school. It was the expressed feeling of this group that these children should have been helped in the elementary school, long before they became advanced problems.

Home tutoring was discussed with the statement being generally accepted that often this experience doesn't change the total remedial picture. Too often the pupil will do well on the one to one basis with the private tutor but does not transfer the learning to the group situation.

The fact was discussed that often the mechanics of reading are mastered, but there is difficulty with the comprehension. Specific skills such as foreshadowing, predicting, inferring, getting the main idea, etc., are being handled very poorly by many of the pupils.

Mrs. W. felt that in some instances there is too much emphasis on word attack skills. That perhaps phonic skills can be overstressed, particularly in the case of the child who cannot handle the fifth step of the phonic approach—blending. If there is no synthesis of the total experience, then it is evident that the phonics skill proficiency does not serve any real purpose.

Vocabulary and word meaning is another area which seems to need much work, since this is the fore step to a good program of comprehension. Additional experiences emphasizing the multi meanings of a word need to be stressed.

Activities for increasing the comprehension of reading material, specific exercises to increase critical thinking in reading must be developed, activities, that is, which go beyond the ones suggested in the basal texts.

Reference was also made to the use of pictures in texts, their overuse for contextual clues in primary grades, and their nonuse for analysis skills in the upper grades being the main points here emphasized.

Reading for pleasure needs more emphasis, the sheer reading for the delight of it needs more emphasis at all ages.

We all agreed that in reading there is a different approach which works for each child and determining which approach is

Dramatic play in the kindergarten

Creative dance practice

the correct one is the most difficult area for all of us. We know
that what works with one child will not work with another. Probably, the safest approach for each individual child is a combination of methods. Then, if one doesn't work, another will.

Some time passed and teachers continued to work out some
of their problems with slow learners. Different approaches were
tried and different methods for determining the exact cause of a
youngster's reading problems.

January 2—Minutes of Primary Meeting

We continued to discuss methods relevant to identification of
reasons for reading problems encountered by certain children.
Whenever and wherever, identification should be as early as possible and as soon as possible in a child's school career. In line
with this, kindergarten teachers are being asked to use increased
criteria for identification of children's abilities: auditory discrimination, vision, eye-hand coordination, muscular coordination, etc.
(see Kindergarten Reading Readiness Chart, Appendix, p. 203).

We have also started to use the Keystone Visual Survey Test
with the #46 Visual Survey Telebinocular. This is an effort to
identify youngsters who may have fusion difficulties which would
hinder reading since these youngsters are not able to fuse both
eyes and thus cannot see the letter properly; far point and near
point difficulties which hinder chalkboard and book work can also
be uncovered with this test.

It is important to note that difficulties that children may have
in these areas, once identified, require medical advice from
opthamologists, not all of whom seem to be aware of the connection between these vision difficulties and reading difficulties.
We do know that some children require help along these lines
and will make every effort to enlist the cooperation of the home
if such difficulties are uncovered.

The test and its uses for diagnostic purposes was demonstrated
by Mrs. W., our reading consultant.

During a meeting held on January 16, this topic was still being
avidly pursued and a new technique for uncovering beginning
reading difficulties was presented which was the result of a
doctoral study in outline form being conducted by Mr. Vincent

Farone which he calls the Primary Informal Reading Readiness Inventory.

It became more and more evident that reading was the major area with which we were going to have to be concerned as far as the slow learner was concerned. It seemed obvious that these children could not really do well in any academic area if they had difficulties in reading. Thus, in late January, we determined to systematically and accurately test and analyze all children identified as slow learners, reading being the criterion, in all our classes. We used every tool at our disposal. It took us two months of devoted, intensive work to complete our analysis. We evaluated the status of some fifty-one children in the primary school. Every effort was made to concentrate on the academic difficulties themselves. Psychological and emotional problems had been carefully assessed and children's difficulties along these lines were being met in other ways. We were concerned with learning difficulties and it was upon these that we focused.

After two months, all fifty-one children had been examined and a detailed report was issued by the reading consultant. We knew whatever we could about the types and kinds of learning difficulties each child possessed. We then set about to outline a detailed program of action for each such child. It would be boring indeed to inflict upon the reader evidence of each and every case explored; we shall instead demonstrate with just a few cases selected at random.

Individualized Reading Programs in the Nongraded Program

Sally L.

Background: Vision 20/20, hearing normal, telebinocular normal. Sally attended summer reading clinic with recommendation for instruction on level five. Frustrated on this level when tested with Informal Reading Inventory, teacher substantiates this finding.

She is unable to read with the use of phonics, even after special summer help. Her maturation is slow and spotty.

Recommendation: An experience approach should be used to build a basic sight vocabulary of interest. In addition, tracing as a method should be used with all new words taught. Work in phonics should not be given.

Bert W.

Background: Vision 20/30 in both eyes. Hearing normal. Results of telebinocular tests indicate difficulty with fusion at near point and far point and steriopsis at near point. Should be rechecked by physician. Parents to be contacted. Frustrated at level seven on the Informal Reading Inventory. Bert is a small boy whose birthday is in December (our entrance cutoff date is December 30). He is also immature. He does not smile or appear happy. He knows initial consonants but not final ones. He needs more work on vowels.

Recommendation: *Phonics A* and Developmental Reading Series *Up and Away.*

Arnold S.

Background: Frustrated on the pre-primer level on the Informal Reading Inventory. Arnold has no word attack skills. He has no recognition of the same word in capitalized form (Down, down). He attended summer reading clinic and made some gains in initial consonants. However, from an analysis of the McKee Phonic Inventory, he still lacks most phonic and structural

elements. He is reading in the third pre-
primer in class and memorizes much of
what he knows.

Recommendation: Arnold has not been able to learn to read
by the phonics approach. A complete ex-
perience approach should be tried with
him. Short interesting stories should be
read to him, and he should dictate these
back to the teacher in his own words. The
teacher should then write them on experience paper for him to copy in his notebook.
He should then take these home to read
and bring back to class again to reread. The
kinesthetic approach should also be tried
with this child. Serious consideration
should be given to keeping Arnold in the
primary school for a fourth year.

There were forty-eight additional miniature case studies of
children showing difficulties with reading. Each child was subjected to a rigorous and thorough examination. We used all our
resources and attempted to determine the sources of their difficulties. Each child was different. Some had difficulties with
comprehension, some with word attack skills, some with sight
vocabulary, etc., but none of them were doing as well as we
would have liked. As soon as a child was thoroughly analyzed,
an individual conference, the second one in each case, was held
with the classroom teacher. Together the classroom teacher and
the reading consultant mapped out a program of attack for the
child. Each program was as different as each child's problem.

The slow learner was up for scrutiny. We never felt that he
didn't have to be a slow learner. We did say that, perhaps, there
were techniques or methods we could try with the slow learning
youngster which would provide him with better skills and proficiency in learning. Maybe we could help him. Maybe zeroing in
on him as an individual as early as possible and designing a hand
tailored program for him would help him overcome his difficulties in learning. Certainly, none could say our efforts were worth-

less. Two pupils, as a result of the telebinocular test, revealed vision difficulties not ordinarily obvious with Snellen Eye Tests. These children were taken by their parents to opthamologists where treatment was initiated which has proven most helpful in solving these pupils' learning difficulties. As for the others, only time will tell whether our increased efforts on their behalf will be of help. Of one thing, we are however certain; it has been our experience in the past, that these children were often overlooked as individuals. Their troubles were permitted to assume unusual proportions and they often entered secondary school as misfits. It is precisely this outcome which we hoped to avoid and we shall continue making efforts in this direction. For us, in the nongraded, the individual was the key. The ability to examine and handle each child as an individual has been our greatest asset.

9

CHILDREN WHO LEARN QUICKLY

Objective: to provide level of enrichment for the rapid learners.

Just as every administrator and teacher has great experience with slow learning children, so do they with fast learning children. These bright children also require special attention from teachers and in most instances they receive this extra attention. The nongraded offered an organizational pattern so designed that the quick learner could benefit even further. Programs could be adjusted within classes that better fulfilled the needs of these children. These programs could be individualized, that is, planned specifically for one child, or could be offered on a group basis, for small groups of children with like abilities.

The fast learner is usually identified rather easily. These children are, if one can generalize, socially mature, physically mature and well coordinated, and relatively free of emotional and psychological problems. In any classroom they may be depended upon to be a healthy element, and quite often they lend spark or dynamism to a group, though they do not necessarily have to be leaders. They are obvious to teachers because the quality of their work is uniformly good and their peer relationships are, also. Often, what brings bright children quickly to the attention of the teacher is that they finish their assignments earlier than other children. This offered us a good clue. If they completed assignments more quickly, then we could do one of two things. We could offer them more assignments than other children, or we could offer them more difficult assignments. Both methods of program adaptation for the rapid learner proved useful. In pedagese we refer to these techniques as enrichment programs for the gifted or the bright. Let's see how this was handled in the nongraded.

We have already demonstrated how children had a sub group in their class which functioned on a level in reading consistent with a pupil's achievement level. In other words, a child capable of pursuing reading skills at level nine worked with a group within his class capable of doing this same type of work Assignments and teaching in reading, therefore, were quite challenging to the bright child since he worked always in reading on his precise functioning level, and the lessons were so designed. This procedure was repeated also in mathematics, where each child worked in his own class with a sub-group of children capable of the same types of learning experiences in mathematics as he was.

All other academic areas were handled differently. They were planned as experiences for the entire class. A specific unit of studies was planned for a number of weeks and certain skills and concepts were expected to be learned through this unit of study. It was within this framework that the largest proportion of individualized adjusted assignments were planned for the fast learner. The skills which were expected at certain levels from each pupil in social studies, science, and language arts were minimal skills. Children capable of doing more advanced work, of learning more refined or more advanced skills, were expected to do so. For instance, a class could be studying Transportation in social studies. The teacher could have decided that one skill which she expected all her children to learn during this unit of study was the use of the topical index. This was a minimum skill. Certain children, through individual instruction, could very easily have been ready for a more advanced library skill, let us say, the use of cross references. This was the exact approach used for enriching the learning experiences of our children who were ready for more advanced work. Remember our district curricula guides classify and record learning skills from the specific to the general, from the simplest to the most complex. The teacher had at her disposal a suggested list of sequential skill experiences in each curricular

area which she could use in order to plan a diversified program
for each child requiring this type of enrichment. Our unit plans,
developed by each teacher before launching a new study area,
had appropriate space for her to show which skills and experiences she planned to teach all the children, and which skills and
experiences she planned for certain individuals only (see Social
Studies Unit of Study, Appendix, p. 273).

Our teachers were consistently aware of this need for provision
for the bright child in these other curricular areas. Their weekly
plans bore evidence of this, also, as did their long and short range
plans. Soon they included a column in their weekly plan books
which showed their enrichment planning for certain individual
children.

**Reproduction of part of one Teacher's
Plan Book showing weekly plans for
sub-groups in reading.**

L. Dean, "Weekly Reading Plans" (Plan Book, Old Bethpage School).

Grade _____   Subject __Reading__

MF+N – Oral reading pp. 97-102. Wkbk – ck Fri's work – new assignment p. 32.
Looking Ahead – Word analysis and reading skills – words on board (pp. 186-
190 Teacher's Ed.) Wkbk pp. 35-36 – letter sound and context clues.
Story Caravan – Silent reading and dramatization pp. 106-113.
Wkbk p. 41 – syllables (ck) wkbk to be done at seats pp. 42-43.

MF+N – pp. 104-108 – Silent reading + questions. Wkbk – Word test p. 33.
Looking Ahead – pp. 102-108 – Silent reading and discussion. Wkbk pp. 37-38.
Story Caravan – Silent reading and discussion pp. 114-120.
Wkbk – Ck pp. 42-43 best endings and locating parts in book.
        New wkbk – pp. 44, 45, 46.

MF+N – pp. 104-108 – Dramatize – talk about woodchuck legend.
        Wkbk – Word test.
Looking Ahead – Dramatize – pp. 102-105. Wkbk pp. 38-39 seat work.
Story Caravan – Dramatization pp. 114-120.
                Check wkbks.

MF+N –   Read – Social Studies
Looking Ahead –   Raynham Hall
Story Caravan –   literature

        Free Reading

Fig. 9-1.

**Reproduction of part of one Teacher's
Plan Book showing weekly plans for
individuals in reading**

AREAS OF INDIVIDUAL NEED AND ASSISTANCE

Keith	Kenneth	John B.	David
Improved mostly in reading this week — Praise! Praise! Praise!	*Reads adequately for him — still needs to be physically close to me*	*Apparently forgotten letter names. Still very pugnacious in line, playground etc.*	*Giving a mighty try! Has mastered the "th" sound in mother rather than mudder. 1 to 1 speech help*
Peter	John S.	Bruce	Gloria
Remove from Bobby S. and John Z. or can be a problem			*Boisterous still at times — always with other teachers*
Beth	Bobby S.	Robt. L.	Gregory
	Behavior poor — irresponsible. Moved to a place by himself there is some improvement		*Much improved in reading — 1 to 1 talk re: being grown up helped*
Mary	Debbie	Cheryl	Laura
	Improved this week!	*Still makes errors with +1 more*	
Susanne	Marilyn	Carol	Allison
	Not quite up to par with + one more concept in math		
Michael	John Z.	Philip	Alan
Tremendously behind, complicated by many absences — doesn't even remember left to right — It's SAD!	*Sly and a constant source of disruption — unreliable — special seat by my desk — Poor coordination — silly, aggressive, exposes himself to physical harm from falling, etc. because of behavior*	*For the 1st time this week he shows improvement in letter names, sounds + sight reading*	*Doing better on letters and gets many more sounds*

I. Price, "Areas of Individual Need and Assistance"(Plan
Book, Old Bethpage School).

Fig. 9-2.

They became concerned, however, with still another aspect of the learning capacities of the bright child. With all their individual planning for the bright child, was there, perhaps, not an additional problem? Were these children, and these children specifically, capable of certain activities which they could pursue by themselves with a minimum of guidance from the teacher herself? And more importantly, were these children not those for whom there should be stress on individual responsibility and self-discipline? Were not these the children who should be provided the time for self-growth, for awareness of potential, for freedom to explore and find out *on their own?*

September 29—Minutes of Primary Meeting

> There is much place in the nongraded program for independent activities. Activities which youngsters can pursue at their leisure during the day when teacher directed instruction is not taking place—painting, clay work, woodwork, leisure reading, enrichment mathematics exercises, language arts experiences should be available in the room and the children instructed in their appropriate use during leisure time. There might very well be centers of interest located throughout the room where children can go and work on some project of interest during their free time. This, too, is an area which will require much exploration and trial and error for all of us. The materials being issued to teachers for their center of interest programs may well be of value in this context also.

Discussions continued, and more and more organized efforts were being made to find out what the bright child might well pursue on his own. The teachers wanted and needed suggestions and guide lines for working out special programs for these children on an individualized basis. Mrs. G., the assistant principal, had in her files a list of special individualized techniques which other teachers had used with success in their classrooms. This list had been collected over a period of years. She distributed it to the teachers (see List of Individualization Practices, Appendix, p. 204).

October 6—Minutes of Primary Meeting

The attached list of Individualized Procedures was distributed and discussed by the group. This list was compiled from the actual classroom activities of teachers in this district and are the beginnings of some excellent suggestions of a specific nature for individual activities for youngsters during class time. They are designed to help teachers reinforce the independent skills. The teachers promised to submit in writing additional ideas of their own for practices which they have developed with their classes this year for individualized activities. We will begin to collect these many ideas and offer them in ditto form as we accumulate them in number.

Thus we began to encourage the planning of additional experiences for children outside the area of regular planned curricular experiences. Bright children were instructed in ability groups in reading and mathematics. They pursued enriched and advanced experiences on a group or individual basis in art, music, science, social studies, and language arts. We were now beginning to open the door to experiences for children which they could explore on their own, with a minimum of planning or guidance by the teacher. Classroom after classroom began to display corners or sections of the room where materials were collected which children were encouraged to use on their own. There were science corners with specimens, microscopes, books, magnifying glasses, etc., for work on science problems. There were sections of the room set up with paints, clay, and crafts materials for children who wished to work in the creative arts. Still other centers housed mathematics manipulative materials and play materials for encouraging additional work in mathematics. The examples are too numerous to list.

It was not enough that teachers demonstrated their interest in children becoming involved in independent activities. It was necessary that children learn how to pursue this type of learning on their own. This problem solving training took much time and effort on a teacher's part; but by the end of the school year, we became more and more accustomed to seeing two or three children in a corner of the class working alone on some project which they had selected from the many the teacher had suggested. A technique which became quite popular was a chart posted in many rooms which listed suggested free time activities for children. For the very young child who couldn't read, this was, of course, difficult. We don't think we shall ever forget one highly creative young woman who made a chart of suggested free time activities for her children with the use of pictorial symbols which the children understood long before they were ready to read words!

Mrs. W., the reading consultant, added to our store of suggestions for independent activities by distributing in November a list of suggested Independent Activities for the Language Arts (Appendix, p. 207). This list of suggestions also proved quite helpful to the teachers. Certainly none of the ideas offered to the teachers or by the teachers for independent activities was earth shattering or shockingly original, nor did anyone pretend that they were. The point of significance was that the need for the bright child to work, think, plan, and create occasionally on his own part of the time was now recognized. Once this recognition became obvious, methods and techniques to encourage independent learning were borrowed freely from all sources. The child who learned quickly was being given every opportunity within our means to learn quickly that which we deemed appropriate for him to learn; but, in addition, opportunity was now provided for him to direct some of his learning by himself, and productively so. This was an extremely important goal for us. We were providing levels of enrichment for the bright child yes, but more relevantly, he was being encouraged to provide some of these enrichment experiences for himself and by himself. Since all real creative work becomes, in the last analysis, an individual process, we felt this aspect of our nongraded program represented very positive growth on our part.

10

THE TWO OR FOUR YEAR
PRIMARY PROGRAM

Objective: to remove the trauma associated with acceleration and retention.

We have tried to show how we provided for the individual differences of all the children. We have pointed out our program adaptations for children who learn slowly and for children who learn quickly. There came a time, however, when still further decisions had to be made about some of these children. They had been exposed to a learning situation which encouraged continual, uninterrupted, sequential learning experiences in each curricular area. It was quite natural, therefore, to find children at different levels of achievement in each curricular area regardless of the length of time they had spent in primary school. It was also quite possible to find individual children who achieved at different levels in different curricular areas. But what about the child who continually produced at an achievement level consistantly lower than we had hoped in all curricular areas; or what about the child who achieved at a level consistently higher than we had predicted in all curricular areas? Were these children to stay with us in the primary school for the allotted three years? The answer seemed quite apparent. If we really were talking about continual progress, then these children were entitled to an adjusted time table. Some of them could be permitted to complete their primary schooling in two years; others could be permitted to complete their primary schooling in four years.

Dr. Robert Anderson,[1] in his speech, talked of the history of graded schools. He said, in essence, when the graded school was imported from Europe in the mid-nineteenth century, the prevailing view in this country was moralistic—"the child could do it if he only tries." The results of a century of graded education have been the "erosion of self-respect, defeat, and failure for the less able, and less than fulfillment of potential by the gifted" who have not been challenged to explore beyond the grade standards. The notion that all men are created equal was regarded not only as a moral principle but as an educational policy.

We at Old Bethpage recognized that realistically since we had eliminated artificial grade level barriers, we were going to have to eliminate also artificial time barriers if we were going to see to it that children be permitted to learn normally and naturally within the scope of their abilities. This meant an adjusted time-table for some children. It meant that children who had successfully completed our standards in all curricular areas in the first two years of their primary schooling were going to be given the opportunity to move quite naturally into the fourth grade. It meant also that children who had completed three years of our primary program and were still functioning well below our standards were going to be given the opportunity to continue quite naturally with a fourth year of primary schooling. Of course, this plan was just the skeletal academic outline. There were other mitigating circumstances affecting our decisions, and for us there always will be. No child was considered simply from an academic point of view.

It should be explained, at this point, that we at the Old Bethpage School treaded extremely carefully this first year before making any decisions about these children. If there ever was a doubt in our minds about a certain child, we gave him the benefit of that doubt and permitted him to continue with a three year program. This rule we followed very simply because we felt that with just one year of the nongraded at our disposal, we did not

---

[1] Anderson, Speech.

wish to unfairly penalize any child who might well not have had sufficient opportunity in one year of our primary school to really prove himself. We feel we will not be on real firm ground in this regard until we have been operating our nongraded for at least three full years.

In our first year, we established for ourselves, together with the teachers, certain academic standards of achievement as the base criterion for time decisions. Roughly this meant, any child achieving on reading level thirteen or above, and mathematics level eleven or above with corresponding proficiency in the mastery of skills and understanding of concepts in the other curricular areas by the end of the first two years of the primary school was perforce an *academic candidate* for the fourth grade. If you will consult our instructional levels table in Chapter 6, you will see that these instructional levels go beyond what we normally expected as achievement from even the above average learner. What we were saying, in effect, was that we did not feel that we could provide this pupil with a suitable instructional program within the third year of primary school consistent with the child's ability. This child would profit best from spending his third year of formal schooling in the fourth grade rather than in the third year of primary school.

Now the situation was quite the reverse for the slow learning pupil. Any child achieving on reading level seven or below and mathematics level five or below with corresponding deficiency in the mastery of skills and the understanding of concepts in the other curricular areas by the end of the first three years of primary school was perforce an *academic candidate* for the fourth year of primary school. If you will consult our instructional levels table in Chapter 6, you will note that these instructional levels go far below what we normally expect as achievement from even a below average learner. What we were saying, in effect, was that we felt that we could provide this pupil with a program better suited to his academic needs in the fourth year of primary school than could be provided for him in the fourth grade. This child could profit best from remaining with us for another year of sequential continual learning experiences in the primary school.

We have indicated the criterion for academic candidacy for adjusted timetables in the primary school. We must remind the reader again that these were just the base criterion we used before considering any child for a two or four year primary school program. Each child was, in addition, subjected to detailed, precise analysis before decisions were made relevant to his candidacy. We paid careful attention to all aspects of a pupil, his psychological, emotional, and social well-being constituting a large part of our decision. We evaluated a pupil from all these points of view, in addition to his achievement potential, before we made any decision as to his next year's placement.

November 3—Minutes of Primary Meeting

The Length of Time Necessary for the Completion of the Nongraded

We do know that it will take some children four years to complete the necessary levels of skills before they can enter the fourth grade. We also know that it will take some children only two years to complete this same level of skills. Our discussion revolved around the recognition of this factor. At what point will we be aware of the youngster who will need a longer or shorter period of time for the nongraded program? We have come to no definitive answer; however, there was general agreement that in most cases the fast learner who will require two years for completion will usually be identifiable by the end of the first year of primary school. In the case of those youngsters who will require four years for completion there seems to be general agreement that we, in most cases, will be able to recognize this fact by the end of the second year. Parents should be notified of these possibilities just as soon as the school can make this kind of prognostication.

We were all intensely interested and involved in this process of evaluation. By midyear, we had determined on a prescribed approach for handling these decisions, but long before this time teachers were bringing pupils to our attention.

November 2—Minutes of Primary Meeting

Paul A. is a youngster who was being considered for acceleration last year before we became nongraded. He was, therefore, placed in a class with a group of older youngsters who function academically at his level. Mrs. Q. reports that Paul is a bright child whose behavioral pattern is very meticulous, careful, and slow and thus he takes too long to complete homework assignments, for instance. The parent, who contacted Mrs. Q., will be told to limit the youngster's time allotment for homework. Paul is making a good adjustment in class albeit he does evidence compulsive behavior patterns. "I think that he will be able to quite naturally move along into the fourth grade with the other children in class."

November 2—Minutes of Primary Meeting

Emilie S. was being considered for acceleration last year before we became nongraded. She was, therefore, especially placed in a class with a group of older youngsters on her academic level. Mrs. Q. reports that Emilie is an exceptionally bright child who is doing extremely well in all areas, socially, emotionally, and academically and will make a good adjustment to the fourth grade.

November 9—Minutes of Primary Meeting

Kenneth G., who was noted for brightness last year, was placed with a group of above average youngsters older than he, since there were no children his age who functioned near him academically. His name will certainly come up for a possible two year program. Mr. T. reports that Kenneth is an immature youngster who is still managing to function well academically. His work habits are not as good as they might be. There is a tendency not to complete work properly or to leave things out. We shall have to carefully re-evaluate this youngster before permitting him to enter the fourth grade.

Here were three children in the beginning of their second year of primary school, with teachers quite aware that their academic potential was such that they might easily qualify for a two year primary program. They began to take a long, hard look at these children long before we had established any base criteria for evaluation.

At almost every primary meeting we held, teachers discussed with us children who were different enough to be conidered for two or four year primary programs.

November 30—Minutes of Primary Meeting

Mrs. H. and Mrs. I. brought to our attention two youngsters, Arnold and Henry, respectively. These two boys are functioning well below level academically. There is no question in the minds of these two teachers that these boys will require a fourth year in the primary school. They are youngsters who are not only having academic problems, but are already exhibiting the acting out patterns of the poor learner and becoming discipline problems. No doubt, their inability to function academically is contributing to their poor behavior.

December 15—Minutes of Primary Meeting

Miss O. reports that she has a little boy named Charles, who came to us from another school and about whom we knew very little. She is beginning to feel that he will complete the primary school in just two years.

January 4—Minutes of Primary Meeting

Mrs. J. reports that she has six youngsters whom she is beginning to feel will not qualify for entrance into the fourth grade at the end of the year. They will still be quite far below academic achievement levels at that time.

By this time, the academic standards described in the first few pages of this chapter had been established and a form was completed.

January 4—Minutes of Primary Meeting

Pupil Evaluation Forms (Figure 10-1.)

There will be developed and distributed next week an "evaluation form" which teachers will be asked to fill out in order to initiate discussions relative to the time it will take a youngster to complete the nongraded primary. If a teacher has a youngster or youngsters whom she suspects will require either two or four years for completion, she will fill out the form and submit it for discussion at our primary meetings.

Thus we began to collect the evidence on these children. The procedure went something like this. A teacher would complete a Pupil Evaluation Form for a child whom she deemed a candidate for a two or four year program. The school nurse-teacher would provide us with complete information on the medical and physical case history of the child. The school psychologist would look in on the child and report any relevant findings or case histories she had accumulated. The speech therapist supplied us with documented case histories for any child whom she had been seeing for speech therapy. The teacher herself was asked to consult the Teacher's Guidance Handbook[2] and to use the checklists and guides contained therein for more specific identification of children's differences. Most specifically, their attention was called to the sections in the book on social, emotional, and general behavior problems, as well as patterns of the slow and fast learner. Finally, the reading consultant was asked to do a thorough work up on each child who was a candidate for a two or four year program and to evaluate his functioning achievement level in reading. Once these examinations were completed, time was set aside at Primary Meetings for complete discussions of each pupil. Finally, decisions were made jointly by all who had some knowledge of the child and his abilities. In all cases, one or both of the administrators had also spent some time observing the pupil in class.

January 26—Minutes of Primary Meeting

Children Who May Qualify for a Two or Four Year Primary Program

It was decided that we present at primary meetings the names of any or all children about whom we have some concern. No decisions will be made as to their placement or the time it will take for them to complete the primary program at this time.

---

[2] Jack Kough and Robert F. De Haan, *Identifying Children with Special Needs* (Chicago, Ill.: Science Research Associates, Inc., 1955).

OLD BETHPAGE SCHOOL
PUPIL EVALUATION FORM

(Use for children who may qualify for a two or four year primary program.)

NAME _____CLASS _____

DATE _____AGE _____yrs. _____mos. _____

DESCRIPTION AND HISTORY—from kindergarten thru present. (Include physical health, emotional health, and social adjustment).

Date _____

Group I.Q. _____

Date _____

Ind. I.Q. _____

ACADEMIC HISTORY

Latest Achievement Scores:
Date _____   _____

Name of Test: _____

_____   _____

Latest IRI: _____
Date _____

                                      _____

Other Test Data:
Date _____   _____

Name of Test:

_____   _____

Teacher's evaluation of child's learning ability, interest, and rate:

_____

_____

Teacher's comments and total evaluation:

_____

_____

_____

Fig. 10-1.

However, we will be "zeroing" in on these children and studying them for the next few months.

March 9—Minutes of Primary Meeting

Formal discussions have begun about youngsters who are recommended for a fourth year or no third year in the primary school. Complete records have been collected from classroom teachers, nurse-teacher, speech therapist, and reading consultant. Psychologist's reports, where relevant, are also included. Final decisions will be made prior to spring parent-teacher conferences so that the matter can be discussed with parents at that time (spring parent-teacher conferences were scheduled in late April). Since all records are of a highly confidential nature, they are not attached to these minutes, but are available for reference in the principal's office.

From January through mid-April, we documented the histories of children who were going to be considered for a four or two year program in the primary school. Our final decisions were made in mid-April. We considered first those children who were already in their third year of primary school and would normally be expected to move on to the fourth grade the following September. There were fifteen such youngsters brought to our attention. It was imperative that decisions be made about these children since time was running out on all of them. They were already near the end of their third year in primary school and, needless to say, none of them were achieving at anything quite what we would have liked to see. We were, however, also quite aware of the many other problems present in offering a fourth year program to a child, and decisions were made keeping these other factors in mind.

March 16—Minutes of Primary Meeting

A lengthy discussion followed the evaluation conference relevant to children who qualify for a fourth year in the primary school. Questions of social stigma and parental disapproval were explored, but it was emphasized that one of the advantages of the nongraded primary is that any youngster required to spend his fourth year in the primary school would be carefully placed with older children and his educational program would consist of curricula content totally new and different for him. It is quite different from former retention methods where the youngster was forced to repeat the same learning experiences the following year. The philosophy and implementation of the vertical curriculum and continual progress certainly are best served through the nongraded primary organizational pattern.

Arnold

Arnold was a candidate for a fourth year in the primary school. His name was first brought up in November, when his teacher, Mrs. H., reported his reading difficulties. On November 30, she reported his poor social behavior and reading problems and nominated him for a fourth year in the primary school (see this Chapter, p. 110).

March 1—Minutes of Primary Meeting

> Mrs. H. reports that although Arnold is having specific reading problems, she finds him alert in general. He is becoming increasingly conscious of his academic deficiencies, resulting in classroom control problems. Although he has been placed under sedation by the family physician, he is still extremely hyperactive. Mr. F., the principal, related the background of parental contacts last year which, he felt, were unsatisfactory in terms of increasing parental awareness of Arnold's problems.

Arnold was one of the pupils for whom an individualized reading program had been worked out by the reading consultant and the teacher (see Chapter Eight, p. 95). He was functioning on level four in reading.

Mrs. H. completed a Pupil Evaluation Form on March 22.

> Arnold is nine years and one month old as of this date. Arnold is a small child for his age. The children accept him and seem attracted to him because of his antics. His academic achievement

has been consistently recorded as poor. There seems to be no progress made in reading. He is still functioning on a primer level. He is unable to determine the sounds that the alphabet letters represent. In mathematics, he shows some clarity in computation, though he is functioning at a very low level. Arnold makes no attempt at written expression, however, his oral expression is good and he is well informed in some areas. His I.Q., on the group Otis, is average. Arnold shows indifference to work because he is unable to cope with it. I feel his ability is much greater than his performance. He is becoming increasingly self-conscious of his academic inferiority. To overcome this, he is constantly drawing attention to himself by clowning. He is a most disturbing influence in the class.

All reports from the other specialists confirmed this report. This pupil could be doing better but was becoming an increased problem as time passed because of his inability to function. This child desperately needed the tools of learning which, heretofore, he had not accepted for reasons unknown. It was our considered feeling that now that we had the cooperation of the home and the family physician, and now that we had a totally individualized reading program especially designed for Arnold, he might well profit from spending a fourth year with us.

As already indicated, fifteen such children were brought to our attention. Three of these fifteen children remained with us for the fourth primary year. Our decisions, as we have tried to explain, because of the fact that we were only in the first year of our nongraded, were quite liberally on the side of normal placement. This restriction will undoubtedly not hold true a few years from now, when we will be more intimately acquainted with each child and his potential through three years in the primary school. But for this year only children who really stood out as deviates were assigned to the fourth year in the nongraded. The other twelve children whom we evaluated all proceeded to the fourth grade, though we made these decisions with serious reservations. These types of problems were to be expected at the onset of any such new program. Here is an example from our files of one such pupil.

Nicholas

Nicholas was first brought to our attention by his teacher, Mrs. L., in December. He was discussed as a possible fourth year candidate in January and was one of the pupils for whom a special individualized reading program was worked out.

Mrs. L. reported on January 26:

> Nicholas is eight years and five months old as of this date. His Informal Reading Inventory places him on the primer level and he is being instructed on this level. His Science Research Associates Achievement Test scores are reading composite 1.6, mathematics composite 2.6, and language arts composite 2.0. This pupil is physically healthy as well as emotionally. He is basically a follower. He is a very slow learner, but a hard worker, puts a good deal of effort into his activities, and seems frustrated during reading.

Mrs. L. completed a Pupil Evaluation Form on February 1:

> Nicholas has no obvious physical or emotional or social problems. He follows anybody who will lead him. He seems to have a speech problem. Functioning on level five in reading and level five in mathematics. Nicholas is a slow learner. Finds it difficult to understand new concepts. Puts great effort into his work. He tries very hard and puts time into his work, though he is frustrated by his reading deficiencies. His work habits are generally poor.

On the same date, the school nurse-teacher reported:

> Private physician reports negative findings. Child is normal in all respects. Height 50¼ inches, weight 57 pounds. Gained two inches and five and one-half pounds since last year. Vision 20/20, 20/30, within normal range. Telebinocular tests—normal, as is hearing.

On the same date, the speech therapist reported:

> Nicholas' speech was evaluated in December 1964. No true defect was noted although there were some substandardisms (i.e., "mudder" for "mother"). Nicholas was able to imitate the cor-

rect pronunciation of these words upon suggestion. He appears to have some phonic confusion about the sounds that should be in certain words, but was not placed in the speech program as he demonstrated ability to articulate all sounds correctly when made aware of them. A conference was held with the teacher, offering suggestions for reading work with Nicholas. He will be reevaluated next September.

The psychologist also took a look at Nicholas and found him to be a normal, average boy. The reading report had indicated that Nicholas's problem was one of auditory discrimination and had suggested that the child be subjected to a rigorous series of experiences to increase his ability with auditory discriminations. This his classroom teacher, with the reading consultant's help, set about to do and Nicholas was beginning to show some improvement in reading. This average child, with no obvious problems and with a new approach to reading, who functioned fairly well in other academic areas, did not seem to us to be a logical candidate for a fourth year in the primary school. We felt that he had more to gain from placement in the fourth grade and made arrangements with his next year's teacher to continue his individualized reading program.

We had still further pressing problems in the case of children who had completed just two years of the primary school, but who seemed ready to go ahead with their groups into the fourth grade. Decisions about these children couldn't be delayed either and so the same rigorous evaluation procedures were instituted for these pupils. There were four such children brought to our attention. After due deliberation, we made our decision. Three of these children were to proceed to the fourth grade, the other was to remain with us for the third year of primary school.

Emilie

Emilie was first brought to our attention on November 2 (see this chapter, p. 109). Her teacher was already beginning to consider her for the two year primary program.

On January 21, Mrs. Q. completed a Pupil Evaluation Form:

Emilie is functioning on the highest achievement levels academically in all areas, although she came directly to me from the first grade last year. Her adjustment has been excellent and she is extremely well-liked, even having been elected an officer of the class. Her group I.Q. is 145 and she is achieving on level fourteen in reading and level eleven in mathematics. Her *Science Research Associates Achievement Test*[3] scores are least two years above top level in all areas tested. She is at the stage where everything is interesting, and she is quite capable of exploring problems on her own. She is absolutely at the top of her class, even though many of the children are older than she is and many of them are quite bright.

It was the unanimous opinion of all of us that this pupil was ready and quite able to make the adjustment to the fourth grade, psychologically, emotionally, socially, and academically without any difficulty. Her one year in the nongraded had given us added testimony to this effect. And so Emilie was approved as a candidate for a two year primary program as were two other pupils. We had reservations about another one of these children and ultimately, made the decision to keep him with us for the third year of primary school. Although he was functioning well in his class (see this chapter, p. 110), Charles did not seem to us, after very careful examination, to be so outstanding that we could not take care of his learning needs very nicely in the third year of primary school. His classroom teacher, Miss O., who initially felt very strongly that Charles should be a two year candidate, had some reservations herself near the end of the school year, so our decision seemed well justified.

During the course of this, our first year of the nongraded, we were quite naturally pressured to make decisions about children who might well have been in their last primary year with us— third year children ready to proceed to fourth grade, and second year children ready to proceed to fourth grade. This condition

---

[3] Science Research Achievement Series (1-2 and 2-4)—Developed by Louis P. Thorpe, D. Welty Lefever and Robert A. Naslund. (Chicago, Ill.: Science Research Associates, Inc., rev. ed., 1963).

existed only during the first year of the operation of the non-graded. This pressure will not be present in the school years to come since we can evaluate children at least one year in advance and reserve final judgment until the completion of the second year. By the close of this year, we already have had brought to our attention three children who were in the first year of primary school, who may well be candidates for a two year program. We will make our decision next spring, but note how much longer we have to evaluate these pupils and make certain of the correctness of our decisions. The same holds true for nine children in their second year of primary school who have already been clearly identified as possible candidates for a fourth year in the primary school. We have another full year to evaluate these children before it becomes necessary to pass judgment.

Certainly, the decisions of four and two year programs for certain children do not have the stigma or glamour, as the case may be, which they had in the past. Indeed, ideally these children will experience a relatively undisturbed education pattern. They will proceed from one level of achievement to another in curricular areas without interruption, repetition, or lapses. They are assured of continual progress and easy transition from one stage to another. In addition, another extremely vital point in the operation of the nongraded is the fact that we have increased advantages in the placement of these children. What we mean is simply this. Consider the above mentioned three children who completed their first year of primary school with such success that their teachers were considering them for a two year primary program. These children have been placed for next year in classes that are interage by composition and contain some children who are older than they are but who are functioning on similar academic levels. There are too in these classes children of their own ages. These bright pupils can work on their appropriate academic levels in certain curricular areas and still enjoy the experience of being with older children as well as children of their own age socially. If we decide to permit these children to enter the fourth grade after this next year, as the case may well be, they already will have the experience of working and playing with older children and their total adjustment will be that much easier.

Conversely, those nine pupils who have been identified as slow learners also have an advantage. For their third year in the primary school (next year) they will be placed in classes which are interage and contain pupils the same age as they are and pupils younger than they are. They will perform academically with mixed age children and mingle socially with both age groups. Subsequently, next spring, when the decision will be made to keep some of these children in the primary school for a fourth year, as well the case may be, these children already will have had one full year to adjust to the younger child and will not feel the stigma nearly as deeply as they might in the graded retention pattern.

Herein lie our efforts at removing the trauma of acceleration and retention, heretofore, met in the graded school structure. Children are enabled to make smooth transitions with a minimum of interruption to their continual progress. We considered this one of the foremost goals of the nongraded school. We feel that we have made giant strides in this direction. All of us are alert to the earliest possible identification of possible candidates and are making provisions for these pupils. We have also instituted the first steps in establishing criteria and procedures for the making of these decisions. Much work is yet to be done, but we are well pleased with the first year's results.

11

CURRICULAR IMPLEMENTATION

Objective: To explore more fully the range of teaching techniques and implementation of curriculum within the class.

Our district, as already mentioned, had created fine curricular guides in all the major subject matter areas. They were sequential in development from kindergarten through grade twelve. Although teachers had been using them for two years before the start of our nongraded program, it was our feeling that the nongraded was going to prove the best organizational plan for implementing these curricula. We think our prediction was correct. Time after time we were present during examinations of these curricula by groups of teachers, which we had never witnessed in the past. The need to provide for individual differences in children created a need to understand and use curricula to much better advantage than had been evident in the past. We are convinced that the scrutiny our curricula were subjected to this past year was a direct consequence of nongrading. Certainly, aspects and portions of our curricular guides had been examined in the past but not with the diligence and urgency and genuine interest which the nongraded fostered. Here are a few examples taken from our records which may help to substantiate our findings.

Reading

September 28—Minutes of Primary Meeting

The general consensus of opinion is that in the area of reading we do an excellent job of skills instruction but are somewhat remiss in the development of the thinking and comprehension skills. This is an area of concentration for us this year. Types and kinds of activities to increase the thinking skills and the conceptualization needs will be studied, explored, and tried in the classroom.

Some of the specific suggestions include:

Mrs. W.'s publication of a list of conversion tables for all available reading comprehension material (other than basal reading materials) will be made available to teachers. The use of these materials at the appropriate levels will give the children more skills training in comprehension.

Teacher use of differentiated materials for increase of comprehension skills. Discontinue total reliance upon basal reading materials for this skill training. In addition to the materials suggested above, texts in other subject areas may be used, also (social studies, science).

Beginning recognition of the fact that there has been too much reliance on picture clues in primary reading. There will be a new emphasis on less use of pictures for contextual clues and more reliance upon the printed word.

Publication of lecture notes which Mrs. G., the assistant principal, took in a class with Dr. Jonas on activities to increase children's thinking.

There is some evidence that some of this lack of understanding on the children's part stems from their home life, where sometimes there is not enough time allowed for independent activities and free choice of activities or freedom of choice or thinking. Youngsters of this type are coddled, overprotected, and most importantly for our understanding, overdirected. There is some evidence that in our suburban culture most of the thinking, planning, structuring, and arranging are done for the children. This, of course, makes it even more necessary that we concentrate on this area in the teaching of reading this year.

We use this example since it represents some important aspects of our discussion. These teachers brought up this topic by themselves. They felt this need on their own. They were genuinely concerned about their children and their skills in reading. As they said, they were doing an excellent job in reading, but they were still not satisfied. They wanted more from themselves and more from their children. We certainly were in agreement with their conclusions but always have felt that administrator-originated ideas never quite get off the ground the way teacher-incepted ideas do. These teachers were thinking; they were concerned; they were going to do something about the problem. They evaluated a situation; came to some conclusions; and planned a program of action—in precisely that curricular area where we would have predicted they were quite content, since this was the area of their greatest strength. But they wanted to improve instruction in certain aspects of reading, and they did.

On October first Mrs. G. distributed to the teachers a ditto of lecture notes she took in class at New York University with Dr. Arthur Jonas.[1] (Figure 11-1.) These notes proved quite helpful in further exploration of thinking and the way children understand. They were distributed to the teachers without comment as was the other material promised them at the September 28 meeting. About a month later, a second set of lecture notes was distributed to the teachers (Figure 11-2). This set dealt with ways and means of improving children's thinking. It was of a practical nature and contained worthwhile suggestions for teachers' use in lesson planning. The teachers continued to be concerned with the problem of reading comprehension and thinking. Much work was done in the classrooms in this area, an area which heretofore had been relatively ignored in the planning of reading lessons.

January 4—Minutes of Primary Meeting

Discussion revolved around the dittoed material prepared by Mrs. G.—*Thinking* and *Suggestions for Improving Children's Thinking*. The teachers gave many examples from their classes of thinking and comprehension experiences which had been quite successful. Recognition of the fact that these experiences must be

---

[1] Louis E. Raths, Arthur Jonas, Arnold Rothstein and Selma Wassermann, *Teaching for Thinking* (Columbus, Ohio: Charles E. Merrill Books, Inc., 1966).

Creative art experiences

Creative art experiences

Independent activity-
loom weaving

real in order for children to feel them, and not artificial, as are many school experiences, was further explored. The normal school day offers many opportunities for experiences in thinking which teachers have not utilized fully in the past (program planning, class elections, class chores, unit activities, etc.). We shall continue exploring this avenue for further techniques for improving the thinking of our children.

October 1, 1964
Old Bethpage School

THINKING

At one of our primary meetings we explored the factors of reading comprehension, conceptual understanding, and critical thinking. We all agreed that this was the area least developed in the schools. In an effort to be of some help, I am reproducing some random notes I have collected on children's thinking which you may find helpful. I have also included a bibliography of particularly meaningful books in this area.

Some definitions of thinking: Please note that all these activities do not take place at the same time or during any particular mental exercise. They occur singly, in groups, or all together but never, once again, in any specific order.

1. Thinking is an act of suspended judgment—we stop, look, and listen.

2. Thinking is collecting data—the procedure of gathering information.

3. Thinking is realizing or recognizing that a problem exists. A problem is a situation involving doubt where the solution is unknown.

4. Thinking is looking for alternatives and possible solutions.

5. Thinking is discriminating among alternatives.

6. Thinking is making predictions—"if, then"—statements, hypotheses.

7. Thinking is organizing data into a structural form.

8. Thinking is appraising values in connection with alternatives.

9. Thinking is the rigorous testing of conclusions and alternatives. Does it work or fit?

10. Thinking is the selection of the best available solution at this moment subject to re-examination.

Responses of the non-thinking youngster: Please note that these are some of the signposts which we can use to detect youngsters in whom the art of thinking is not finely developed—and can be used diagnostically.

1. The youngster who responds impulsively, without any thought.

2. The youngster who responds dogmatically, in his own way, in a loud or assertive manner.

3. The youngster who misses the meaning, misinterprets, doesn't conceptualize, or doesn't understand.

4. The youngster who responds consistently each time, who stays in a rut, whose responses reflect a contentment with the status quo condition.

5. The youngster who lacks concentrative ability, who has a short attention span, whose mind wanders, or who just doesn't pay attention.

6. The youngster who is afraid to state his own opinion, who is fearful, hesitant.

7. The youngster who is overdependent and not self-directed, who will not do his own work, who always wants help, wants to be told, is basically lazy and doesn't wish to do his own thinking.

8. The youngster who doesn't want to learn, who is happy with rote assignments, who says, in effect, "tell me what to do and I'll do it."

If you can learn to identify children in these categories, and remember they may display more than one of these sets of characteristics, you can help develop techniques for guiding these children to think. Interestingly enough, as they are encouraged to think more and more, their behavior also undergoes a change.

It is important to emphasize further that youngsters who fit these characteristics occasionally are not really consistent non-thinkers. It is those children who repeat these characteristics frequently with whom we must be concerned.

Children actually improve in their thinking when teachers teach thinking. Many research studies and doctoral theses have been published which proves this statement valid (Berken, Wasserman, Jonas, Fawcett, Lewis, Rothstein, Glaser, Watson, Bloom, Blooder, and Chess).

Books which have been published which are particularly helpful in teaching teachers to recognize children who do not think and which discuss techniques for teaching are listed below.

Raths, Jonas, Rothstein, and Wassermann: *Teaching for Thinking*
Dewey, John: *How We Think*
Russell, David: *Children's Thinking*
Piaget, Jean: *Thinking*
Wing, Kimball: *Teaching Thinking*

Vocabulary: It is important to note that the following phrases are used interchangeably when discussions about the development of thinking are held. They really all mean the same thing.

Reflective thinking
Critical thinking
Analytical thinking
Problem solving

Fig. 11-1.

November 1, 1964
Old Bethpage School

Suggested Techniques for Encouraging Thinking

These are just suggestions offered which may be used in lessons stemming from any curricular area. These techniques have been used efficaciously and have been proven to be effective in developing thinking in youngsters. Some of the techniques you have often used in the past. The point to be emphasized here is that all these techniques should be used frequently and often, with groups or individuals.

1. Plan lessons which make use of the techniques of making comparisons. Anything may be compared for similarities and differences (books, natural objects, inanimate objects, animals, etc.).

2. Plan lessons which make use of the technique of collecting data or materials.

3. Plan lessons which make use of the technique of organizing, classifying, and sorting data or material. Things can be classified according to rank, size, shape, order, color, etc. In more advanced groups, the use of visual aids, graphs, charts, lists, and rules which the children make or those which are prepared professionally should be encouraged.

4. Plan lessons which make use of the technique of observing and listening, the increased awareness of all the senses which are natural to human beings.

5. Plan lessons which make use of the technique of criticizing and analyzing for good and bad points inherent in each situation.

6. Plan lessons which make use of the technique of interpreting data, the reading of charts and graphs, facts to be investigated, taken apart, real sources, primary sources, etc., determined, logic or illogic uncovered.

7. Plan lessons which make use of the technique of looking for assumptions which we make all the time. Some of our simplest statements or explanations bear assumptions which we should be able to examine.

8. Plan lessons which make use of the technique of self-analysis, individual goals, objectives, plans, and evaluation.

9. Plan lessons which make use of the technique of problem-solving—for instance, in everyday activities there are real problems for children to solve (seating arrangements, planning for the day, housekeeping chores, supplies and inventory, A-V aids, discipline, classroom arrangements).

10. Plan lessons which make use of the techniques of outlining.

11. Plan lessons which make use of the technique of using our imagination.

12. Plan lessons which make use of the technique of problem-solving in the scientific method sense: hypothesis, collection of data, testing, evaluation, etc.

13. Plan lessons which make use of the technique of making hypotheses about future events from available data and then watch our predictions come out.

14. Plan questions which make use of the technique of answering questions after oral or silent reading which have the children respond true, false, or don't know.

15. Plan lessons which make use of the technique of summarizing, paraphrasing, or synthesizing experiences.

Fig. 11-2.

Thus reading, the area we as administrators would have least selected as an area of concentration, came in for its share of analysis and a group of teachers set up for themselves a goal in instruction, the improvement of thinking and comprehension skills. Once teachers were provided the time and the opportunity, other problems of curricular implementation and adaptation were brought to our attention.

Language Arts

November 16—Minutes of Primary Meeting

Discussion *re* role of correct usage, grammar, punctuation, spelling, and handwriting and the actual usage of these skills in real situations. How much transfer is there really? What is the result of learning spelling words in isolation, or for that matter, handwriting practices, if there really is not real carry-over?

December 7—Minutes of Primary Meeting

It was suggested that the words in the *Multi-Level Spellers*[2] be supplemented by words which the children use in their social studies and science units of study in addition to words that they use in language exercises and creative writing.

December 15—Minutes of Primary Meeting

There was some discussion relevant to the accepted procedure for the teaching of handwriting. Most specifically, were we to be bound to the technique illustrated in the Zaner Bloser text, for instance? The basic formation of all letters is the circle and the straight line. Is there specific relevance to the order in which

---

[2] Morton Botel, *The Multi-Level Speller* (State College, Pa.: Penns Valley Publishers, Inc., 1959).

these two geometric forms are to be used in the formation of a
single letter? Mrs. W. promised to provide us with the necessary
research background before we come to any definite conclusion
on which course of action to follow since she was active on the
committee (district) which explored this area of study last year.

December 20—Minutes of Primary Meeting

The discussion continued which started last week on the best
techniques for teaching manuscript. Mrs. W. presented all the
materials developed by the district to-date in the area of penmanship. This material was offered to the teachers for their perusal. We shall obtain for the teachers the teacher's edition of the
Zaner Bloser texts in manuscript since this is the method which
the district committee recommends for classroom instruction after
their careful research into the problem. It is also to be pointed out
that there has not been much research done on penmanship since
the 1930's.

The entire area of penmanship and the language arts came up
for examination. Teachers had questions about handwriting, very
specific questions, questions relating to their everyday teaching
techniques. If there was a better way to do it, they wanted to
know about it. This interested us tremendously, since the two
of us have always been pretty much of a mind with regard to
penmanship and spelling. We have always doubted the need for
penmanship drill and training. Here were the teachers themselves questioning these same basic instructional techniques in
this area, and we had never moved a muscle. Spelling was another area where we felt that daily drill was unnecessary. The
memortization of lists of words has never impressed us as being
particularly meaningful as a learning experience. The teachers,
some of them, were coming to this same conclusion and beginning to plan for spelling in a more realistic manner. Curriculum
adaptations and changes and interpretations were occurring every
day. All of them were pursued professionally. Questions were
asked, techniques explored, studies made, and finally after due
deliberation, conclusions were reached. This was truly the improvement of instruction as we had never dared hope it would

occur. We earnestly believe that these changes can be laid at the doorstep of the nongraded program.

Creative Music

The area of music illustrates our contention even further. We had a fine music curriculum guide in the district and available to us was the full time service of a vocal music teacher. In the time honored tradition (one with which we do not fully agree) she circulated among all the classes on schedule. Certain classes had vocal music experiences twice a week, others just once a week. These lessons were designed to make youngsters conversant with the elementary theories of music, music appreciation, and vocal singing. We had both felt for a long time that the area of creative music had always been neglected.

October 27—Minutes of Primary Meetings

Mrs. K., a kindergarten teacher with one of our other schools, on sabbatical leave, is involved in a creative music workshop at the Bank Street School which so stimulated her thinking with regard to creative music experiences for the young that she offered to share some of her experiences with this group. The group was very receptive to her discussion and found it quite profitable.

The essential heart of the message which Mrs. K. tried to get across to all of us is that we have not freed the young child for creative music experiences. On the whole, their musical exposures are stereotyped.

She suggested that we draw on the children's environment and ritual experience to give them activities in creative music.

Mrs. K. demonstrated some of her knowledge and we distributed to the teachers sample lessons which she had developed in this area. The lessons are quite exciting and could be the source of much excellent learning for all our children. (Figures 11-3 and 11-4.)

October 28, 1964
Old Bethpage School

Sample Lesson: *Creative Music,* an experience in spontaneous music which may be helpful for auditory discrimination (reading readiness and beyond) and listening skills development as well.

This material was collected by Mrs. K. for the kindergarten and primary grades, but it has excellent potential for any age level.[3]

Motivation: Have one youngster come to the chalkboard and draw a large scribble design.

Activities:

1. Individual youngsters volunteer to demonstrate the design on the chalkboard with their bodies. They are told to act out the pattern and that they may use any body motions or movements necessary. A number of youngsters may take turns demonstrating, till ultimately all the youngsters join in creating and interpreting as they go.

2. Individual youngsters volunteer to demonstrate the design on the chalkboard with rhythm instruments of their choosing. They are told to sound out the pattern and that they may use one or as many rhythm instruments as they wish. A number of youngsters may take turns demonstrating, till ultimately, all the youngsters have had some experience with an instrument.

Culmination:

The children each using one instrument band together to play the pattern on the chalkboard. The point to be emphasized here is that

---

[3] Hugh McElheny, *Sample Creative Music Lesson,* Bank Street College of Education, 1965.

experience will prove that sounds need not be discordant, that they always make music, and that music need not be melodic. After a number of experiences, the final performance can be taped for the children for a permanent record with their own title.

Fig. 11-3.

October 28, 1964
Old Bethpage School

Sample Unit: *Creative Music,* an experience in spontaneous music which may be helpful for auditory discrimination (reading readiness) and listening skills development as well.

This material was devised by Mrs. K. for the kindergarten and primary grades, but it has excellent potential for any age level.[4]

Motivation: During a unit of study on "Good Breakfasts" the children would already be accustomed to thinking in terms of their home kitchens. The children then would be asked to go home and listen for all things which make sounds in their kitchen. One would hope that some of the items in the list below would be brought up by the children during the post discussion. If not, the following technique could be used to encourage further discussion. "I'm making scrambled eggs for you for breakfast. Can you think of a sound that would tell you I'm making scrambled eggs?" The children could think up examples such as that above and all guess the answers.

Spontaneous Music Observed in the Kitchen (many others not listed)

1. Running water
2. Coffee perking
3. Electric toaster popping
4. Electric dishwasher
5. Electric refrigerator running

---

[4] Nan Kay, *Sample Creative Music Unit.*

6. Electric can opener
7. Electric mix master
8. Electric blender
9. Hand egg beater
10. Sound of dialing a telephone number
11. Telephone ringing
12. Food frying in a frying pan
13. Whistling tea kettle
14. Grating food on a grater
15. Pouring liquid into a glass
16. Pouring liquid from a can
17. Sound of food cooking in a pot with steam opening on top of cover
18. Electric timer with bell on oven
19. Sound of a steam iron
20. Electric floor polisher
21. Sound of scraping food off plate
22. Sound of cold cereal when milk is poured on it
23. Sound of salt shaker
24. Sound of opening cellophane bags
25. Taking ice out of ice cube trays
26. Rattle of dishes and glassware
27. Opening and closing of doors, doors of cupboards, and closets
28. Mixing with a wooden spoon
29. Sound of silverware being put in or taken out of drawer
30. Opening and closing of drawers
31. Sound of chopping in a wooden bowl or board
32. The pop of opening soda bottle
33. Sound of carbonated drink being poured into glass
34. Electric switch clicks
35. Exhaust fan whirring sound

Activities:

1. Set out rhythm instruments and have youngsters simulate sounds from the kitchen.

2. Have youngsters act out the motions of the sounds they remember (toast popping, coffee perking, etc.).

3. Collection of kitchen implements (for display) which make sounds and demonstrations.

4. Blindfold testing of recognition of sounds that teacher makes with various kitchen implements.

Culmination:

It would be hoped that as many motions and sounds as possible would be explored by the teacher and the youngsters. The basic understanding being that all *sounds are music.*

The children could compose a "Symphony of Breakfasts" or "Sounds and Rhythms of the Kitchen." The children would decide the form it should take and its name and perform for themselves or others.

This type of unit could be expanded to other areas of the environment giving the children as many experiences as possible with the sounds and rhythms in motion.

Fig. 11-4.

A number of teachers ventured forth. Some tried the lessons as they were presented, still others made up their own variations. We visited a kitchen band in one class which produced music with the use of an egg beater, a whisk, some pots and pans, a grater, a garlic press, and various other sundry items taken from mamma's pantry. It was an exciting lesson and certainly was the beginning of an awareness on the children's part that music was everywhere. None of the curricular adaptations which we discuss in this chapter took over like a house on fire nor do we mean to imply that they did. However, each teacher absorbed something new, a new concept, a new idea, a new way of looking at things. This type of learning is infectious. Teachers talked about it among themselves and the overtones were generally much larger than the initial exploration. Our teachers were trying, they were full of ideas and methods and means of expanding their teaching; and curricula were coming up for more and more scrutiny and question. Who knows, someone may yet ask in the years to come, why is it that creative music experiences are really not stressed in our music curriculum?

Creative Dance

Still further interest in creativity came as a result of the New York State Teachers Association's North Nassau Zone Conference which we all attended in early fall.

October 6—Minutes of Primary Meeting

> Three of the teachers in this group attended the Creative Dance Workshop, conducted by Dr. Emil Rivera with a group of school children whom he had brought along to present the technique itself. The teachers were very pleased with the workshop and felt it had many practical applications for them in the classroom. This led to some further discussion of the need for exercises in class which provide for experiences in rhythms, muscular coordination, and which relieve tension. Creative dance is particularly meaningful in this context. Also mentioned were such activities as creative dramatics, the wearing of masks, and puppetry. Some mention was also made of the technique of acting out, being especially helpful to the shy child, who when assuming a fictional role can sometimes be helped to overcome his basic shyness. In addition, the hidden talents of certain children can sometimes be uncovered and, of course, the obvious factor that dramatics and the dance are natural activities for the release of tension.

The attendance at this workshop stimulated some very fine experiences in these classes. One teacher, Mrs. B., who had formerly taken ballet lessons, decided to try creative dance with her little ones. The project became a year long activity. Every Friday afternon, you could walk down the hall and watch these little ones dancing out stories to appropriate music played on the phonograph. They loved it and looked forward to the activity eagerly. It became such a big activity in their lives, that tights were the order of the day for Fridays in Mrs. B.'s class. Around February, Mrs. B. had convinced the high school industrial arts department to make a portable barré for her children which they used for exercises. It was a joy to behold these children in action and to watch how they learned to express emotion through the dance. We personally were entranced by one little boy, a gentle soul really, who physically resembled one of the old 1920 Chicago hoods, as he assumed "position one." Perhaps, the best tribute that could be paid Mrs. B. and her dance-a-story afternoons was the fact that we received not one parental complaint all year about the fact that the children did all their dancing in bare feet. Incidentally, Mrs. B., herself, is now back at ballet school so stimulated was she by dancing with her children.

Units of Study

We have been blessed in our school with a truly outstanding librarian. She has been an essential part of our school program and naturally she played an important role in the nongraded. Many of the classroom units of study were conducted in large part through the auspices of the librarian and she was called upon to supply needed help and guidance in the implementation of all units of study. This is in addition to her regular lessons in library skills and literature appreciation. Long before a class had started a particular unit of study, this wonderful woman had collected all the materials, books, texts, and audio-visual materials which they might need for this area of study. A good deal of the success of our program was due in large part to her cooperation and work. Like all good evangelists, she was ever on the watch for opportunities to spread the good word. Here is one such example.

September 29—Minutes of Primary Meeting

> Mrs. H. made a presentation on research library techniques, indicating that the children should be trained to use the supplementary books in the classroom as an initial source of reference (as she kept them up-to-date in each class), going from those to the books, vertical file, filmstrips and records in the library. The last stop should be the encyclopedia. Teachers must be cautioned about using the encyclopedia too soon in solving a problem or finding information to avoid the danger of pupils using this source exclusively. Mrs. H. emphasized the importance of children knowing *why* they are researching a topic as well as *what* they

are researching. Failure to orient children properly limits their proper use of the card catalog and other sources. The teacher's guidance is required in the development of research skills.

Library research skills were an essential core of the social studies and science curricula in our district. None of us, who had ever thought about it, were convinced that we were doing as good a job as we could in this respect and our librarian agreed with us wholeheartedly. She was an integral part of our efforts to improve this instructional area. However, a further development occurred right after school opened which gave the three of us the opportunity we had been waiting for. Before long the area which received the greatest focus during the school year was the implementation of units of study in social studies and science. Happily this was just the area we were most interested in stressing, so we were quite elated.

It all came about through a supervisory technique we used which involved a private conference with each teacher on tenure at the beginning of the school year, where together the teacher and administrator explored her personal teaching strengths and weaknesses and outlined an individualized program of action for the school year. It was during these conferences that we noted that a number of our teachers expressed serious concern about their ability to implement properly a social studies or science unit of study in the primary classes. This was our clue. Note, that at our September 29 primary meeting, when this topic was first discussed, this fear did not seem apparent.

September 29—Minutes of Primary Meeting

This group of teachers will follow the scope and sequence unit topics as outlined in the State-suggested revisions. These topics will lead to much more interesting and meaty social studies units.

They will also, where possible, introduce other units of study which may be pertinent to their classes.

They will make a conscientious effort to begin to introduce the multitudinous skills of the social studies unit development program at the primary level (i.e., research skills, committee work, audio-visual group techniques, interview techniques, picture collection, dramatic play). We are firmly convinced that the primary teacher is amply equipped to introduce this type of social studies unit approach and that we will explore these techniques with the children this year.

Individual, independent activities designed to instill in the children the independent learning skills so essential to their learning will also be studied this year. Specific suggestions include— art corner with materials, leisure reading corner, science corner with materials, etc.

Finally, this group will conduct an active program of team planning during the professional hour where they will plan (on paper) the new units discussed above for use in their class. This group development will broaden the scope of the unit development of each topic. Specific suggestions for activities will be exchanged though, of course, the program will be carried out individually by each teacher in her classroom.

The multi-disciplinary approach to the teaching of social studies was also briefly discussed, since it is essential to any properly developed unit.

Armed with our private conferences with certain teachers and the written unit plans presented to us by still other teachers, we began to see that there really was need for further understanding in the implementation techniques of units of study. We put it up to the teachers, did they feel that this area merited further study? We received an unqualified affirmative response. Whatever help we could offer, they wanted. Our decision was to offer, on a voluntary basis, a six-session workshop (during professional hours) on unit development and implementation. We split our primary teachers into two groups and Mr. F., the principal, worked with one group of teachers while Mrs. G., the assistant principal, worked with the others.

October 19—Minutes of Primary Meeting

Mr. F. announced the proposed double series (one run by Mr. F. and one by Mrs. G.) of workshops on unit development and implementation for the primary teachers. These will be held every two weeks, for a period of 12 weeks, during the professional hour. These workshops are planned to be highly practical in nature and to explore all the aspects possible for the development, execution, implementation, and evaluation of a unit of study. The teachers responded well and felt that if the workshops were practical in nature, they would be eager to participate.

We have included the outline of the Workshop on Unit Development for your perusal. The expanded notes for each separate session are included in the Appendix on page 210. The workshops were worthwhile, we feel. The quality of unit class presentations have proven to be greatly improved as a result of them.

OLD BETHPAGE SCHOOL

Overview of Workshop on Unit Development

Session   I. Establishing Objectives
Session II. Selecting Appropriate Content
Session III. Methodology
    and
Session IV.
Session   V. Materials For Instruction
Session VI. Culminating Activities

Fig. 11-5.

(Appendix, pp. 210-213, pp. 269-272)

Our emphasis during these workhops was upon practicality. We considered the factors of concept versus fact learning, quantity and type of content necessary for a child's learning, the degree of teacher-directed activities, individual versus group work and a host of other topics. We all worked together to plan one unit of study for a primary class, from its conception to its culmination. The practical and real everyday problems of classroom management and children's reactions were constantly kept in mind. Throughout, we were always aware of the admonition that educators are emphasizing these days—the explosion of knowledge is so fast and great that we must constanly reevaluate what we teach children. Certainly, social studies and science are leading examples of this problem, what with the content of these two subject areas shifting with every day, so that the generalizations and relationships, and conceptualizations inherent in these studies assume greater importance than the facts. We had been terribly aware of the gross importance of this precept to present day teaching, and had even discussed the problem with our teachers in former years. It was the nongraded, however, which permitted us to introduce the topic meaningfully. For this we were grateful.

Anderson has said that "there must be an adaptable curriculum operationally defined."[5] We feel that we have made sharp inroads in this direction, and after just one year of nongrading. We have taken our basic and excellent curricula and begun to translate them into action. The words are now taking on newer and deeper meanings. We are fitting the grand precepts in each curricular area to the children themselves. We are, in a word, making them workable. This, for us, is curricular implementation at its best and we hope to continue in this path.

---

[5] Anderson, Speech.

12

MATERIALS AND ACTIVITIES

Objective: to encourage the use of differentiated instructional materials and experiences.

Curricular implementation and adaptation to individual differences required that a teacher select a specific method of teaching to suit her purposes. Once she had selected the most appropriate method to teach what she wanted to teach, she had then to select from among the varied materials and tools that which best enhanced the precise method of her choice. She then often found that she had to offer this same knowledge more than once in order to assure that her children had mastered that knowledge. This necessitated that the teacher select more than one activity in order that she vary the approach used in presenting this knowledge. Let us suppose that a teacher was concerned with teaching children about the wheel. She planned one lesson which was a simple discussion with the children about said wheel. Another time she showed the pupils a film (incidentally, Walt Disney has produced one such which is excellent). Still another time, she brought to class a wheel and had the children try it out on their own. Needless to say, the ideas were endless. It was this type of diverse and varied approach to the presentations of lessons to which we refer when we speak of diversification of materials and activities. It is an important point, because it is precisely this variety of approach which stimulates the learning of children, which makes learning for them the truly exciting adventure it ought to be. Just think of the few examples we have given you and contrast them with the time honored tradition of having children read portions from a text aloud, one after the other, while the teacher holds her copy in front of her, and makes appropriate comments. And consider the dullness when this procedure is repeated day after day until all two hundred seven pages of the text are completed. Variety for variety's sake is not our purpose. Variety which truly excites the minds of children and stimulates them and challenges them is what we are referring to. And, of course, our ultimate question always, did the nongraded in any way cause teachers to plan for new and different types of activities using new and different materials to enhance the learning experiences of children? It did. Once again, the need to recognize the differences among children, *inherent in the nongraded*, necessitated that teachers explore in greater depth than previously the many techniques, methods, materials, and activities by which any lesson could be presented to any child or group of children.

Reading Experiences

Recent research studies have brought to light some interesting facts. It has been noted that boys and girls approach learning differently. Boys tend to analyze words by breaking them into parts. Girls tend to view the word as a whole. Interesting in light of the individualized approaches we designed this past year for pupils having reading difficulties (Chapter Eight). In many of the cases of pupils with reading difficulties we found it was necessary to alter their approach to reading just along these very lines. Still further are the findings which indicate rather clearly that well adjusted children do not require a phonics approach to the teaching of reading, while the maladjusted child profits from this approach because of the security and structure which it provides. Once again, our own experiences with adjusted programs for pupils with reading disabilities bore out this fact.

October 19—Minutes of Primary Meeting

Pacing

There was discussion relevant to the pacing of reading instruction at the beginning stages of reading instruction and reading experiences. There was disagreement about when formalized instruction should begin. Mrs. C. stated that the immature youngster who is average or above average will have to start a bit later, but will catch up without any difficulty. The slower child will have to start later and his overall pace will always be slower. Mrs. W. mentioned also the female-oriented world of the primary boy child and the adverse effects on his learning rate. This is an accepted fact and we shall try whatever we can to help these children.

October 20—Minutes of Primary Meeting

After an earlier discussion which Mrs. E. and Mrs. G. had, it was decided to try the technique of creating daily experience charts with the children relating to their direct experiences only (at home or in school) and upon completion of the chart, having the story dittoed by the teacher (primary type) and a copy distributed to the child for the formation of his own book.

Thus the child, who is having difficulty with beginning reading, builds a vocabulary which includes the basic words necessary for the primer, in addition to other words stemming from his own environment and interest. He also has in his possession a book with illustrations, cut outs, etc., which is his and his alone and which ultimately he can pace with ease. Mrs. E. is quite pleased with the results of this approach thus far and finds it a very efficacious tool for learning with the young child who has phonics difficulty. This was the method which Mrs. G. had used once with a slow first grade and she recommended it enthusiastically.

Flexible Grouping

Many were the problems which we discussed during the course of the school year relevant to varying the materials and activities for instruction in the classroom. One such avenue which reaped excellent rewards was discussions centering around flexible grouping. The present day approach to instruction emphasized that children be exposed to working in a number of different group arrangements during the day. In addition, as has already been described, pupils might well be working on their own. A child, during the course of a normal school day at our school, could have worked with one group of children in reading, still another in mathematics, the whole class for a social studies lesson, and completely independently on a science problem. This type of switching was planned in order to accommodate the changing interests and capabilities of a child, but it required skillful planning and maneuvering on the teacher's part, and, of course, raised some difficulties.

October 20—Minutes of Primary Meeting

> There was discussion relevant to the movement of pupils within the class during the day for their different activities (reading groups, mathematics groups, social studies groups, etc.). This is a normal part of the organization and movement pattern of the nongraded class which will take some time to get accustomed to. However, there are some techniques which can be used to cut down on the actual physical movement of the youngsters, if this poses a problem. For instance, the original seating pattern of the class can be planned according to reading groups, thus eliminating at least one change of seat for this activity. The movement itself, from one group to another, from one seat to another, from one part of the classroom to another, is highly beneficial to the physical needs of children. It provides them with some freedom of movement during the school day. It also provides a normal and natural change of pace in the day's activities which is beneficial to the learning situation.

We evidenced some difficulties in adjustment. This much freedom of movement was, of course, difficult for some teachers to adjust to. However, by the spring semester movements of this sort became the accepted pattern of classroom management. As has been previously noted, centers of activities were also created around many classrooms which provided opportunities for children to learn, to explore, to play, and to create on their own. Room arrangements became more and more flexible and tables and chairs were easily shifted for different planned activities. Incidentally, our budget for the 1965-1966 school year included, at the behest of the teachers themselves, an order for ten six-foot project tables for use in the classroom. Now that more and more activities were being encouraged in the classroom, the teacher demanded more furniture to provide their children with a place to conduct their projects and activities. Individual desks and chairs were no longer answering all the needs of the classroom teacher or her pupils.

Instructional Materials and Texts

Materials for instruction came up for inspection this past year also, as they had never in the past. Follow this short history with us if you will.

November 23—Minutes of Primary Meeting

The group was alerted to the fact that supply and text orders are to be determined in the near future. Specific requests should be forwarded to the office. Teachers pointed out the need for more visual aid material in the area of "Community Helpers" and "Old New York City," as well as any available material on primitive civilizations or cultures other than the North American Indian. Texts and reference books are needed in this critical area also and we will look for suggestions from all in this regard.

November 24—Minutes of Primary Meeting

Requests for materials and texts have been coming in to the office. Teachers are to continue putting their requests in writing and are requested to place particular emphasis on their search for materials in our deficient filmstrip areas and on the new topics in social studies recommended by the New York State Education Department.

December 1—Minutes of Primary Meeting

In general, it was felt that there are a sufficient number of volumes to use for story time, and for children to use for browsing. These volumes are kept in the library and removed in batches at a time to the classrooms on an alternating schedule by Mrs. H., the librarian. A recommended list of books for primary children, which appeared in the *School Library Journal*, will be directed to Mrs. H.'s attention and we shall endeavor to purchase those titles which we do not already possess.

December 7—Minutes of Primary Meeting

Mrs. W., the reading consultant, introduced to the group the new phonics and comprehension material which we have just received: *Practice Readers*,[1] *Reading for Meaning*,[2] and phonics workbooks. She explained their use and distributed same. She also distributed to the teachers a dittoed list of the words which appear in all our basic reading series (the district uses three). The materials had been particularly ordered to accomodate the individualized reading programs being planned for children having difficulty in reading. (Chapter 8).

February 15—Minutes of Primary Meeting

Mrs. H. introduced to the group prepared ditto materials with supplementary reading activities on the primer level which emphasize phonics and comprehension skills which she has obtained from the Jenn Publications. The material is quite good and we shall order some for the school, but do caution that the children not be asked to color these exercises, but rather check or circle the appropriate selections. The latter method is all right, but the former is not since the pictures are too small for primary children's hand coordination in coloring.

February 16—Minutes of Primary Meeting

Mrs. W. has just completed a list of all reading materials—basal and supplementary, which are appropriate for our twelve reading levels. This should be particularly helpful to our primary teachers.

March 9—Minutes of Primary Meeting

The only topic discussed at this meeting was the completion of budget and orders. Instructional supplies were determined as the group continued their perusal of catalogues and materials for next year's budget orders.

The librarian, always a key resource figure in instructional books and materials made her presence known repeatedly also.

---

[1] Charles C. Grover and Donald G. Anderson, *New Practice Readers,* (St. Louis, Mo.: Webster Division, McGraw-Hill Book Co., 1961).

[2] W. S. Guilier and J. H. Coleman, *Reading for Meaning,* (Philadelphia, Pa.: J. B. Lippincott Company, 1955).

November 7—Minutes of Faculty Meeting

Mrs. H. displayed a number of newly received books for children and professionals. She provided a thumbnail sketch of the professional volumes. The children's books were too numerous to discuss but were on view in the library.

Mrs. F. suggested that when teachers write for materials from commercial companies that they request two of everything. The free materials are often quite excellent and thus Mrs. H. would have one copy available for others in the school's vertical file.

Mrs. H. announced that she had obtained a free film entitled, *Lunchroom Manners*,[3] which will be shown at Friday's assembly.

Mrs. H. distributed dittoes on the Dewey Decimal System and the list of magaines (over fifty) on the school's subscription list. She indicated that the revised list of filmstrips as well as the greatly amplified list of materials in the vertical file have been run off and are being collated by the Parent Teacher Association. Lists of phonograph records are being started this week.

Mrs. H. closed by suggesting a correlation between literature and science or social studies—using fairy or folk tales related to the unit under study. She would be glad to recommend specific related titles. She did caution that many of the books in our library on these topics have readability levels beyond the comprehension of our primary children, having been ordered at a time when we were running a kindergarten through sixth grade school. However, she suggested that even these books could be used by the teacher in terms of picture analysis and story content.

Certainly, attention to materials was constant. A new world was opening. There was a wealth of material available in all media which could help a teacher teach. She had but to find it and request it. (Wherever possible, budget—wise, we have always filled any worthwhile request.) We, ourselves, were constantly on the lookout for worthwhile material which could help teachers help children. We have always felt that one of the prime responsibilities of the administrator is to act as a resource

---

[3] Distributed by Group 5 Savings Bank Association, I Hanson Place, Brooklyn, N. Y.

person and bring to the teacher's attention any new, relevant, and significant materials or texts on the market. Unfortunately, this is a time consuming process, since so much of what is being produced today we find worthless and we spend many hours sifting the wheat from the shaft.

Teacher-Made Materials

If you can recall back in Chapter 7 we discussed special programs for the immature and extended readiness pupils. Although we purchased at that time extra supplies and materials for these children, we found one of the richest sources of materials for these programs came from the teachers themselves. This is why we deem it important to mention at this time. Often, the inspired teacher, who is creative to boot, will design her own materials for use with children. Here is one such case.

September 22—Minutes of Primary Meeting

> The meeting continued with an exploration of the materials available and which can possibly be ordered to aid in giving the immature child gross manipulative experiences in the arts, reading, and mathematics. Some specifics were discussed and Mrs. G. volunteered to comb the catalogues and purchase these items as soon as possible. Certainly, elementary items such as creative wood toys, plastic forms, and puzzles are quite necessary, not to mention kindergarten blocks.

One month later, at a primary meeting held on October 20, Mrs. E. met us all with a pleasant surprise. She wasn't waiting for the manufacturers to ship our order.

> Mrs. E., because of her own intense interest in the extended readiness child and program, has developed an excellent set of materials (all homemade) which she brought to the meeting for demonstration to the other teachers. Each item was specifically created to provide the needed additional experiences in the precise areas of weakness which the children display (auditory discrimination, left to right eye movement, small muscle movement, motor coordination, etc.). Some of the materials displayed were

puzzles made from magazine pictures, squeegees which the children can use by themselves (placing pictures in order of sequence), copying peg board designs from pictured diagrams, corn meal pans for letter formation, sand shakers with varying pitch, sandpaper letters and numerals for kinesthetic experiences, copying of bead shapes and many more. Each item was of great usefulness to the primary teacher and need not necessarily be used for an extended readiness program.

Teacher-made materials became evident, we might say, in almost every classroom in the nongraded. The teachers took great pride in their ingenuity, but not nearly as much as we did. We know that the nongraded challenged them to create materials for which they had somehow never felt the need in the past, and we are grateful that they rose to the occasion.

Field Trips

What about experiences? Were the nongraded teachers exploring new types and ranges of experiences which they could make available to their children? Well certainly we have already demonstrated that individual children were now being given an opportunity to explore new and varied experiences on their own through the use of center of activity corners in each room in the sciences, the arts, the social studies, music, and the language arts. Concerted effort was being made at all times to increase the variety of experiences for all the children in class also. Take field trips, for example. Our district provided free bus transportation for trips within a twenty mile radius of the schools. More importantly, however, other than neighborhood walks, and local trips to the fire house, and post office, we had not seen too much evidence of field trips at the Old Bethpage School for one simple reason. The teachers felt that the longer trips were too physically taxing to the primary child, and rightly so. Thus, many of the excellent trips we could have planned to New York City were out of the question, except for some physically mature nine year olds.

January 4—Minutes of Primary Meeting

Teachers felt that most trips which require two to two and one-half hours of traveling time are too physically tiring for the primary child. "Well," some said, "why can't we find out about worthwhile trips locally other than to the community resources which we have used in the past."

An investigation started and shortly thereafter, a list of some twenty suggestions was compiled and distributed to the teachers. We found, to our pleasant surprise, that there were some fine experiences available right here on Long Island which would make for meaningful field trips for primary children. Late spring saw many of our classes off and away. One class visited a local dress manufacturer during a unit of study they were conducting on Clothing. Another class studying Food, visited a candy factory (they got free samples), a milk farm, a duck farm, and a bread bakery. A class involved in a Transportation unit took themselves off to the Long Island Railroad roundhouse and had themselves an exciting and informative time. Still another class, studying Shelters Around the World, visited the many local builder sources, tile manufacturers, roofing manufacturers, lumberers, etc., and watched the construction of a house in a local development from start to finish as an example of shelter construction in an industrialized society. We are strong believers in realistic, primary, firsthand experiences for children. We greeted this increased interest in field trips as a welcome change in approach.

Center of Interest

Probably the area which received the greatest amount of attention and time in our schedule was what we called the Center of Interest (not to be confused with the previously discussed Center of Activity corners in each classroom). This name and procedure we borrowed, on invitation, from Mrs. Reba Mayer and her nongraded teachers at Public School 89, Queens in New York City.

During our investigation into the nongraded the previous spring, we had visited for a full day with Mrs. Mayer, and the result was a very profitable trip. We were so impressed with this teaching approach that we introduced it formally to our teachers early in the school year.

September 29—Minutes of Primary Meeting

The administrators launched this meeting with the topic of Centers of Interest. After much study and visitation last year, it was found that the Center of Interest, as a classroom technique, was an excellent and recommended experience for the nongraded. It is particularly effective with interage classes.

The Center of Interest is a simple technique which we saw effectively demonstrated at Public School 89 in Queens. The teacher starts each day with a total group discussion of some small topic, the circus, the drought, the fair, the zoo, etc., and then small groups of children explore this topic through some specific activity assigned to them by the teacher. These topics are not to be confused with units of study in social studies or science which are long range by nature. They are of a much shorter duration (fifteen minutes often being enough time for the discussion and the one activity though, of course, if a teacher wishes she can extend the topic through a few days. After the discussion, the activities which the children may explore are reading, drawing, dramatic play, free play, language arts activities (creative writing, experience charts, etc.), arts and crafts construction, etc. A group is assigned an activity conversant with its abilities. Youngsters who have not yet learned to read would, of course, be assigned activities consistent with their abilities (drawing, construction, dramatic play, etc.). More advanced youngsters could work in the other areas.

The Center of Interest serves as a unifying focal point and ties all the children together before they spend the larger part of the school day in other group or individual activities in the curriculum areas. It serves many purposes and seems to us to be exceptionally meaningful as an experience for the nongraded classes.

It was suggested that the teachers try this technique and see how it works out. The following materials are being offered to the teachers to help with ideas during this trial period—*120 Independ-*

ent Activities,[4] *Spice,*[5] and our own list of individualized activities which may be transposed to service groups instead of individuals.

The teachers were not as excited about providing this experience for the children in their everyday planning as we had hoped, but they agreed to give it a try. Some of them learned to use the technique to exceptional advantage. Others used it only on certain days.

October 26—Minutes of Primary Meeting

Mrs. M. suggested that the Center of Interest as an activity requires some form of evaluation (most probably at the end of the school day). This is an extremely important realization and all the other teachers found that they were in agreement. Educationally, the need for evaluation is a rule in almost all activities, but is particularly meaningful in relation to the Center of Interest. It has, in addition, a social purpose and a motivational purpose for future activities. It also provides children with experience in the development of self-direction and discrimination in critical thinking.

The teachers continued their discussion by exploring some of the topics which they have used for their Centers of Interest. Fire Prevention, UNICEF, Halloween, Breakfast Club, Science Experiments, the October Calendar, Our Wishes, the World's Fair, National Elections, and Autumn. The teachers indicate that there is no lack of ideas for Centers of Interest, but that it may well be absorbing too much of the actual school day. However, as time goes on more and more effort may well be directed toward activities during the Center of Interest which will fulfill the instructional needs of children (i.e., children who need more experience with subtraction, may be assigned work in subtraction during their Center of Interest time directly related to the topic of the day—which might be, let us say, Running a Food Store).

There was general agreement that these activities must be quite structured and well planned and organized. It should not be

[4] Isobel Willcox, *120 Activities for the Independent Work Period* (Teachers Practical Press, Inc., 1964).

[5] Mary E. Platts, Sister Rose Marguerite, and Esther Shumber, *Spice, Suggested Activities to Motivate the Teaching of the Language Arts* (Benton Harbor: Educational Service, Inc., 1960).

an activity of free choice. Other activities described were drama, puppetry, dance, art, and creative writing.

After a number of months had passed, we were fortunately able to arrange for some of our teachers to spend a day at Public School 89 in Queens. The sophistication and critical judgment displayed in their discussions about the nongraded and the Center of Interest in particular was marked proof of the growth we had all made from the "greenhorns" we had been in early September.

January 4—Minutes of Primary Meeting

Discussion centered around the use of the Center of Interest as demonstrated at Public School 89 during our recent visitation. It was felt that too much time was spent by these teachers in motivating these lessons. It was suggested that our use of this technique be developed a bit differently. First, that the motivation not take longer than five to fifteen minutes at the start of the school day. Second, that the class then break into groups for carrying out various activities stemming from the topic for that day's Center of Interest, and that these activities might well be in various curricular areas (language arts, dramatics, music, art, etc.). Third, that the topics for Centers of Interest might well come directly from class units of study in social studies and science. Teachers will continue to report some of the successful experiences they have had with their youngsters with the Center of Interest.

Here was an exciting process taking place. Our teachers not only demonstrated the ability and interest in making curricular adaptations in techniques, methods, materials, and activities, but also were competent enough to make their own adjustments within the scope of new activities to which they themselves had just been introduced, and tailored them to suit their own needs.

There was marked evidence, of which we have given you some sample in this chapter, of the increased use of varied materials for instruction at the Old Bethpage School. The experiences and activities in which children were participating in each classroom were on the way to making learning the volatile, creative, and self-fulfilling task that we had always envisioned it as being. Much of the credit must go to the nongraded program.

13

PARENT EDUCATION

Objective: to help parents adjust to the ideals and philosophy of individualized goals for children inherent in the nongraded.

We've talked about children. We've talked about teachers. We've talked about program. It comes time now to talk about parents, an integral part of any school program. Our jobs would be relatively simple, we suppose, if we could plan and work in some sort of isolation, outside the context of the community in which our work is taking place. But this is never the case. We knew from the moment we started to plan for the nongraded that we would have to make extensive plans to educate our parents to a clear understanding of our program and our goals. We set about doing just this.

Orientation

We had an orientation plan for the preceding spring. This began with an opening announcement to the community at large and to the parents of the Old Bethpage School in particular that our school was going to be nongraded during the following school year. Immediately we followed this anonuncement with an invitation issued to all parents of the school to attend an evening orientation session. This first evening orientation session was held in May. We presented our case at that time. We reviewed the literature of the nongraded (in brief), described the nongraded and its philosophy, and explained *exactly* how the nongraded was going to operate in our school. We demonstrated all our points with the help of the overhead projector and charts which we had prepared in advance. These charts were designed to show our grouping patterns (Chapter 3) and the differences between graded progress and nongraded progress (see Appendix, Nongraded Brochure p. 222). We ended the meeting with an open ended question and answer period. There were many questions and we tried to answer them all. We had planned this first orientation session as a sort of private get together, just some staff and administration from the school and the parents. It was our feeling that this would make the whole procedure less formidable and more relaxed. The parents, we felt, would have many intimate questions which they would feel freer to ask if there were no outsiders present.

In June we held the second Evening Orientation meeting with the parents. At that meeting, we had present some outsiders, administrators from other schools, who were successfully operating nongraded plans. We felt that the parents by this time were quite prepared to ask specific questions from professionals who had already demonstrated their ability at running a successful nongraded school. Again, at the conclusion of the talks, we closed with an open ended question and answer period. The questions came fast and heavy.

Knowing full well, that our meetings had not reached our entire public, or even answered all the questions of the parents who attended the meetings, we also prepared a brochure on the nongraded which was sent home with every child in the school. This brochure, entitled "Why—Nongraded Primary?" was an exhausting labor. Mr. F., the principal, wrote the text: Mrs. G., the assistant principal, proposed the format and the key questions, and Mrs. S., editor of the school newspaper, made the charming illustrations throughout the brochure. (see Appendix, p. 225). The sub-title of the brochure indicated its content—*An earnest attempt to answer the ten most frequently asked questions about the Nongraded Primary.* These were the ten questions about which we judged our parents were most concerned:

1. What is the Nongraded Primary?
2. In what ways is the Nongraded Primary different from the graded school?

3. What happens to the "slow" child in the Nongraded Primary school?
4. What happens to the "average" child in the Nongraded Primary school?
5. What happens to the "bright" child in the Nongraded Primary school?
6. How are the children going to be grouped into classes?
7. Does the Nongraded Primary require a different curriculum or different materials?
8. How will we know about our children's progress if we don't know what grade they are in?
9. How will the children know what class they are in?
10. Why does the administration and staff of the Old Bethpage School endorse the Nongraded Primary?

It is almost unnecessary to point out, we are sure, that from the moment of the original announcement of our plans to nongrade through the remainder of the school year, the administrators' doors were completely open to visitors. And visitors we had. Many were the parents who made appointments, or dropped in to see us with further questions which we zealously attempted to answer. We should mention here, too, that we had successfully solicited the cooperation of the Executive Board of the Old Bethpage School Parent Teacher Association in advance. These mothers proved to be wonderful allies. Many were the questions they fielded for us. Many were the parents they talked to and helped orient. We had held an informal orientation meeting with these seventeen mothers prior to our first public announcement and had, at that time, presented all our plans. They were then, as always, very supportive and we could never express our gratitude properly to this group.

Once the school year started, we felt that continued efforts at parent education had to be made. We employed the following techniques. Two evening meetings were held in addition to our regularly scheduled P.T.A. meetings. The first, near the beginning of the school year, was combined with our traditional "Open School Night, Meet the Teacher" evening. This meeting was always the best attended and this year proved no exception. After we completed the staff introductions that night, we opened the

meeting to questions which all of us together attempted to answer. In addition, each teacher met with her parents for one
hour in her classroom for further orientation. She explained to her
group her plans for the school year, and gave them an overview
of the curriculum for the year. This was a procedure we had used
effectively in the past and had no reservations about using this
time. We discussed the proposed "Meet the Teacher" evening
with the staff in advance since we had noted that they seemed
to be more nervous about the prospect than they had appeared
in the years past.

September 21—Minutes of Primary Meeting

> The major topic for discussion was the handling of questions
> relating to the "Meet the Teacher" meeting scheduled for Wed-
> nesday night. We envision a certain number of queries from
> parents when the teachers meet with their parents in their class-
> rooms for a group discussion. We feel relatively certain that many
> of the questions this year will relate directly to the Nongraded
> Primary. We reviewed the question of interage grouping, sub-
> grouping within the class, cycling of social studies and science
> topics. We determined on uniform philosophical responses to all
> the parents, knowing full well that we, ourselves, were just getting
> our feet wet and need time to really develop our thinking and
> our operation. Many of our parents need reassurance that their
> youngsters will be learning as much, if not more, than before and
> this fact needs stressing also.

We closed the building that night, all of us, with a huge sigh
of relief. Discussions held at subsequent Primary Meetings revealed that the questions teachers had been asked in the confines
of their classrooms proved to be basic and they had had no difficulty in making suitable responses. In the late fall we held our
second evening meeting directed at the Nongraded Primary
which we called, Nongraded Progress Report Number One (see
Appendix, p. 235). We had six staff members including ourselves
present for a panel (the school psychologist, one teacher, the
reading consultant, and librarian). This was a successful program
as our enthusiasm was genuine and it was beginning to come
across to the audience. There were questions that night, but they

didn't seem to have the nervous intensity which we had met at previous meetings.

Throughout the rest of the school year, we also continually published. We published a series of one page items which we called *News of the Nongraded* at monthly intervals from November through May which were distributed to each parent through the children (see Appendix, p. 233). These were just informal little vignettes designed to keep parents alert to the happenings at school. Our P.T.A. published its newspaper, *The Ptarmigan*, six times a school year, and no issue went to press which didn't contain some interesting article or two on the nongraded. The district publications (of which there are two) also included one article (see Appendix, p. 239) on the nongraded which was distributed throughout the school district. Educational reports on our progress were prepared for the Assistant Superintendent of Schools in late spring which were presented at the end of year Evaluation Meeting with the Superintendent of Schools and the Board of Education. These documents, being evaluative by nature, are not included here, because we have attempted in our book not to evaluate, but rather to report. We leave judgments up to the reader.

Just as our office doors were open during the previous spring so were they all during the school year. To our knowledge no parent who wished to see us or any member of the staff was ever denied an audience. We met with all of them and continued to explain and answer questions. These were our efforts at indoctrination to the overall philosophy and goals of the nongraded primary.

Parent-Teacher Conferences

The other large area of concern was the awareness we wished parents to have of one essential hard core fact of nongrading. We wanted parents to accept and understand that each child competes with himself, not his class or some other group of children. This was the significant factor of nongrading—*the essen-*

*tial concept of the individuality of each child, and the individual
goals which we had established for each child consistent with his
native abilities.* This brings us to the topic of reporting to parents.
Certainly our reports to parents represented a shift from past
efforts. Certainly parents required a new orientation. We had
endeavored to explain these new individual goals for children
in our meetings and our publications, but it was the reporting
itself which was to reflect our new emphasis. Briefly, we followed
the following plan for reporting to parents. The school year was
divided into four quarters. At the end of the first quarter, there
was an individual parent-teacher conference held. At the end
of the second quarter there was a report card issued. At the
end of the third quarter, we once again held an individual parent
-teacher conference. At the close of the school year we issued the
closing report card. Our district conducted one week of parent-
teacher conferences in the fall and one in the spring. The schools
are closed for one-half day two weeks out of the year to accomplish this. It is the responsibility of each teacher to see every parent during this period of time. Special arrangements are made to
accommodate working parents and conferences are also held, if
needed, one evening during Parent Conference Week.

October 13—Minutes of Faculty Meeting

Each teacher has received a guide to conducting parent-teacher
conferences, which was discussed at this meeting (see Appendix,
p. 242). Questions were broad in nature since specific questions
will be pursued during our Primary Meetings. The emphasis
during the fall parent-teacher conference is upon the exchange
of information. It is an informal get together which is designed
to help both the teacher and the parent better understand the
child. Attached to the guide for parent-teacher conferences is an
excellent compilation of a study made in Omaha, Nebraska, on
the most frequently asked questions which schoolmen encounter.
A quick look at these questions may be helpful in better preparing
yourself for the questions of your own parents.

November 2—Minutes of Primary Meeting

Emphasis during fall parent-teacher conferences is on securing
information from the parent pertinent to insuring an optimal

learning situation for each child. Reports to parents at this time should be specific only if possible. Actual reading level, math level, and spelling is to be reported. I.Q. information is only available to parents by special request and then only through the auspices of the school psychologist, Miss C. Actual SRA scores are to be used with parents only if the teacher feels that it would be helpful in describing the achievement level of a youngster only. The only other information which may not be revealed to the parents is reading or curricular levels of the other pupils or groups in the class. This information is not relevant to the particular child under discussion, since the parent is to be told only about the achievement level of his own youngster and nothing about his performance in relation to other pupils. Each child's abilities and talents are individual and are to be discussed individually.

In the case of a child who represents a behavioral difficulty, there is also a procedure which is to be used. The child's social behavior should be described. Then together the parent and teacher may determine on a particular course of action which they may cooperatively pursue to help the child make a better adjustment. All suggestions should be specific and not generalized since, in general, parents are looking for specificity. If possible, the teacher is also cautioned not to attempt any lay diagnosis of the reasons for the youngster's behavior. We deal with the symptoms and help to eradicate difficulties, but we do not deal in analysis. Too often, our honest attempts at lay analysis are strongly resented by parents and create more problems for us than less.

At the completion of the week's conferences we polled the teachers to find out how many of the questions they were asked directly related to nongrading. Below is a list of the questions we compiled from the teachers:

1. Will younger children, who are in interage classes with older children, complete the nongraded primary in two years?
2. What will the nongraded primary do for my child?
3. How is the nongraded different from our former program?
4. In what way is the learning situation different this year from last?
5. Isn't it difficult to handle so many different groups in the same class?
6. Many questions relating to achievement test scores.

7. Many questions relating to homework and parental help at home.
8. Will my child have the same teacher next year?
9. Will my child be in the same group next year?
10. If my youngster completes two levels of reading during the first year of primary school, where will he be put next year?
11. Parents of children in classes where switches had been made (of other pupils) questioned the reasons for these switches.
12. Parents of children who had been switched made very favorable comments on the nongraded program, feeling that the changes were highly beneficial to their children and questioned why this was not done more freely in other schools.

The general consensus of feeling, after the fall parent–teacher conferences, was that the teachers were able to handle the questions with dispatch, although parents did show more concern than usual because of the newness of the program. The conferences were felt to be a little more difficult than they had been in the past. As to how effectively we were beginning to get our message of individual children and individual goals across, many had some serious reservations.

All too soon, the spring brought the second week of Parent-Teacher Conferences. It was our custom to use the second Parent -Teacher Conference as the true reporting device. Where our emphasis during the first conference was upon getting to know the child, the emphasis during the second conference was on complete and accurate reporting of a child's achievement levels in all areas, accompanied with the teacher's thorough appraisal of this child's potential. Thus parents of children who were underachieving, for example, were definitively and completely alerted to this fact. We attempted to be very specific during this conference and there was a detailed explanation provided of any and all individual programs which had been designed expressly to help any one child. Home cooperation or non-cooperation, as the case might be, was solicited. We wanted all our parents truly aware of the potential of their children and of their performance. Plans were reviewed and specific programs explained. The emphasis once again was upon keeping the parent aware of his individual child, his needs, his interests, his abilities, and his performance. Our meetings with teachers carefully outlined procedures for conducting these conferences and we enlisted the aid of the school psychologist at one faculty meeting to carefully document ways and means of handling ticklish situations with special cases. In certain instances, where we could predict that there might be difficulty with a parent, due to the unique nature of a pupil's problem, one of the administrators or the school psychologist sat in on the conference.

The spring conferences went smoothly, and we make this judgment because of the relative paucity of parent requests for conferences with administration following the week of conferences. This was in rather marked contrast to the flood of requests we received for private conferences following our fall Parent-Teacher conferences.

Report Cards

Report cards were issued in January and June. Due to the pressure of time, we never prepared a report card which we felt was adequate as a reporting device for the nongraded. The report card allowed space for indicating the precise level at which a pupil was achieving in each curricular area, with appropriate space for anecdotal comments, in addition to space for comments upon the social aspects of a child's behavior (see Appendix, p. 251).

January 4—Minutes of Primary Meeting

> The primary report card was discussed since we wished to place a new emphasis on specific identification of level achievement and weaknesses and strengths in curricular areas on the cards. Mr. F. will prepare on ditto a suggested list of topics to be handled under each curricular area on the report card. This list will hopefully be of help to each primary teacher in the preparation of her report cards.

This dittoed material, *Instructions for Completing Report Cards* (see Appendix, p. 259) was distributed to the teachers on

January 12 and contained the exact terminology which teachers could use to describe pupils' achievement in each curricular area in addition to designating the precise level of achievement. After the report cards were sent home with the children, we asked that teachers forward to the office all report cards on which parents had taken the trouble to add written comments in addition to their signatures. All of these comments were read.

February 9—Minutes of Primary Meeting

> We were most interested in determining the quality of parental comments on this, the first report card issued since we became nongraded. We read all of the comments and related them to the specific children and their adjustment, as we knew it, to the school program.
>
> In general, the comments were favorable and indicated a high degree of cooperation that existed between home and school. In those instances where there were unanswered questions left in the parents' minds, the teacher was contacting the parent by phone or in person for a conference.

We had no way of gauging reactions to the June report cards since they were distributed on the last day of school. These report cards, however, also reflected our new reporting techniques and were specific in reporting to parents the actual performance level of their children. There also was indicated on the report card the pupil's next year's room number.

Thus, the techniques we used to help parents adjust to the ideals and philosophy of individualized goals for children inherent in the nongraded—a planned series of information meetings, four in all, a planned series of articles describing activities even further, an explanatory brochure, and new techniques for reporting to parents in conference or writing. We used them all. How successfully we leave for you to determine when you read our next two chapters.

14

INTERNAL PROBLEMS

As we have promised, we are devoting these two last chapters to the difficulties which we encountered during this first year of the nongraded school. This chapter will attempt to describe what we euphemistically call "internal" problems, that is, problems related directly to the school, the program, the children, and the staff. There is no way for us to assess the significance of each problem. Nor are we able to determine whether they are problems of a long or short range nature. We can only describe our efforts at meeting these problems as they arose and our plans for the future. Let us look first at a problem which was rather foreboding and which raised its ugly head before we had even started operating in September. These events all took place in May of the previous semester during our grouping sessions.

Teacher Tension

Naturally, our teachers were nervous about their new program. We were prepared for this condition, and really were in no better condition ourselves. In May we began to group our children for the nongraded. Here is a description as it appeared in the *National Elementary Principal.*

> We drew up a "master paper plan" for grouping in each class based on the cumulative totals now available from the Profile Cards (i.e., twenty-seven youngsters to be instructed at level eight in reading, etc.). It was a beautiful plan, if we do say so our-

selves; we even used different colors to designate different chronological ages. Each class had three contiguous reading groups, and
no class had an age span of more than two years . . .[1]

We had predetermined that we would keep interage grouping
at a maximum of two years in each class as a cautious first step
toward the ultimate "true" interage grouping (i.e., 1-2, 2-3).

> We called our first group meeting with the teachers. The pur-
> pose of the meeting was to designate actual class placement for
> real children according to the "master paper plan." All hell broke
> loose. Our heretofore well-mannered, staunch friends panicked.
> For the first time the specter of actual, real, honest-to-goodness
> interage grouping reared its head, and they weren't having any.
> The school psychologist, Miss C., normally quite busy with
> final reports at this time of the year, was now quite busy holding
> the hand of almost every teacher in the building. The news
> spread quickly. We closed the door, took out pipe and cigarette
> respectively and talked. We both went home and chewed the cud
> some more. Mutual decision next morning: scotch our beautifully
> colored "master paper plan" and start from scratch. The "master
> paper plan" we developed the next day (want to talk about pro-
> ducing under pressure) kept us at the same basic grouping
> structure but reduced our original seventeen interage classes to
> six, leaving eleven classes without interage groups. . . . We got the
> word out fast—only six interage classes. The building visibly re-
> laxed, nerves untensed, and smiles returned once more to the
> faces of our friends.[2]

So it was that one of our prime goals in the nongraded—true
interage grouping based on the needs and abilities of the children
—was not immediately realized. The morale of our teachers
was so important to us that we felt we could not sacrifice it for
an ideal concept. Although we were firmly convinced that total
interage grouping was necessary for the nongrading, we bowed
to the emotional needs of our teachers. Our grouping (see Chapter 3) does not represent the best of all possible worlds. It
is our considered judgment that this condition will change. We
feel in time tensions and emotional reactions to total interage

---

[1] L. Glogau, *Make Me a Nongraded.*

[2] Ibid.

grouping will decrease. We are planning to make adjustments and changes each year, but *gradually*. In time we feel the teachers will greet true interage grouping as a perfectly normal and natural process, as normal and natural as the old grade labels.

Teacher tension, of course, did not disappear with the readjustment of the number of interage classes. There was much evidence (during the course of our first year) of their worry and concern.

November 3—Minutes of Primary Meeting

General Problems

The discussion revolved around certain problems which have arisen in the interage classes. The discussions which we have held to date have been marked by a good deal of frankness. There is good recognition that some of our problems come from the newness of the program itself and we will make the necessary adjustments in time. For instance, the clear recognition of the differences inherent in the levels of achievement when there are younger children in the classroom is one such problem, as is the necessity of learning different pacing and timing for the younger child, especially for those of us who have been teaching one grade for a long time. The re-grouping and sub-grouping for different activities all through the day is one practice which the teachers report they are beginning to find an easier technique and that some of our former suggestions have proven helpful in this regard. The need for materials and lessons to be of a high interest order to hold the interest of the younger child is another problem. There is also a new alertness to the lack of skills on the younger child's part and the fact that they require training in all curricular areas. An addition recognition which is being made is the shorter attention span of the younger child and the need to adjust the program to his level. Also stressed was the need for using different research techniques for children for whom there is an insufficient amount of appropriate reading material, by substituting picture books, picture collections, the vertical file, filmstrips, records, etc.

November 17—Minutes of Primary Meeting

The nongraded primary does offer an opportunity for teachers to more easily observe the differences among children and they must adapt their program, lessons, and materials to this range of differences.

It is evident that as the awareness of individual differences increases so does the need for differentiated planning, materials, and program. This type of approach demands more and more of the teachers' time for preparation and planning. It does not seem that our current organizational pattern permits this type of preparation time under optimum conditions.

This brings us to the next and very important problem which we faced in the nongraded, and one for which we have found no solution.

Teacher Planning and Meeting Time

As the year progressed and as we became more accustomed to the nongraded, this spectre of time continued to haunt us.

December 17—Minutes of Primary Meeting

Long and lengthy discussion revolved around the institution of any new program. Some very pertinent points being made by these teachers who have interage classes. Many of the issues raised have implications for next year's program and grouping.

It is understood that this is a year of extreme pressure.

Many problems which are coming up regarding the children in these classes were in existence before but somehow it is the very structure of the nongraded itself which is making these differences in children apparent to the teacher. The needs in adjustment of program and grouping and techniques are particularly demanding in the first year. Strong suggestions were made that there be some effort put forth by the district to help the classroom teacher do a better job by freeing her from the clerical burdens. Some specific ideas offered are: the machine scoring of standardized tests (the SRA tests this year took twenty hours per teacher for hand scoring), increased clerical help in the office so that they might be able to help in the preparation of teacher made materials, the use of teacher aides (library, recess, audiovisual), elimination of all extra duty assignments during the school day, increased use of student teachers (we average about two per semester), increased use of Future Teachers of America from our high school, and the proposal of closing school early one day each week for professional preparation time.

What happened was simple to understand. Certain teachers, most of them that is, began to make their adjustments to nongrading and interage classes. As they made this adjustment they became increasingly aware of the amount of time now needed for classroom preparation. Although these teachers had an excellent reputation for classroom proficiency, they were beginning to make new and increased demands of themselves. They needed more and more time for the preparation of lessons and planning for the individual needs of their children. Traditionally a good part of this work is done at home or after school by the conscientious teacher. However, what is the point of no return? Should there not be more time made available to allow these teachers time for preparation during the professional school day? We think yes. How we are going to accomplish this goal, we do not know. These are decisions which rest with our superiors and the Board of Education. We have made them aware of the problem, and hope that they will consider it carefully and arrive at some solution. It is an important area of concern. We should not like to see the enthusiasm and interest in differentiated planning, which this year has brought forth, thwarted because of lack of understanding of the nature of the time problem itself. Our teachers are not asking anything for themselves, they are asking for their children.

It would be unfair, we feel, not to mention two additional difficulties encountered which are directly related to this same general theme of tension and time. It is an area we do not like to stress, naturally, but it should be mentioned. It is our firm conviction that there are certain teachers, for reasons or reason unknown, who cannot make the adjustment to the philosophy and requirements of nongraded teaching. These teachers are in the minority, but they do exist. In the natural course of events these teachers will eliminate themselves from the school. The pressures are too intense for them to handle, and they will protect themselves by leaving the nongraded school, without any effort on the administrators' part. This is fortunate, because these teachers are good people and it is hard watching them attempt an adjustment of which they are incapable.

The second fact which should be mentioned here is another touchy one which we would be content not mentioning, but must in the interest of fairness. It seemed to us, and still does, that one of the most natural and normal consequences of nongrading would be efforts by teachers themselves at the elimination of the self-contained classroom. If there is so much need for increased planning and preparation, what would be more natural than teachers grouping together to do just this? Yes, we are talking about team teaching—to us the most logical next step in nongrading. Suffice it to say, that our teachers have, except for one case in passing, never even considered the possibility of team teaching as a partial solution to their time and planning problems. Once again it is our belief that in time, quite gradually, team teaching will evolve from our nongraded. We certainly feel the need. For us the self-contained classroom is as antiquated as grade labels. We shall, however, wait on our teachers before making any dramatic moves in this direction.

Primary Meetings

Still on the topic of teachers' time, we ourselves were faced with an enormous problem. We wanted to meet with three groups of teachers (six, six, five) once a week for an hour. This meant that for three hours every week our teachers had to be free to meet with us during the school day. Our district provides for two professional meeting hours per week after or before the school day on Mondays and Wednesdays. We couldn't use that time for a number of reasons. We have a fourth grade and a kindergarten, ten teachers in all, plus some six other special teachers to meet with occasionally. There were only two professional hours in all per week and we required three just for Primary Meetings. The district made certain inroads on these meeting hours also, with special programs, special television programs (we have closed circuit television in the schools and our own station) special meetings, and in service programs. We, ourselves, needed to hold full faculty meetings throughout the year, though we held these to a minimum. And so it became mandatory that we arrange for meeting with our primary teachers during the course of the school day. We arranged these hours by having all the special teachers scheduled to meet with the classes of those teachers with whom we were meeting (see Figure 14-1). This sounded like the only solution, but made us very unhappy. In the course of arranging for primary meetings, we were destroying, to some extent, the foundations of our philosophy of special teacher schedules. We began to arrange for special teacher schedules which were open by nature, that is, not precisely scheduled by the hour and day. Special teachers were being encouraged to act more in the capacity of consultants to teachers than to children. But in one swoop, we were reverting to our old tightly scheduled special teacher routine which meant that each special teacher met with certain classes each day. We did not know any way out of this bind, and at this moment still do not. Our time for primary meetings is arranged exactly the same way for the coming year, even though we are meeting teachers on alternate weeks only. This problem arose because we have twenty-two primary classes next year and this means one additional primary group per week to schedule. This increase in primary classes came about when our fourth grade classes moved to a neighboring school.

In addition to a special teacher schedule which is now too rigid for our standards, we encountered another problem of interesting consequence. This problem we are happy to announce we are meeting and solving. However, it is interesting to note how one difficulty and one solution often creates another. By having the special teachers conduct classes during Primary Meetings, we eliminated all possibility of their *ever* being present at Primary Meetings. Other personnel, speech therapist, psychologist, reading consultant, etc., were able to adjust their duties so that they were present at least at some of the meetings, but

OLD BETHPAGE SCHOOL SPECIAL TEACHER SCHEDULE

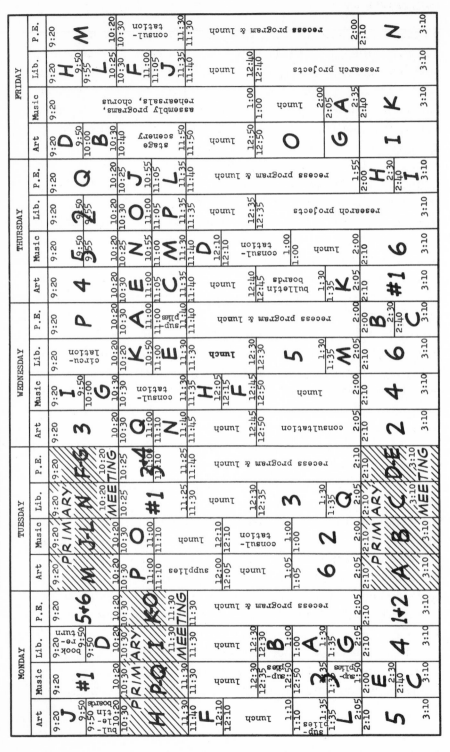

Fig. 14-1.

the special teachers (art, music, physical education, etc.) were never able to be there. Result? You can guess. While all of us were discussing, arguing, studying, adjusting, and embracing the nongraded, the special teachers were almost totally isolated. They weren't catching the flavor or the taste of our adventure. They became the last hold outs of the nongraded, *through no fault of their own*. Their lack of exposure to the primary meetings caused them to be the last staff members to make the adjustment to the nongraded philosophy and goals. Add to this, the fact that their directors (music, physical education, etc.), who worked at the district level, had no exposure at all to nongrading and you can see the extent of the rift which was caused in understanding between these special teachers and ourselves. In time, during the course of the school year, we became aware of what was happening and began to make overtures to correct this dichotomy. Happily we can state that we have now arranged for a more amicable meeting of the minds. By the end of the year, some of our special teachers had become our most enthusiastic supporters.

You may well ask why do we continue with Primary Meetings if the cost is so high? We tried in the first chapter to show you the many reasons why we feel these meetings are so essential to our success, why we consider them the essential core of our program. But we were also interested in learning how our teachers felt. We asked them for their reactions to Primary Meetings. They confirmed everything we felt and when it came time to evaluate the Primary Meetings and most specifically to decide whether provision should be made for holding them next year, our teachers said:

February 23—Minutes of Primary Meeting

We are of the opinion that Primary Meetings on a weekly basis should be continued during the 1965-1966 school year. They are most especially important at the beginning and close of the school year. The meetings serve a valuable purpose. The possibility of alternate week scheduling is suggested. New agenda items to be included in the coming year will be: team planning, demonstration lessons, teacher observation, and team discussion.

Pupil Inventory

The final difficulty which we faced last year is also one which we did not resolve in our first year of operation, nor did we expect to. The nongraded requires a very difinitive method for the identification and inventorying of a pupil's achievements. It requires a knowledge and specificity about each child which was not somehow necessary under the graded situation. Teachers must know exactly what skills a youngster has mastered in each curricular area before he can proceed from one sequential learning level to the next. This system implies three prerequisities: the recognition and identification of a pupil's achievement level, the organization of each curricular area into levels of achievement with appropriate identification of exact skills at each level, without reference to grade labels and finally, a system for recording each pupil's progress within each achievement level. We had made a good beginning in the identification of the child's achievement level in each curricular area. We had made a good start in the identification of skills at each level, (although still somewhat grade oriented) most precisely in reading and mathematics, and in broader terms in social studies, science, and language arts. Where we were notoriously weak was in a method for recording the skills or difficulties at each level of a pupil's attainment. In other words, a child could be working at level eight in reading, but we had no precise instrument designed for recording or checking off the skills at level eight as he mastered them. We, the administrators, felt this lack seriously. The teachers did not. They were so absorbed with recognition, identification, and provision for individual differences within each curricular area that they had no time to even think about techniques for keeping accurate records. Every time we brought the topic up for discussion everyone agreed in principle, but that's where the matter ended. There wasn't any time for them to devote to this additional responsibility.

January 23—Minutes of Primary Meeting

Following a decision to have the teachers meet in small workshops periodically to develop Flow Sheets (the name which we selected to call these records) in the various curricular areas (social studies, science, mathematics, language arts, and reading), there was much discussion centering around two main concerns: one, the amount of time necessary to develop and use the Flow Sheets; and two, the actual need for the Flow Sheets.

The actual need for a Flow Sheet, which will more accurately record the actual skills of each youngster in each curricular area, becomes a real need in the nongraded operation. It is a technique for establishing some standards or criteria for proceeding from one level to another in each curricular area. It reduces the teacher's need to discover each and every facet of a pupil's learning pattern for herself. It is an instrument which is also helpful for the planning of lessons with sub groups based on actual and real needs in the skills.

The time needed for the development of Flow Sheets is, of course, quite extensive, even though we will be using the district curricula in each area as the take off point for the development of criteria and the progression of same. The time needed to fill out Flow Sheets will be offset by the time saved in learning about children and their academic needs. As teachers begin more and more to use any and all records available to them about each pupil, they will recognize their value, since often the records reveal factors or facets of a youngster's learning situations which would take a good deal of time to unearth for oneself.

The time needed was so extensive *that we never found it.* This entire Flow Sheet situation is a grand example of a principle which we have learned in operating a school. If teachers aren't ready for something, no amount of coaxing or wheedling is going to work. Every time the topic of Flow Sheets came up for discussion, every one agreed they would be nice to have, but no one could find the time to design them. Of course, this was partially true and partially not true. By this we mean, if the teachers had really felt the need for Flow Sheets, they would have found the time to make them. In December, Mrs. W., the reading consultant, made another gallant effort.

December 19—Minutes of Primary Meeting

Mrs. W. introduced a set of curricular level follow-up cards which she procured from the Mineola Public Schools. There were two examples—one, an individual card for each child, and the other a card on which the teacher could record the progress of up to twelve children in each curricular area (a group card). It was felt that format of the large group card was easier to read and to handle, but we would prefer using this format with the individual child. It was also felt that the areas describing each particular instructional level were too detailed for our use. We would prefer a more simplified approach. Mrs. W. also produced some excellent Flow Sheets from a California district which she loaned to one teacher for her private study.

Need we say again, that this was simply an intellectual exercise. The sample Flow Sheets were analyzed, but no one had any intention of working on them for our school. Talk of Freudian slips, another charming incident in this sequence of events, was that the teacher who had been given the sample California Flow Sheets, when asked for them one month later, forgot she had them and couldn't even find them. Along about this time, we reluctantly decided that the two of us and the reading consultant would develop these Flow Sheets on our own. We announced our intentions to the teachers, feeling if their objections were to the production of the Flow Sheets themselves (from the point of view of being too time consuming), we would remove this stumbling block by producing them ourselves. We were greeted with a dismal lack of enthusiasm and so we dropped the entire matter. It was not until the next to the last week of school, that two teachers came to us privately and on their own to say that they felt that the development and use of Flow Sheets was indeed necessary in the nongraded. Now we have two more allies for our continued struggle this coming year. We frankly are quite pleased that we even made two converts this year.

This story of Flow Sheets is especially interesting in light of the teachers' disdain for the district report card which we used (see Appendix, p. 251). It did not suit the needs of the nongraded school they said.

January 27—Minutes of Primary Meeting

> There is still a general feeling that this written report card does not communicate to the parent well enough. The parent will not know how the child is functioning academically. For instance, a comment such as "he knows his initial letter sounds" has no real meaning when taken out of context. Is this good or poor achievement for this child?
>
> *Once again we came to the conclusion that Flow Sheets with specific criteria and goals should be the basis for reporting to parents in either a check list or graph form.*

They were unhappy about our system of reporting to parents. They felt all its inadequacies, as did we. They felt Flow Sheets were the answer, but were still totally unready to really do something about it. We hope that the new school year will see a change in this attitude. We certainly will be in there pitching.

We have attempted, in capsule form, to outline for you those matters about which we felt concern during our first year of operation: teacher tension, teacher planning and meeting time, Primary Meeting schedules, Pupil Inventories, and Report Cards. Wherever and whenever it was possible, we attacked a problem at its roots. In some cases we were successful, in others, not. We hope, of course, that in the years to come, we will be able to lick our as yet unresolved problems. We need an extraordinary amount of patience and a "little bit of luck."

15

EXTERNAL PROBLEMS

In this the final chapter of our story we shall endeavor to describe what we have chosen to call "external" problems. By "external" problems we mean those problems over which we have less control or influence than those directly relating to the school. They are for the most part concerned with attitudes: the attitudes of children, parents, and professionals.

Follow-up

Before proceeding to a description of these problems let us note one important factor in passing. No doubt you have asked yourself what happens to our children when they leave the nongraded primary and enter the fourth grade? In all honesty we do not know, though every effort has been made to facilitate this transition. We have plans for following the history of the total group as they make their adjustment to the fourth grade. We shall also be carefully evaluating the progress of certain individual children for whom special instructional programs have been designed. There are certain factors which need explanation. The school to which our children are going for their upper elementary education is the next closest geographically. It is staffed by an excellent group of professionals with whom there has been good articulation. It is a school which is participating in a grant for the experimental study of team teaching and the Knapp Library Foundation. It is, therefore, a school whose philosophy is very much directed toward the individualization of instruction for children. Finally, ours is one of two pilot demonstration projects in nongrading for the district. It is expected that as the years proceed more of the schools in the district will be nongraded. This, of course, will make the transfer from our building to others even smoother for our children. But as for the present, we feel that every effort will be made to accommodate our children at the precise level of achievement which they have attained in each curricular area. The follow-up study which is planned at the Central Park Road School during the 1965-1966 school year will give us the evidence which is needed to evaluate our children and their adjustment.

Staff Orientation

Still another factor which we feel we need mention is the indoctrination techniques being employed in the district to promote the better understanding of the nongraded among those schools still operating graded patterns. This past spring an invitation was issued to all teachers in the district to visit one of the two pilot nongraded schools. This invitation was accepted by some thirty teachers, each of whom spent one full day at the school (substitutes were provided for their classes.) These teachers on the whole submitted reports in writing to the district office which were highly favorable. This coming school year will see the district offer a voluntary in-service workshop on the nongraded. These are the total plans to date for orientation of other staff members of the district and we respectfully submit that they are inadequate. Administrators, for instance, have not participated in any of these programs thus far. If the district seriously wishes to further the cause of nongrading, more and specific orientation plans are going to be needed. The one factor which we consistently ran into all during our first year was the woefully inadequate amount of time which we had been granted to establish the nongraded. It is our feeling that more time must be granted to indoctrinate both the staffs and the parents.

February 13—Evaluation Meeting

There is an overall feeling that this is the year which tries men's souls. If we can but survive the changes and the pace, we will all be better for it professionally and the children will reap immeasurable harvest from our growth. However, there is a strong note that the program should be sharply and clearly studied and reviewed by other staffs in the district for *two years* before its inception. Also, that parent indoctrination will take at least two years, since elimination of the graded concept and its consequent status use by parents is a difficult concept to get across.

Parent Attitude

The topic which received our greatest attention during the school year is one which we can broadly categorize as parent attitude. We shall examine specific examples of parent attitude in relation to nongrading as we proceed. We have shown you evidence repeatedly throughout this volume of the basic pattern of our community. We are blessed with wonderfully alert and aware parents who are truly supportive of education, yes. But they are parents who, through no fault of their own, are caught in the suburban syndrome. Enough studies by social science researchers have been made in this area for us not to have to belabor this point. The results of the suburban syndrome are many, the only ones with which we are concerned are those which directly affect our children and their performance in school. Needless to say, the only reason which we have for examining this larger sociological problem is that it has serious repercussions for our school and its operation. Listen as our teachers discuss in broad terms their pupils. (And bear in mind at the same time some of the previous discussions which you have read about the immature child, etc.)

January 25—Minutes of Primary Meeting

A Question of Values

Over and over again we come back to the theme of the values our children hold. Teachers report that some of our children lack initiative, drive, and self-direction. They lose interest quickly; they do not complete tasks; they do not make decisions; they are over-dependent upon the teacher. We are, of course, talking about responsibility. How much or how little children are encouraged to have.

We know that in the modern suburban community a lack of responsibility seems to be the norm for many children. Parents are dedicated and devoted to their children, wish to give them the best, and wrap their youngsters in tender loving care.

Mr. F. asked whether it might not be possible that we perpetuate this condition ourselves by providing continued loving care in school? Is it possible that we ourselves do not ask enough of our children in school?

Miss O. posed an interesting problem when she talked of parents abrogating many of their responsibilities at home and expecting the school to do most of the work, but at the same time being resentful of efforts the school makes which may be construed as strict.

Mrs. G. suggests that the teacher's self-image may be an important factor. If it is important that children love you, then many classroom decisions may be made with this goal in mind. If the goal of the classroom teacher is respect, then quite a different series of decisions will be made in the classroom. Self-direction and purpose may well be emphasized with children holding the teacher in high esteem and beginning to emerge as responsible individuals fulfilling their roles and carrying out their responsibilities. The end result well then may be love for a teacher, even though this was not the immediate goal.

Certainly this question of responsibility is extremely important and will merit much careful analysis.

The immaturity of some of our children and how it affected their school progress, and the attitude a teacher needed to affect in order to handle this problem, absorbed a good deal of our time and efforts, and will continue to do so as we proceed with the nongraded program.

When you have parents deeply concerned with their children, you have parents deeply concerned with the education of their children. This concern is honest and real. It is our contention, and in this we have the complete concurrence of every professional in our building, that some of this concern was misdirected.

When parents misdirect their concern they directly affect our
school, our staff, and our children.

Grade Label and Status

November 16—Minutes of Primary Meeting

> It is obvious now that we have removed the tangible status of
> grade, that we have not replaced this symbol with anything
> meaningful that the parent can use as a status symbol. Our
> hope is that time will produce a more healthy emphasis on the
> development of the individual child and parents will come to
> accept this.

As you can see a concommitant problem arose which we called,
for lack of a better name, grade label and status. It became apparent that our old grade labels gave our parents security. They
knew, or thought they knew, where their children were and how
they were progressing. A third grader could be counted on to be
a third grader and no nonsense. We destroyed this security when
we eliminated the grade tags. More, we substituted nothing in its
place. We offered the parents no status symbol to which they
could attach any significance until they discovered one for themselves. This made for a fascinating story and we still do not
know how unique our experience was.

We had six interage classes. Some were basically first and
second year in composition and some second and third year in
composition. What some of our parents did was quite simple.
They made the assumption that all younger children in these
interage classes were bright and automatically *candidate for a
two year* primary program. Nothing could have been further from
the truth. Interestingly enough none of the parents of the older
children ever made the assumption that their children were slow
and automatically candidates for a four year primary program.
Nothing which we did or said during the course of the school year
ever changed this attitude on the part of certain parents. During
the very last month of school we were still being visited by

parents who insisted that their children be placed in the fourth grade after just two years in the primary school. Needless to say, these were children for whom we had no such plans.

Ruth E.

This youngster's parents have expressed to the teacher during the parent–teacher conference their desire to have Ruth placed in the fourth grade next year, reducing her attendance in the nongraded primary to a total of two years. Our evaluation indicated that this is not a wise decision in Ruth's case. Conferences will, therefore, be held with the parents by both the teacher and administrators.

Note, this pupil's name had never even been submitted as a possible academic candidate during our two or four year evaluation sessions. When the parents were asked by Mr. F. why they had assumed that Ruth was going into the fourth grade, they gave as their explanation her placement in an interage class with older children. This is but one example from our files of requests of this nature. We have documentation for at least two handfuls more.

Interage Classes

The interage classes caused us concern all during the course of the school year. At the beginning of the school year, we were deluged with requests by parents to have their children transfered out of these classes. The excuses were different in each case, but the basic reasons were really the same. Interage classes completely eliminated the possibilities of grade labels, and there was no way to identify a child by grade. Also, it was considered a social disgrace for pupils from two formerly different grades to be housed in the same class. It implied, for the parents, and for the children to some extent, that some of the children were underachievers and this made them uncomfortable.

Irene

One such case (from among many) is rather typical and illustrates our point. There was in one of our interage first and second year classes, a little girl named Irene. Remember we never felt that Irene needed to be shifted. It was her parents who came to us repeatedly with this request.

October 15, Mrs. P. completed a movement form:

Child is presently under pressure for higher achievement and consequently seems somewhat tense, dissatisfied, and restless. Normal intelligence. Adequate social competence in dealing with adults and children, has been reported to be distant in class with the children because she doesn't feel she belongs in this class. Child normal physically. Parents have been dissatisfied with child's placement in interage class from the beginning; have pressured child into working after school to improve so that *she will be moved.*

Our investigation, which included a psychological and reading evaluation of this child as thorough as we could make them, substantiated the fact that Irene was in her proper class and with her proper group. The parents were so insistent that Irene be moved out of an interage class that they subjected the child to much forced learning at home which she, of course, did not really absorb. We need not report, we are sure, the kind of work which went into adjusting this poor little girl's attitude in class and the time which we needed to convince the parents.

Once parents began to accept the fact that we weren't going to shift children so easily without good cause, they began to see in interaging and the nongrading a new use. Once again they devised an approach which would substitute for grade status in the nongraded.

November 30—Minutes of Primary Meeting

The mobility and fluidity provided us in individual learning situations makes our pattern of movement a commendable one.

However, it does bring up other problems. A child who is subjected to parental pressure for scholastic achievement is now quite often under intensified pressure since parents see in our movement pattern an opportunity for children to advance to higher levels of academic achievement throughout the school year.

Teachers gave us increased evidence of this type of pressure being brought to bear on children to make them perform. Where in the past the end of the school year was the evaluation time for each child, now children could proceed from one academic level to the next throughout the school year. Time after time children were being asked, by some parents, to do just this before they were really ready. The thinking was easy to understand. The faster a child moved through the academic levels the greater became his chance to complete the entire program in two years. Thus in a way the nongraded was making life more difficult for some children. We don't think we need point out that parents, who placed pressure on their children for better academic performance, had behaved in exactly the same manner before. Our only concern was whether they were being encouraged by the nongraded to pressure their children even more. It is a moot point and we do not have the answer. In private conferences with parents, however, we carefully explained a child's potential and tried to have parents become more aware of the fact that we were the people who should be most directly concerned with the child's learning program and his rate of learning.

This parental concern with pupils' achievement which we encountered is not unique. It exists in most suburban communities. The ultimate goal for most children is a college education; the better the student, the better the chance for college entrance, and the better the opportunity for placement in a status college. There is nothing unusual or unnatural about this concern. Our only fears rested with this concern when it worked to the *detriment of the individual child*. When we were presented with evidence of this kind, we felt we had to make precise overtures to correct the situation.

Homework

One area to which we devoted much time was that of homework. We selected this topic of concentration because we reasoned thusly: if parents are concerned with their children's education; if some of them wish to check the day by day progress of their children; and, if these parents are more comfortable when they can help their children; would it not be best if we directed this interest and concern by providing a planned homework program? Homework helped fulfill these prerequisites. It kept parents alert to a pupil's functional level of achievement in the various curricular areas, and it gave some of them an opportunity to help their children directly. There was no sense kidding ourselves. These parents worried about their children. These parents wanted to be a part of their children's learning program. Would it not be most beneficial to all concerned if we allowed them to do just this, by providing them with a planned home study regime? We reasoned, "Yes."

November 16—Minutes of Primary Meeting

> Since many of our parents' questions on Open School Night revolved around homework, its philosophy, its execution, the parents' role, etc., it is felt that a full faculty meeting will be necessary with this item as number one on the agenda.

November 18—Minutes of Faculty Meeting

> Mr. F. opened the meeting with a statement to the effect that opinion and practice in the area of homework vary widely, and that this very variation can create problems.
>
> Teachers' opinions on the topic varied widely also. Some teachers felt that a consistent policy of homework would be helpful to pupils when they reached the secondary school level and were suddenly faced with the necessity for completing homework each night in many curricular areas. They further felt that ever present *parent pressures could be properly channeled when home assignments are instituted by the school rather than the parents.* Others felt that homework assignments should be op-

tional with the teacher, determined largely on the basis of class and individual needs and a unified policy toward homework would represent an attempt to placate parents. Time limitations prevented a full exploration of the topic. It was decided to continue discussion at a subsequent meeting.

Mr. F. distributed to all the teachers some dittoed notes which he had prepared called *The Problem of Homework* (see Appendix, p. 269). This material stressed certain essentials for homework assignments which are elementary to any good program: assignments should be individualized when possible; assignments should require a realistic amount of time; assignments should be checked and corrected by the teacher, etc. At a subsequent meeting which was held on homework, we decided that we would continue to allow each teacher the right to make her own decision about assigning homework. Further, those teachers who did make such daily assignments were cautioned to follow the suggestions offered in ditto form "Characteristics of Good Homework Assignments" (see Appendix, p. 272). However, we tried to emphasize to the teachers how much simpler their every day class responsibilities would be if they would use the simple strategem of homework with their children. Most of our teachers understood our reasoning and went along with our proposals. There were those, of course, who did not. It should be noted here that the teachers who planned for a systematic assignment of homework for each child (as individualized as possible) throughout the school year, consistently maintained the best rapport with their parents. There is no other variable to which we can attach this significance and importance. The teachers who assigned well planned homework on a daily individual basis, which was checked the following morning had consistently less difficulty of any kind with their parents. We carefully catalogued during the year the types and kinds of complaints parents brought to the front office. It astonished us, over and over again, that these teachers, *even if they had interage classes,* were brought to our attention less frequently than others. We plan, therefore, to emphasize this need for homework in our meetings with teachers this year again. We shall also, once again, offer an evening PTA education program on homework and the parents' role. We have found it is necessary to reinforce one particular aspect of homework responsibility with parents each year, the difference between helping a child and actually doing his work.

The Future

We leave to the social scientists the reasons for some of the attitudes of parents. We concern ourselves only with the symptoms which seem to adversely affect the children. It seems hardly necessary to point out that many of the suburban parental attitudes we have found to our extreme liking. For example, their consistent support of quality education in our district. We do not wish the reader to leave us feeling that suburban parents possess attitudes which are injurious to education. They do not. In some certain selected instances their attitudes are misguided, albeit well intentioned. Robert Anderson in his speech to the parents pleaded with them to "succeed with your children, not through them."[1] He felt that one of the greatest gifts a parent could give his child was the capacity to accept his innate ability with grace while working toward the goal of being a productive, well motivated human being. We couldn't agree more.

In those instances then where we feel change is necessary we have one of two alternative courses of action. It behooves us to *change parental attitudes* or *to adjust our program.* In other words there will be times when we will attempt to change parents, or times when we will attempt to change ourselves.

When we speak of parent pressure, resistance to interage classes, and grade status symbol, for instance, we should like to change the parental attitude. This we have started to do, and shall continue to do with formal and informal meetings throughout the coming school years. In the past we have invited noted sociologists and educators to our P.T.A. meetings to speak with

---

[1] Anderson, speech.

parents about suburban mores and values. We have inaugurated parent workshops for pre school children. It is our hope that persistent repeated exposures of this nature will result in attitudinal change.

On the other hand, when we speak of parent cooperation, help and orientation, for example, we shall have to make the changes. We shall have to make adjustments in our programs and plans. New understanding about the role and importance of homework, for example, will have to be reemphasized with our own staff. Pleas for more study and visitation of the nongraded by our own district people will have to be made to fully insure their understanding of the nature of nongrading, its values, its problems, its rewards, and the inordinate length of time required to orient both parents and staff to these concepts.

Efforts at adjusting the attitudes of our parents to the needs of our children and our school we shall continue to make in the forthcoming years.

In the forthcoming years we shall continue to make efforts at adjusting our program wherever and whenever we deem it important to the success of our children or our school. We need an extraordinary amount of patience and a lot of luck.

APPENDIX

A. LEVELS OF READING SKILLS[1]

This is a list of achievements to be attained at each level of instruction. It will serve as a guide for teachers in determining each child's readiness for the next level.

Level 1—Kindergarten and Level 2 are considered the initial readiness and adjustment levels.

	Word Recognition Skills	*Comprehension Skills*

Level 3 – Reading Readiness	A. To build visual discrimination.
	  1. Observing differences and similarities in shapes of things, differences in size of things, colors, pictures, differences between letters, words.
	  2. Observing likenesses and differences between letters (beginning sounds) and words.
	B. To build auditory discrimination.
	  1. Identifying sounds – whistling, tapping, singing.
	  Identifying differences between sounds.
	  2. Rhyming – recognizing words that rhyme, saying rhymes.
	  3. Hearing similarities and differences between beginning sounds and words.
	C. Identify and read own name.
	D. Matching capital and small letters; letter names.
	E. Observing and understanding left and right sequences.
	F. Classifying objects into categories (foods, animals).
	G. Sequential order – draw or place pictures in sequence of events, retell story in sequence.
	H. Eye-hand coordination (pasting, coloring, cutting, following lines).
		A. Retention—remember main characters and events in a story, etc. Memory of orientation of forms.
		B. Follows directions (to do or find specific things) games, printed material.
		C. Listening ability (attention span).
		D. Understand opposites (top, bottom, stop, go).

---

[1] Belle Warshavsky, *Reading Skills* (Old Bethpage School).

	Word Recognition Skills	Comprehension Skills
Level 4 — Pre-Primer	A. Uses context clues to figure out unknown words. B. Recognizes 2 words out of 3 that rhyme in pictures and orally, rhyming phonograms. C. Structural analysis — plural function of *s*. D. Visual discrimination—recognizing similarities and differences in beginning letters, words, position and detail of objects. E. Auditory discrimination — recognizing similarities and differences in beginning sounds, words, phrases, sentences. F. Learning names of all letters, capital and small. G. Use configuration clues.	A. Read silently without symptoms of tension such as finger pointing, lip movement, etc. B. Understanding main idea of a story. C. Following a sequence of ideas in a story, and arrange pictures in sequential order. D. Identify the speaker in a story, in conversation. E. Follow a simple series of directions for work sheets. F. Deciding which words tell opposite idea, as in-out, stop-go. G. Make inferences. H. Contributing to group-dictated story based on picture sequence. I. Classifying ideas, e.g., toys, colors. J. Recognize most of the vocabulary in three pre-primers. K. Read independently with interest and understanding.
Level 5 — Primer	A. Auditory and visual discrimination — initial consonant sounds and blends, final consonant sounds, median consonants, rhyming phonograms and their vowel sounds. B. Configuration: in isolation and by comparison. Notes general configuration of words, looking for striking characteristics such as tall letters or two letters alike. C. Nouns and verbs with *s* ending. D. Blending the first consonant of a word with the rhyming or last part of another word to make a word (look-book). E. Recognition of inflectional variance formed by *s, es, ing, ed, 's*.	A. Read and answer questions. B. Locate answers to questions. C. Draw conclusions based on events in a story (what will happen next). D. Interpret ideas implied but not directly stated or pictured. E. Note details — color, size. F. Follow one-step and two-step directions. G. Recognize emotional reactions and motives of story characters—happiness, sadness, anger, etc.

Word Recognition Skills	Comprehension Skills

F. Recognition of known parts in compound words.
G. Recognition of variants ending in *s, ed, ing.*
H. Uses picture clues in recognizing words.
I. Uses context clues to determine word.

Level 6 — 1/2 Book

Word Recognition Skills

A. Show increased competency in short vowel sounds, magic *e* and all consonants in initial and final position.
B. Be able to blend words which have common vowel digraphs for reading.
C. Recognize blends and digraphs in initial position.
D. Homonyms (to-two-too)
E. Synonyms (too-also)
F. Recognition of contractions.
G. Hearing and seeing rhyming phonograms.
H. Hearing and seeing the endings *ed, d, ing, 's.*
I. Hearing and seeing syllables in words.
J. Blending first consonant of a known word with last part of known word to make another known or unknown word.

Comprehension Skills

A. To interpret ideas implied but not directly stated or pictured.
B. To understand relationships of time, place, number, manner.
C. To understand that a phrase/sentence is a meaning unit.
D. To use punctuation as a guide to meaning—period, comma, exclamation point, question mark.
E. To follow oral and written directions.
F. To locate information.
G. Strengthen memory based on observation association, visual imagery, sequence of events.
H. To use picture dictionary (knows letters in order of alphabet).
I. Use of pronouns.
J. To identify main idea of a story.
K. Make judgments related to cause and effect.
L. Make judgments related to outcome.
M. Visualizing characters associated with book titles.
N. Use books carefully, find table of contents, find pages readily.
O. Apply reading ability to other content areas.
P. Reads silently without vocalizing or lip movement.
Q. Show increased attention span especially in independent reading.

Word Recognition Skills	Comprehension Skills

R. Read orally with expression and good phrasing, and use of punctuation.

S. Use of new vocabulary in meaningful context in sentences, original stories, rhymes and riddles.

T. Classification—Add a word that belongs (cat, dog, cow, rabbit).

Level 7 — 2/1 Book

A. Review of blending first and last consonants of words, phonograms and first consonant of a known word with last part of a known word to make another known or unknown word.

B. Hearing and seeing special last consonants in words.

C. Visual-auditory perception of qu, thr, scr, spr, str, squ.

D. Variability of consonant sound, hard and soft c, g.

E. Silent consonants—ck, igh, wr.

F. Y as long i or short i.

G. Short vowels followed by r, l, w.

H. Recognition of vowel digraphs, ee, ea, oo, au, ie, aw, ai, oa, etc.

I. Dictionary—alphabetize to first letter.

J. Hearing differences between short and long sounds of a, e, i, o, u, in printed words.

K. Applying final e rule to new words with vowel a, e, i, o, u.

L. Hearing and seeing the suffix er, y, ty, est, ion, etc.

M. Hearing and seeing the words of hyphenated compounds (snow-white).

N. Hearing the difference between the ar, or, ir, ur, and er.

A. To continue to develop ability to read for details, to recall, to discuss and interpret story facts, to locate specific information in answer to questions, to support one's own ideas, and to follow more complex printed directions and independent reading.

B. Forming sensory images; reproduce in own drawing.

C. Perceiving relationship, time, place, manner, sequence.

D. Interpreting main ideas.

E. Understanding make-up of a book.

F. Develop listening skills.

G. Meaning of comma, period, question mark, exclamation point.

H. Write simple poems.

I. Finding subjects and predicates of sentences as— Who did something? What did they do?

J. Indexing or identifying things included by a general term — colors may be blue and yellow.

	Word Recognition Skills	*Comprehension Skills*

Level 8 —
2/2 Book

A. Continue vowel sounds, vowel digraphs, suffix y usage.
B. Homonyms (rode-road, so-sew).
C. Hearing the syllables er and ly in words.
D. Hearing syllables in two and three syllable words.
E. Applying final e rule to words.
F. Root word plus n, en, er, est.
G. Double final consonant before adding an ending, or suffix.
H. Changing y to i before adding an ending or suffix.
I. Dropping an e in adding an ending or suffix.
J. Recognition of prefixes—com, ex, in, en, el, up, de.
K. Recognition of dipthongs on, ow, oi, oy.
L. Vowel letters stand for more than one sound.
M. Silent vowels as visual clues.
N. Visual clue to vowel sound usually follows the vowel letters in a word.
O. Rules for vowel sounds.
P. Recognition of most phonograms.
Q. Dictionary — words represent more than one meaning.
R. Using sentence context to determine appropriate meaning.

A. Develop skill in critical reading.
B. Forming sensory images.
C. Understand main idea of sentences.
D. Skim for requested phrase to locate answers to questions.
E. Understand mood of characters.
F. Phrase and sentence meaning and simple definitions.
G. Interpret ideas implied but not directly stated.
H. Making inferences.
I. Making Judgements and drawing conclusions.
J. Perceiving relationships—cause and effect, past and present.
K. Summarizing and organizing ideas.
L. Refining listening skills.
M. Locating information, as using a table of contents in a book and using a diagram of a baseball field.
N. Telling difference between fact and fantasy.
O. Relevancy (deciding whether an idea is or is not in a selection.
P. Distinguish among comparisons such as good, better, best.

Level 9 —
3/1 Book

A. Continues use of techniques learned in first and second year.
B. Uses long and short vowel marks.
C. Form plurals of nouns ending in f or fe such as calf, life.
D. Builds new words and recognizes syllabic units of y, ly, er, est.

A. Interpreting main idea of paragraphs.
B. Distinguishing between fact and fancy, relevant and irrelevant.
C. Making judgments and drawing conclusions.
D. Comparing and contrasting.
E. Locating information.
F. Following directions.

Word Recognition Skills	*Comprehension Skills*

E. Add prefixes in front of word and understand how prefix changes the meaning of words: un-happy.

F. Can divide two-syllable and three-syllable words in syllables and principles of syllabication.

G. Hear such suffixes as less, ness, ment.

H. Understand purpose of glossary.

I. Understand meaning of homonyms, synonyms, and antonyms.

J. Recognize common homonyms, synonyms, and antonyms.

K. Alphabetize according to second letter.

L. Identifying root word in inflected and derived forms.

M. Hearing the schwa sound represented by "a" in (a)gree.

N. Applying phonic skills to new words with "vowel plus an r"—c(are).

O. Recognize as sight words and associate in sound groups: though, although, ought, fought.

P. Identify the sound represented by ou in trouble.

Q. Identify the ing, ful, ed syllable in two-syllable words.

R. Identifying syllabic r in two syllable words by adding r to the root .

S. Hearing syllabic l and n in two-syllable words.

T. Hearing short and long vowel sounds in first syllables of two-syllable words.

G. Identifying and reacting to the mood or tone of a passage, story, or poem.

H. Classifying.

I. Map reading and interpretation.

J. Definite and indefinite terms—few, many, etc.

K. Abstract of three degrees—ex., carrot, vegetable, food.

L. Shades of meaning—ex., talked, chatted.

M. Figurative language.

N. Multiple meaning of words.

O. Identifying shifts in the use of a word from telling actions to telling the name of a thing.

P. Visualizing events in a story.

Q. Listing ideas that go together (one point outlining).

R. Identifying and understanding the point of a joke.

S. Interpreting the relationship between analogies as horse is to gallop, as frog is to hop.

Level 10 —
3/2 Book

A. Selection of meaning appropriate to a given contextual meaning.

B. Finding descriptive words.

A. Using reference books to find answers to questions.

B. Learning how to take care of books.

Word Recognition Skills	*Comprehension Skills*
C. Recognizing word forms by adding prefixes.	C. Using outline form to organize the main points of information.
D. Recognizing word forms by adding suffixes ish, ful, ily, er (of agent), ness, less, ier, ious, ous, ant, iest.	D. Relating places, events and time.
E. Identifying root word in inflected and derived forms.	E. Relating facts to a generalization.
F. Relation of vowel sounds and syllables.	F. Interpreting relationships between ideas.
G. Principle for determining vowel sounds in accented syllables.	G. Drawing conclusions from related facts.
H. Alphabetizing according to first, second, third letter.	H. Drawing conclusions about the relationship between cause and effect.
I. Division of alphabet into three parts.	I. Skimming to locate information quickly in a table of contents.
J. Identifying vowel sounds represented by a, be, de, ex, in — in unaccented first syllables.	J. Interpreting main idea of paragraphs, sentences, stories.
K. Changing word endings by er, est (happy—happier).	K. Ability to read for detail.
L. Identifying the roots of words changed by adding a suffix (carry—carrier).	L. Ability to recognize sequence and events of story.
M. Hearing accents in two and three syllable words.	M. Distinguishing between fact and fancy, relevant and irrelevant.
N. Use a glossary to get meanings of words.	N. Interpreting idioms and unusual language.
O. Syllabicate, using three steps: (a) place accent mark, (b) mark short or long vowels on accented syllable, (c) mark off suffixes.	O. Comprehending phrase and sentence meaning.
	P. Forming sensory images.
	Q. Critical reading.
	R. Perceiving relationships — time, place, seqeunce, analogies.
P. Understand and apply principle of schwa sound. and accuracy and comprehension.	S. Develop ability to read longer units with speed, accuracy, and comprehension.
	T. Following three or four steps in written directions.
Level 11 — 4/1 Book	
A. Context — associate exact meaning of word used in context.	A. Comparative and superlative forms of words.
B. Identifying the prefixes— a(sleep), dis(obey).	B. Understand abstracts.
	C. Figurative language.
C. Identifying and interpret-	D. Similies.
	E. Understand climax.

Word Recognition Skills	*Comprehension Skills*

ing the suffixes ness, ment, like, ship, ful.

D. Identifying contractions with two letters left out—he'll.

E. Identifying common unaccented first and last syllables.

F. Identifying shifts of accent in homographs, 'rek-rd or re-'kord.

G. Identifying the root word of the accented syllable in a word of more than one syllable—pay-ment.

H. Compound words: cobblestones, merrymaking.

I. Possessives — mother's, Jones'.

J. Using number of vowel situations in a word to estimate the number of syllables it has.

K. Syllables — words ending with le; exceptions in syllabication.

L. Accent—effect on vowel sounds—rules and identification of accented syllables.

M. Alphabetizing to third letter of words.

N. Using guide words to locate words quickly in the dictionary.

O. Identifying the names of pronunciation symbols.

P. Interperting high and low marks to show stress.

Q. Interpret the slant line used to show beginning and ending of pronunciations.

R. Interpreting the hyphen used to separate syllables.

S. Deciding that the first and third syllables of a three or four syllable word are likely to be accented.

T. Applying vowel rules to the syllables of words.

U. Using guide words to locate dictionary entries.

F. Infer meaning from characters' behavior.

G. Emphathize.

H. Drawing conclusions from related facts.

I. Summarize paragraphs.

J. Put ten ideas in sequential order.

K. Interpreting main idea.

L. Recognizing emotional reactions, motives, and inner drives of story characters.

M. Inference skills.

N. Recognizing connotations and denotions of words.

O. Recognizing story problem or plot structure.

P. Interpreting figurative, idiomatic and picturesque language.

Q. Identifying elements of style.

R. Identifying author's purpose.

S. Identifying character traits.

T. Generalizing.

U. Summarizing and organizing ideas for purpose of remembering.

V. Skimming.

W. Evaluating information.

X. Outlining.

Y. Note-taking.

Word Recognition Skills	Comprehension Skills

Level 12 —
4/2 Book

A. Continuation of 4/1 skills.
B. Prefixes con, com.
C. Apostrophe — possession, contraction.
D. Concept of terms—singular, plural.
E. Alphabetize to the fourth letter.
F. Concept of noun, verb.
G. Meaning—selection of appropriate meaning — synonyms and antonyms.
H. Pronunciation — diacritical marks, phonetic spelling, use of syllabic divisions, accent mark.
I. Locating guide words by estimating what part of the dictionary the first letter of a word is found.
J. Identifying the heavy black type used for dictionary entries.
K. Using illustrations to interpret dictionary definitions.
L. Identifying the italicized entry word in an illustrative sentence following a definition.
M. Using a base word to locate dictionary help on the meaning of a derivation.
N. Using an index to locate information in a textbook or encyclopedia.

A. Interpreting and organizing two point outlines.
B. Interpreting charts of information, maps, time relationships, signals for sequence of ideas, context clues, poetry, fables.
C. Following directions—steps in a science experiment.
D. Visualizing a character from clues planted in a story.
E. Evaluating the author's purpose for writing an article.
F. Interpreting author's mood toward the topic.
G. Evaluating the effect of the selection on a reader.
H. Interpreting cause relationships in sentences.
I. Identifying the antecedent of a pronoun.
J. Using personal pronouns correctly.
K. Relevancy and irrelevancy.
L. Main idea.
M. Using reading study skills to do a three-page unit.
N. Taking notes.

This material is a compilation of skills analysis as developed in *A Guide for Instruction in Reading for the Plainview Public Schools,* issued September 1961, Plainview, N. Y.; The Public Schools, pp. 13-53; Emmett S. Betts and Carolyn Welch, *Phonic Skills Thinking Abilities,* New York, N.Y.: American Book Company; *Reading Level Card—Levels 1-12,* Mineola Public Schools, Mineola, N.Y.; The Public Schools; in addition to original work.

B. SCOPE AND SEQUENCE CHART
FOR THE SOCIAL STUDIES

Level	District Guide	Suggested Revisions [1]
Kgn.	Becoming Acquainted with School Personnel Becoming Acquainted with School Plant Our Home and How We Live in It Our Families and Their Members	The Family — Role of Its Members The Family — Its Role in the Economy The Family — Comparison with a Family in Another Culture The School Environment — Contribution of Education Map and Globe Skills — The Classroom and School Holidays — Patriotism and Our American Heritage
One	Working Together in Our Classroom The Community Safety and Health Holidays	The Family — Comparison with Family of Yesteryear (American) The School — Comparison with Schools of Yesteryear (American Agrarian) The Neighborhood — Community Resources Which Service Us Agrarian Community Today — Types of Farms Map and Globe Skills — The Neighborhood and Its Geographic Features Holidays — Patriotism and Our American Heritage
Two	Food Clothing Shelter Safety and Health Holidays	The Local Community — Either Plainview — Old Bethpage, Nassau County, Township of Oyster Bay, or Long Island The Economy — Industries Political Science — Community Services (Who Provides Them, Who Pays for Them) Transportation — Connection with Larger Community Communication — Connection with Larger Community Service Organizations—Service Groups, Religious Groups, etc. Comparison with Other Community in U. S. (Urban or Rural) Map and Globe Skills — Community and Its Connection to Outside World, Larger Geographic Terms (River, Mountain, etc.) Holidays — Patriotism and Our American Heritage

[1] *Tentative Flowchart of the Elementary Social Studies Program* (modified) (Albany, N. Y.: State Education Department, 1965).

Level	District Guide	Suggested Revisions
	How and Where We Obtain Food	Biographical and Historical Approach to Study of Greatness of Our Country
	How We Obtain and Care For Our Clothing	Discoverers and Explorers; Examples: Columbus, Hudson, La Salle, et al.
	What Kinds of Homes We Have	
	How We Travel	Colonial and Revolutionary Leaders; Examples: Smith, Williams, Franklin, Adams, et al.
Three	How We Communicate	
	Indians (As Related to Food, Clothing, and Shelter)	National Leaders; Examples: Washington, Jefferson, Madison, Hamilton, et al.
	Holidays	
	Animal Care	
	Plainview and New York City (Incidental)	American Freedom Leaders; Examples: Paine, Marshall, Lincoln, Tubman, Addams, Washington, Riis, King, et al.

Industrial and Scientific Leaders; Examples: Whitney, McCormick, Edison, Bell, Carver, Salk, Ford, Rockefeller, Carnegie, et al.

Arts Leaders; Examples: Thoreau, Longfellow, Poe, Lewis, Hughes, Foster, McDowell, Gershwin, Handy, Anderson, Homer, Whistler, et al.

Immigration — The Basis of Our Country's Population

Contributions of Sub Cultures—Negro, Indian, Puerto Rican, Irish, et al.

Map and Globe Skills — Routes of Explorers, etc., Origin of Immigrants, etc. World and Globe Emphasis

Patriotic and American Citizenship and Traditions — Holidays, etc.

C. KINDERGARTEN Check Sheet for READING READINESS

DATE
_____

NAME	SCHOOL

SENDING TEACHER	RECEIVING TEACHER

TOPICS	BELOW AVER.	AVER.	ABOVE AVER.
AUDITORY RHYMING			
AUDITORY BEGINNING SOUNDS			
VISUAL GROSS SHAPES			
VISUAL – MATCHING WORDS AND LETTERS			
LETTER NAMES			
SPEAKING VOCABULARY			
LISTENING VOCABULARY – COMPREHENSION			
FOLLOWS DIRECTIONS			
ATTENTION SPAN			
RETENTION (MEMORY)			
EYE-HAND COORDINATION			
INTEREST IN LEARNING TO READ			
GROSS MOTOR COORDINATION			
FINE MOTOR COORDINATION			

ADDITIONAL COMMENTS:

Old Bethpage School
October 1st, 1964

D. LIST OF INDIVIDUAL PRACTICES—
PRIMARY SCHOOL:

1. One hundred sheets of mathematics puzzles and games, one per sheet, kept in a file called "Mathematics Activity Sheets." Children use these sheets when they complete their regular mathematics assignment. They keep a record of the Activity Sheets completed in their personal folder.

2. Folder listing additional topics for research in Units of Study (Social Studies, Science, Language Arts) currently being carried on in the classroom. Children select these topics for enrichment in research during free time.

3. Poetry Envelope. Children compose poems on topics of interest to them in their spare time. At a certain time the poems are reviewed, rewritten, or corrected and then published in a Class Poetry Book.

4. File of pictures (funny, fantastic, exciting) to be leafed through and used for creative writing.

5. Crossword puzzles based on any subject (curriculum or seasons or holidays)—made by children and solved in spare time.

6. File of *outline maps* of states and sections of United States as an outline (no states) and showing all states—to be worked as desired.

7. *Reading Designs*—Circle graphs to be used to chart recreational reading of library books "Watch your designs become well rounded!"

8. Collection of odds and ends of colored construction paper and other scraps for quiet art work (cut paper designs, etc.) after assignments are completed—collage work.

9. Magazines brought in to be examined and cut up (Life, Look, National Geographic, etc.) for scrap books.

10. Pictures collected (old birthday, Christmas, and other greeting cards) to cut apart and make new pictures.

11. Collection of the "beginnings" of stories—one intriguing sentence or part of a sentence.

12. (Number Corner). Table is set up with various types of number readiness materials for children's use. Certain children are en-

couraged to make use of these materials. Ex. abacus, flannel board with numbers, group recognition charts, pencils and paper.

13. (Oral expression-library corner-reading readiness). Child reads book by reading pictures during free time. Afterwards he relates the story read to the class at story time.

14. Readiness corner—materials, bolton frame, zipper frame, hook frame, snap frame, lacing boot. Child practices those in which he lacks skill. After skill is thoroughly learned, he checks this off next to his name on a chart.

15. Use children's outside interests as a basis of conversation and class discussion.

16. Have a section where we exhibit "Things we make at home to share."

17. Keep a file of materials for building auditory and visual discrimination as a preparation for reading in Grade I.

18. Make use of special abilities. Ex. One child could use and explain a microscope very well. Last week a five-year old played the piano for the group with both left and right hands. School songs were sung with him. He has picked up those songs on his own.

19. A third grade teacher finding that she was having large classes year after year and, therefore, not finding the opportunity to have personal contact with her children, invited them to write notes to her and leave them in a designated drawer in her desk. The results were delightful. The children poured out their hearts to her and reported family events, their own feelings, on seeing the first robin in spring, etc. Two collections of these notes were used in the New York Times Magazine to illustrate the freshness and originality of children's speech.

20. Write individual reports of great names in social studies. Biographies of famous men.

21. Arts and crafts projects (specific topics) used to go along with (particular) unit of study.

22. Writing of articles for class newspaper.

23. Crossword puzzles for class newspaper. (makeup)

24. Science collection (rocks, instruments, etc.). Collections of all sorts that children contribute to.

25. Book report cards—trains.

26. Art, reading and writing. Children make up own stories—put into book form—either dictated to teacher or written independently—to aid in reading vocabulary, primarily.

27. Creative Writing—Teacher clips out interesting pictures from ads—*New York Times Sunday Magazine Section* is very good source. Children write stories independently or with help. Very good results.
28. Art Work—children are allowed to use paints and clay independently during work time when assignments are finished.
29. Make own book covers—and for some, book reports on favorite skills. Read independently.

OLD BETHPAGE SCHOOL

E. INDEPENDENT ACTIVITIES LANGUAGE ARTS [1]

1. Write experience stories.
2. Select a magazine picture and write a story about what is seen in the picture. Who are the characters and what are they doing?
3. Alphabetizing groups of words.
4. Crossword puzzle on a ditto in relation to spelling and new reading words.
5. Put groups of sentences on the board with no capitals, punctuation marks, etc. Have children copy the sentences making the proper corrections.
6. Find a certain number of 2, 3, or 4 syllable words using the dictionary (within a time limit). Write words correctly by showing the syllables, accent. Then use these words in original sentences.
7. Use vocabulary list in reader to find words with certain vowel or consonant sounds.
8. Classify games: list of words to be placed in certain given categories, groups of 4 words. Child crosses out what does not belong; assigns category to those left; phrases or word cards to be placed under cards with headings of where, here, there, now, then, how, etc. or lists may be written on paper under such headings and checked against a key.
9. Give simple word, child writes as many homonyms as he can. Compare the list with others in the group. Check spelling with dictionary, add to class list.
10. Assign a section in content area text; each child is required to read whole selection but makes up at least 2 questions based on paragraph assigned to him. Follow with discussion period.
11. Have a collection of small pictures. Children write labels for each picture. Discussion of best label.
12. Give 4 or 5 letter word. Child changes to new word by changing one letter each time.
13. Illustration of a book for giving oral book report.
14. Matching works on cards with definitions on another card.
15. Cut short stories from magazines. Divide into parts. Paste on cards. Assign sections to different individuals to read silently, then to a partner, in preparation for oral reading to a group.

---

[1] Prepared by Mrs. Belle Warshavsky, Reading Consultant.

16. Take short story. Cut off ending and have child write own ending, or begin a story and have child complete the story.
17. Writing news for class newspaper.
18. Composing riddles for rest of class to solve.
19. Choosing correct word to complete a sentence.
20. "Fill in the missing letter game"—gives spelling practice,, using vocabulary list as guide; also good to make children notice small differences in words as want, went.
21. Cut pictures from magazines beginning with phonic elements they have studied and then organize this into booklet form.
22. In connection with a unit of study (food, transportation, etc.) drawing pictures with one line or even one word stories to be organized into a movie (on rollers in a large cardboard box).
23. Matching words, fill in opposites, true-false, drawing pictures that illustrate small stories.
24. Make a picture dictionary. Make a personal dictionary of new words learned.
25. Give each child a supplementary reader at his independent level. Ask him to find compound words or words with magic, silent, or double vowels, etc. Find words and list them under appropriate headings. The same can be done for syllabication rules (vowel consonant/cv, v/cv, c/e).
26. Each child has a set of vowel cards. Teacher or leader calls a vowel and they all have to choose vowel card they think it is.
27. Cut out all the ads in the newspaper and classify them according to ads for things we wear, eat, use at home, use outside home, and the like.
28. Rate the ads in the newspaper as one, two, three, according to your opinion of whether it presents the product honestly and well or not.
29. Take an article and cross out every word that is absolutely not necessary. Leave only those words that are essential to this story.
30. Copying letters or stories from board.
31. Making calendars at seats; greeting cards when in season.
32. Working on projects related to science, social studies, etc.
33. Clay or handwork in connection with class or individual project.
34. Sewing: Prepare papers with long dashes. The children use wool and tapestry needles. They go over the dashes. Later on, they make their own pictures and go over them with wool.
35. Creative writing—give an interesting title, give an interesting topic sentence to enlarge upon; give an idea to develop; give a situation which is to be solved.

36. Additional reading in research books, historical novels, biographies, and other texts to substantiate a fact, to separate opinion from fact, to make a report, etc. (Notetaking during reading and not recopying author's words without comprehension).

37. Give a ditto sheet with a printed passage—determine the number of words which suggest sound, number of words which create a picture of a thing in the mind. Follow with discussion of interesting styles of writing, etc.

38. Outlining material for reporting.

39. Book reports, summaries of stories, etc.

40. Circling words in a column which are like the word at the top of the column.

41. Drawing a line from a word or phrase in one column to the same word or phrase in another column.

42. Marking out picture which does not belong with a given sentence.

43. Drawing a line from a word, phrase, or sentence to the correct picture.

44. Coloring simple objects to match the color word printed under each.

45. Combining number and color directions as "color the first one green."

46. Cigar box containing construction paper fish with staples near mouth. On each fish are words presenting difficulty, or arithmetic facts, etc. On a wooden pen holder (the fishing pole) tie a string with a magnet. Two children play to see who catches most fish. Saying the word on the paper fish means you have caught the fish.

47. Arrange an attractive library corner with many supplementary readers, games, etc.

48. Making scrapbooks of flowers, animals, birds, machines, houses, etc.

49. News bulletins and weather reports.

50. Making puppets and utilizing them in creative play.

F. SIX-SESSION UNIT WORKSHOP

As a result of individual supervisory conferences held between staff members and the principal at the beginning of the school year, it was possible to determine that a fairly large number of teachers felt that they would profit from a series of workshops related to approaches to unit teaching. Some teachers felt that they were well equipped to plan and implement units in the social studies, but were less certain of unit applications in teaching science. The staff was polled as to the desirability of holding such workshops. Our teachers felt that such workshops would be valuable if they were practical in nature rather than structured in theoretical terms.

It was decided that a series of six workshops would be held during normal professional hours. The total staff was subdivided into two groups. The assistant principal conducted these workshops with the teachers of the kindergarten and lower nongraded primary classes, while the principal worked with the upper nongraded primary teachers and the fourth grade teachers.

The workshops deliberately were highly practical in nature. The assistant principal's group selected a social studies topic to develop, and the principal's group selected a science topic. Each teacher was provided with a blank unit development form which was filled in as the workshop progressed. Prepared background data was furnished to all staff members prior to each session. Cooperatively, a practical unit grew out of each group meeting. These workshop sessions involved special teachers as well as classroom teachers. The school maintains a vertical file of sample units that can be used by teachers in planning for their own classes.

The workshops were favorably received by the staff. There were many evidences of change taking place within the classrooms, particularly, in terms of increased emphasis upon conceptualization and pupil-initiated activities.

The following overview was developed jointly by the principal and assistant principal for the workshop sessions:

Session I   *The Establishment of Objectives*

a. Characteristics of a Good Unit—adaptation to the child's interests, needs, and abilities; differentiated materials and activities; relationship to what precedes and follows.

b. Skills—related to the specific unit; need for teacher supervision; reinforcement of the skills through practical applications; as they relate to characteristics of a good unit.

c. Attitudinal Appreciation.

d. Concepts—developing children's perceptive abilities; role of inference and generalization; meaningful applications.

Session II   *The Selection of Appropriate Content*

a. In Relation to Objectives—need for selectivity; developing cooperative endeavor; stimulating critical thinking, problem solving.

b. Integration and Correlation — determining what can be interrelated with the unit and what is best taught separately.

c. Role in Total Social Studies or Science Program—expanding horizons concept of content selection; repetition of topics at increasing levels of conceptual sophistication and with varied approaches.

d. Multidisciplinary Approach—structuring units to provide integration of history, geography, anthropology, sociology, economics, psychology, civics, and philosophy; role of sub-disciplines in providing a broad base for understanding.

e. Content as Related to Pupils' Interests—modifying content and committee assignments based upon cooperative teacher-pupil planning; need to plan for first-hand as well as vicarious experiences; relating content to that which is already known and understood.

f. Post-Hole Theory—choice of broad exploration as opposed to selection of particularly significant content for in-depth exploration.

Sessions III & IV   *Methodology* (Pupil and Teacher Directed Activities)

a. Selecting and Planning Units—criteria to be used; discriminating between essentials and superfluous materials; relationship to practical considerations of time, availability of materials, maturity level of the children.

b. Orientation Phase of a Unit—activities appropriate to this aspect of the unit; use of a single text to establish an overview for launching committee activities.

c. Information Gathering Activities—reading, observing, interviewing, discussing and pooling information; role of library; outlining and summarizing.

d. Summarizing and Presenting Data—varied forms that can be used; value of group approach as compared to individual presentation; establishing criteria cooperatively; role of the teacher during reporting sessions.

e. Activities to Foster Creative Expression—range of media: dance, music, art, written expression.

Session V

Materials of Instruction (Pupil and Teacher Use)

a. Modifying Materials To Stated Purposes—use of multiple-text approach, periodicals, and vertical file materials; determination of the best tool to fulfill need.

b. Relating Materials To Learning—range in readability of materials; the role of picture analysis; audio-visual aids that can be utilized by pupils themselves.

c. Adaptation of the Classroom—possible arrangements of classroom furniture to meet needs at various stages of the unit development, bulletin board displays and activity centers, accessibility to research materials, classroom climate as an asset or liability in fulfilling goals.

d. Use of Audio-Visual Aids—tape recorder as an instructional tool; use of the overhead projector for large group presentations, use of radio and television broadcasts, varied ways of using motion pictures, using filmstrips for correlation with other areas.

e. Community Resources—ways of taking the children out into the community; techniques for bringing members of the community into the classroom.

Session VI   *Concluding the Unit*

a. Types of Culminating Activities—presentations, displays, preparation of food, field trips.
b. Role of Unit Evaluation—of the unit plan itself; of content and organization; in terms of original goals; role of evaluation by pupils and teachers.
c. Leads to New Work—need to relate what has been learned to what is about to be learned; forms this may take.

G. SOCIAL STUDIES SKILLS: A GUIDE TO ANALYSIS AND GRADE PLACEMENT[1]

Eunice Johns and Dorothy McClure Fraser

Helping young people develop and use skills effectively is one of the central purposes of social studies instruction. Indeed, without an adequate command of skills, it is doubtful that students can gain the insights concerning their society or develop the habits of intellectual and social behavior that constitute the ultimate goals of the social studies program. Skills are tools for learning both in and out of school. The student who develops a command of social studies skills during his school years and carries these skills into the adult years has laid a firm basis for continued learning throughout his life.

The chart which appears in the following pages has been developed as an aid to social studies teachers who desire to improve their teaching of social studies skills. It represents an illustrative analysis of major skill areas that should be developed in social studies programs. It is organized in two parts, as follows:

Part One. Skills which are a definite but shared responsibility of the social studies

      I. Locating information
     II. Organizing information
    III. Evaluating information
    IV. Acquiring information through reading
     V. Acquiring information through listening and observing
    VI. Communicating orally and in writing
   VII. Interpreting pictures, charts, graphs, tables
  VIII. Working with others

Part Two. Skills which are a major responsibility of the social studies

      I. Reading social studies materials
     II. Applying problem-solving and critical-thinking skills to social issues
    III. Interpreting maps and globes
    IV. Understanding time and chronology

---

[1] Helen M. Carpenter, Ed., *Skill Development in Social Studies,* National Council for the Social Studies (Washington, D.C.: The Council, 1963) pp. 310-27.

The chart also suggests a tentative grade placement for three levels of emphasis on each sub-skill that is identified: (1) introducing the specific skill, through planned readiness experiences; (2) developing the skill systematically; and (3) reteaching, maintaining, and extending the skill as necessary.

Thus, the chart outlines a planned, sequential program for skill development, one that cuts across subject lines and bridges the gap between the elementary and the secondary school. It may serve as a reminder to every teacher that effective teaching of skills should be part of a cumulative program running from the early school years through high school. It may help the teacher plan so as to reinforce whatever command of skills his pupils have already attained at the same time that he leads them to a higher level of performance.

The chart may also be used by groups of social studies teachers and their colleagues in other fields as a point of departure in formulating their own analysis and plan for the social studies skills program in their own school system. When teachers thus clarify their own purposes for teaching skills, become sensitized to their pupils needs for skill development, and identify ways of meeting those needs, major benefit to the instructional program will result that could never come from uncritical acceptance of an already formulated program.

Throughout this *Yearbook* the point has been made that pupils develop skills most effectively when there is systematic instruction and continuing application of the skills. The following principles of learning and teaching have been emphasized as a basis for the social studies skills program:

1. The skill should be taught functionally, in the context of a topic of study, rather than as a separate exercise.

2. The learner must understand the meaning and purpose of the skill and have motivation for developing it.

3. The learner should be carefully supervised in his first attempts to apply the skill so that he will form correct habits from the beginning.

4. The learner needs repeated opportunities to practice the skill, with immediate evaluation so that he knows he has succeeded or failed in his performance.

5. The learner needs individual help, through diagnostic measures and follow-up exercises, since not all members of any group learn at exactly the same rate or retain equal amounts of what they have learned.

6. Skill instruction should be presented at increasing levels of

difficulty, moving from the simple to the more complex; the resulting growth in skills should be cumulative as the learner moves through school, with each level of instruction building on and reinforcing what has been taught previously.

7. Students should be helped, at each stage, to generalize the skills by applying them in many and varied situations; in this way, maximum transfer of learning can be achieved.

8. The program of instruction should be sufficiently flexible to allow skills to be taught as they are needed by the learner; many skills should be developed concurrently.

In applying these principles, teachers should keep two cautions in mind. First, although it is possible to make a general plan for continuity in skill development, it is impossible to set a particular place in the school program where it is always best to introduce a specific skill. Many factors enter into the final decision of the teacher as he works with a specific class, and the general plan can serve only as a guide to what seems to be good practice. True continuity in skill development is that which is developed within the learner, not that which can be blocked out in a general plan. Furthermore, it can never be assumed that a child has gained command of a particular skill merely because he has been exposed to it. Review and reteaching of skills that have been stressed at an earlier grade level are often necessary, even with the most capable students.

Second, the suggested grade placements indicated in the chart which follows are based on a combination of current practice and the subjective judgments of many teachers, including the authors. Both of these reflect what young people seem to be able to achieve within existing patterns of instruction. It is possible that pupils could achieve earlier and more effective command of many aspects of social studies skills if new patterns and approaches for instruction were employed. More systematic and intensive readiness experiences, for example, might enable children to profit from systematic instruction in skills at an earlier age. If so, they would gain an earlier command of tools that could enhance their learning through the rest of their school years. On the other hand, it is possible that present practice calls for instruction in some skills before the learner has developed the necessary related concepts. If so, he may not only fail for the moment but be handicapped in later efforts to gain control of the particular skill. Almost no research evidence exists to guide the proper grade placement of skill instruction. Evidence of this kind is urgently needed as a basis improving the teaching of social studies skills. It is the hope of the authors that their efforts in preparing this guide to the analysis and grade placement of skill instruction will stimulate such research in the years immediately ahead.

The chart follows:

Skill	Introduce through planned readiness experiences	Develop System-atically
I. Locating information		
A. Work with books		
1. Use title of books as guide to content	EP	LP
2. Use table of contents	LP	
3. Alphabetize	LP	
4. Distinguish between storybooks and factual books	LP	
5. Choose a book appropriate for the purpose	LP	
B. Find information in encyclopedias and other reference books		
C. Make efficient use of the dictionary		
1. Alphabetize a list of words according to the first letter	LP	
D. Read newspapers, magazines, and pamphlets with discrimination		
1. Recognize these materials as sources of information about many topics, especially current affairs	LP	
E. Know how to find material in a library, both school and public		
F. Gather facts from field trips and interviews		
1. Identify the purpose of the field trip or interview	EP	LP
2. Plan procedures, rules of behavior, questions to be asked, things to look for	EP	LP
3. Take increasingly greater initiative in the actual conduct of the field trip or interview	EP	LP
4. Evaluate the planning and execution of the field trip or interview	EP	LP
5. Find acceptable ways to open and close an interview	LP	
6. Express appreciation for courtesies extended during field trip, interview	EP	LP
7. Record, summarize, and evaluate information gained	EP	LP
G. Be selective in using audio-visual materials	EP	

EP = Early Primary
LP = Late Primary

	Introduce through planned readiness experiences	Develop Systematically
H. Use maps and globes in developing geographical skills	LP	
II. Organizing information		
A. Compose a title for a story, picture, graph, map, or chart	EP	LP
B. Select answers to questions from material heard, viewed, or read	EP	LP
C. Classify pictures, facts and events under main headings or in categories	LP	
D. Arrange events, facts, and ideas in sequence	EP	LP
E. Make a simple table of contents	LP	
III. Evaluating information		
A. Distinguish between fact and fiction	EP	LP
B. Compare information about a topic drawn from two or more sources to recognize agreement or contradiction	LP	
C. Consider which source of information is more acceptable, and why	LP	
D. Draw inferences and make generalizations from evidence	EP	LP
E. Reach tentative conclusions	EP	LP
IV. Acquiring information through reading		
A. Read to find answers to questions	EP	LP
B. Select the statements that are pertinent to the topic being studied	LP	
V. Acquiring information through listening and observing		
A. Listen and observe with a purpose	EP	LP
B. Listen attentively when others are speaking	EP	LP
C. Identify a sequence of ideas and select those that are the most important	LP	
D. Relate, compare, and evaluate information gained through listening and observing with that gained from other sources of information	LP	
E. Adjust to a speaker's voice and delivery and to the physical conditions of the situation	LP	
VI. Communicating orally and in writing		
A. Speak with accuracy and poise		
1. Develop an adequate vocabulary	EP	LP
2. Choose the appropriate word	EP	LP
3. Pronounce words correctly and enunciate clearly	EP	LP
4. Talk in sentences	EP	LP
5. Keep to the point in all situations involving oral expression	EP	LP

	Introduce through planned readiness experiences	Develop System- atically
6. Develop self-confidence	EP	LP
7. Exchange ideas through discussion, either as leader or participant	EP	LP
8. Respect limitations of time and the right of others to be heard	EP	LP
B. Write with clarity and exactness		
1. Apply the skills being developed in printing, writing, spelling, punctuating, capitalizing, and arranging written work	LP	
VII. Interpreting pictures, charts, graphs, tables		
A. Interpret pictorial materials		
1. Recognize these materials as sources of information	EP	LP
2. Note and describe the content of the material, both general and specific	EP	LP
3. Interpret by applying related information, and use the material as one basis for drawing conclusions	EP	LP
VIII. Working with others		
A. Respect the rights and opinions of others	EP	LP
B. Understand the need for rules and the necessity for observing them	EP	LP
C. Take part in making the rules needed by the group	EP	LP
D. Accept the role of leader or follower, as the situation requires	EP	LP
E. Profit from criticism and suggestions	EP	LP
F. Distinguish between work that can be done most efficiently by individuals and that which calls for group effort	EP	LP
IX. Reading social studies materials		
A. Understand an increasing number of social studies terms	EP	LP
X. Applying problem-solving and critical-thinking skills to social issues		
A. Recognize that a problem exists	EP	LP
B. Define the problem for study	EP	LP
C. Review known information about the problem	EP	LP
D. Plan how to study the problem	EP	LP
E. Locate, gather, and organize information	EP	LP
F. Interpret and evaluate information	EP	LP
G. Summarize and draw tentative conclusions	EP	LP

	Introduce through planned readiness experiences	Develop System- atically
H. Recognize the need to change conclusions when new information warrants	EP	LP
I. Recognize areas for further study	EP	LP
J. Use problem-solving techniques in meeting personal and societal problems	EP	LP
XI. Interpreting maps and globes		
A. Orient the map and note directions		
1. Use cardinal directions in classroom and neighborhood	LP	
2. Use relative terms of location and direction, as near, far, above, below, up, down	EP	LP
3. Understand that north is toward the North Pole and south toward the South Pole on any map projection	LP	
B. Locate places on maps and globes		
1. Recognize land and water masses on a globe and on a variety of maps — physical, political, chalkboard, weather, etc.	LP	
2. Learn to make simple sketch maps to show location	LP	
C. Use scale and compute distances		
1. Use small objects to represent large ones as a photograph compared to actual size	EP	LP
2. Make simple large-scale maps of a familiar area, such as classroom, neighborhood	EP	LP
D. Interpret map symbols and visualize what they represent		
1. Understand that real objects can be represented by pictures or symbols on a map	EP	LP
XII. Understanding time and chronology		
A. Develop an understanding of the time system and the calendar		
1. Learn to tell time by the clock	EP	LP
2. Use names of the days of the week in order	EP	LP
3. Use names of the months in sequence	EP	LP
4. Use calendar to find dates of special events and to determine length of time between important dates	EP	LP
5. Associate seasons with particular months both in northern and southern hemispheres	EP	LP

	Introduce through planned readiness experiences	*Develop Systematically*
6. Understand the relation between rotation of the earth and day and night	LP	
7. Understand the system of time zones as related to the rotation of the earth	LP	
8. Understand the relation between the earth's revolution around the sun and a calendar year	LP	
9. Use such indefinite time concepts as past, future, long ago, before, after, meanwhile	EP	LP
B. Develop an understanding of events as part of a chronological series of events and an understanding of the differences in duration of various periods of time		
1. Recognize sequence and chronology in personal experiences, as the school day, weekly schedule, etc.	LP	
2. Learn to arrange personal experiences in order	EP	LP
3. Comprehend sequence and order as expressed in first, second, third, etc.	EP	LP

H. THE NONGRADED BROCHURE

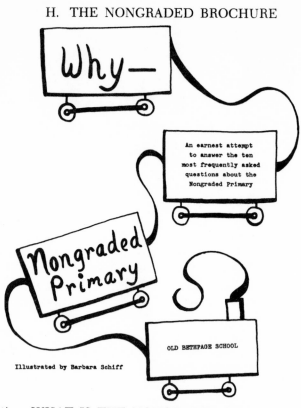

An earnest attempt
to answer the ten
most frequently asked
questions about the
Nongraded Primary

OLD BETHPAGE SCHOOL

Illustrated by Barbara Schiff

Question: WHAT IS THE NONGRADED PRIMARY?

"The nongraded unit has been defined as a pattern of elementary school organization designed to insure full recognition of individual differences . . . by the elimination of arbitrary grade classifications and grade expectations. The nongraded unit has also been described as an organizational arrangement that permits educational progress for all . . . The nongraded unit is, in short, an administrative device for putting into practice a democratic philosophy that emphasizes the value of the individual child." [1]

Stated another way, "the essence of the nongraded [2] primary school is simply a plan in which children beyond the kindergarten . . . and

---

[1] Louis T. DiLorenzo and Ruth Salter, "Co-operative Research on the Nongraded Primary," *Elementary School Journal*, LXV (Feb. 1965), 269, © 1965 by The University of Chicago and published by The University of Chicago Press.

[2] The term nongraded is substituted for "ungraded" in all quotations from this source.

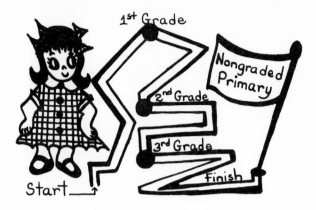

below the fourth grade . . . are grouped together in classes which have no grade level designations. Such an arrangement eliminates the administrative labels of "first grade," "second grade," and "third grade," and the three-year course of study becomes a more flexible program with fewer time limitations . . . A child who enters a nongraded primary class following kindergarten enters into a class with no label except "primary." For the next three years he continues to live and to work in a classroom which has no label except "primary." He continues to do the same work as he would in a typical first, second, or third grade class, but at his own rate of speed. The following September, the child will continue in the primary school and pick up where he left off in June." [3]

Question: IN WHAT WAYS IS THE NONGRADED PRIMARY DIFFERENT FROM THE GRADED SCHOOL?

Differences between the graded and the nongraded organizational pattern are many and varied. The comparison below will serve to highlight a few of these differences.

Graded Structure	*Nongraded Structure*
1. Schools are designed to cover and inculcate a specific body of subject matter.[4]	1. Schools are learner-centered—designed to develop the learner as an individual and as a member of society.[4]

[3] Carol Greenberg, *The Ungraded Primary—Meeting Individual Differences,* January 1962 (unpublished paper), p. 9.

[4] John I. Goodlad, *Planning and Organizing for Teaching* (Washington, D.C.: The National Education Association, 1963) pp. 56-57.

Graded Structure	Nongraded Structure
2. Individual differences merely determine one's chances in the race to cover prescribed material. They are not taken into account in planning the program or the organizational structure.[4]	2. Differences in many aspects of development are recognized and used in planning highly individualized programs.[4]
3. Nonpromotion is the primary mechanism by which students who progress slowly are adjusted to the system.[4]	3. Provision is made for both differentiated rates of progress and variations in kinds of program, according to individual needs and abilities.[4]
4. Decision about grade placement are made at the end of each school year.[5]	4. Decisions about placement in a group take place throughout the school program.[5]
5. Grade placement depends on meeting of fixed annual standards set for the whole group.[5]	5. Individual standards are based on the physical, mental, social and emotional status of the child at any time.[5]
6. Specific bodies of content are assigned to specific grades.[5]	6. Content is viewed as cumulative as well as sequential.[5]
7. Content assigned to the following grade is "Off Limits."[5]	7. When child is ready for the next step he goes to it; it is not the exclusive domain of the teacher of next year's work.[5]
8. Subject matter should be identified and rigorously prescribed.[4]	8. Focus should be on ways of knowing and thinking. Emphasis is on the individual.[4]

Question: WHAT HAPPENS TO THE "SLOW" CHILD IN THE NONGRADED PRIMARY SCHOOL

In the graded school, the slow learning child who is unable to achieve up to the standards of the particular grade is frequently compelled to repeat that grade. Such retentions are made in the

---

[5] Robert G. Scanlon and David Trachtenberg, *The Non-Graded School: Its Background and Current Status* (New Paltz, N.Y.: Mid-Hudson School Study Council, 1965) pp. 27-28.

face of increasing evidence that children do not increase learning through retention. On the contrary, these youngsters usually do better when promoted.

In the nongraded primary school retentions will no longer take place. Instead, some children may require four years to complete the primary program. While a child may spend an additional year in the nongraded primary school, it does not represent retention. The child makes continuous progress at a slower learning rate.

The manner in which a child progresses through the school can be illustrated as shown below:

GRADED PRIMARY

Kgn.————Gr. 2

    Gr. 2————Gr. 4

After leaving kindergarten, the child makes insufficient progress to warrant promotion at the end of Grade 2. He repeats Grade 2 (also repeating much work he has learned) and completes Grade 3 prior to promotion to Grade 4.

NONGRADED PRIMARY

Kgn.———— ———— ————Gr. 4   (Case #1)

The child has made less than normal progress in the first and second years of the program. During the third year his rate of learning increases, making it possible to promote him to Grade 4 after three years in the nongraded primary school.

Kgn.————————————Gr. 4   (Case #2)

The child makes less than normal progress each year. At the end of the third year the child has not completed the work necessary for promotion to Grade 4. He requires an additional year in the nongraded program. He doesn't repeat a grade, but continues making slow progress.

Question: WHAT HAPPENS TO THE "AVERAGE" CHILD IN THE NONGRADED SCHOOL?

To the child whose progress corresponds approximately to the levels of difficulty which have been defined for the first, second, and third grades, the nongraded program may seem to have few direct advantages.[6]

It is anticipated that the nongraded program will "provide teachers with added opportunity to meet the individual instructional needs of children. It will provide groups of learners where each child competes with himself—not with the class or some other group of children. It will place and move children into learning situations where satisfaction and self-development come through progress and success. It will provide goals and levels of work, instead of grades, to assure a developmental instructional program of sequential experiences for all children. By eliminating the pressures of grade-level barriers and predetermined time and subject matter schedules, it will further break down the practice of identical demands for all children.[7]

The difference between the graded and nongraded organization can be illustrated as follows:

GRADED PRIMARY

Kgn.———   ———   ———Gr. 4

The child progresses at a rate which permits completion of expectations for each September to June period. If a child gets off to a slow start in academic work, has a prolonged illness or an emotional block to learning, he may become a candidate for retention.

---

[6] Greenberg

[7] Edward W. Smith, Stanley W. Krouse, Jr., and Mark M. Atkinson, *The Educator's Encyclopedia* (Englewood Cliffs, N.J.: Prentice-Hall, Inc., 1961) p. 142.

NONGRADED PRIMARY

Kgn.————————————————Gr. 4

The child has a three-year block of time to complete the necessary work. A slow start in school or prolonged illness becomes far less damaging to his educational career. Time lost can be made up during the three-year period of time. The greater individualization of instruction provided in the nongraded program enhances the child's opportunity to regain lost time.

Question: WHAT HAPPENS TO THE "BRIGHT" CHILD IN THE NONGRADED SCHOOL?

The nongraded primary school provides special advantages for bright children. Teachers increasingly recognize and encourage ver-

tical growth of bright children through provision of stimulating tasks and enriched curriculum experiences not provided for the slower, less mature child.

The advantages of the nongraded program can be illustrated as shown below:

GRADED PRIMARY

Kgn.—————————— ——————————Gr. 4

A bright pupil has been accelerated or "skipped." While he has high mental ability, social, physical, and emotional maturity, there is still a one-year "gap" in his education. Careful analysis of his needs and skillful teaching will narrow this gap. It can never be completely eliminated.

NONGRADED PRIMARY

Kgn.————————————————Gr. 4

The same pupil in a nongraded school is never accelerated. He may, however, master all levels in a shorter period of time. He thereby gains a year without any gaps in his education. He enters Grade 4 with children who have been in his class for some time in the latter part of the nongraded primary program.

Question: HOW ARE THE CHILDREN GOING TO BE GROUPED INTO CLASSES?

Children will be grouped into classes using the same criteria as in the past:

a. Metropolitan Readiness Tests and Informal Reading Inventories.
b. Teacher recommendations.
c. Children's cumulative records.
d. When necessary, recommendations of special personnel such as the school psychologist, nurse-teacher, speech therapist, reading consultant, etc.

To better meet the needs of our primary pupils, we will organize our classes so all youngsters will be assigned to a group in which they can work comfortably and experience success. Pupils will be grouped so as to reduce the range of reading ability within any

given classroom, thereby increasing the possibility of more individualized instruction. Added factors include consideration of leadership, emotional stability, physical maturity, mental ability, physical handicaps, and chronological age.

Children in any given class will represent, to the degree compatible with other grouping criteria, any three contiguous levels in reading ability. The large number of classes that will be in the nongraded primary school indicates that we will have more than one class containing any given group of levels.

By placing children in classes where their needs can best be met, it is anticipated that some degree of multi-age grouping will be used. In such classes, younger but mature and rapid-learning pupils will be grouped with older children. It is expected that the chronological age range in any class might increase from the present eleven months to about eighteen months.

A child whose learning rate changes might find himself in a class where no group is functioning at his level. In such cases, pupils should be transferred to a class where their needs can be met. Such reassignments would be made upon joint agreement of the principal, school psychologist, and classroom teacher. In such cases, parents would be notified prior to the actual change. The necessity for moving children from one class to another can be reduced by careful initial placement of the children.

Question: DOES THE NONGRADED PROGRAM REQUIRE A DIFFERENT CURRICULUM OR DIFFERENT MATERIAL?

In the Plainview-Old Bethpage Schools curriculum reform has already preceded the nongraded program. We already have curriculum

guides which place stress on conceptualization and upon the vertical development of skills and content in all major instructional areas.

Similarly, stress has been placed on the use of multiple textbooks and other resource materials in our present program. We have consistently supported development of an outstanding library program. It is anticipated that the nongraded program can be effectively carried out with materials on hand. There will be no budgetary increase created by the adoption of the nongraded program.

Question: HOW WILL WE KNOW ABOUT OUR CHILDREN'S PROGRESS IF WE DON'T KNOW WHAT GRADES THEY'RE IN?

"A complete and accurate record will be kept of each child's work and progress. This record calls for a continuous inventory of each child's progress in many areas of experience, including reading, mathematics, social studies, science, and language arts. This also records the development of a child's attitudes, appreciations, and skills.

"The flexibility of the educational program that is characteristic of the nongraded primary school demands parent-teacher conferences that are purposeful and timed in terms of the movement of children through various levels of their educational experiences." [8] At the parent-teacher conferences, your child's teacher will indicate the

level at which he is working in the various curricular areas. Each child's progress will be reported according to his individual growth, taking into consideration his potentialities and capabilities. In this type of reporting, no grade level expectancies are considered nor are children compared to other children of the same age or same number of years in school.

The parent-teacher conference provides an opportunity for communication between the teacher and parent in which the teacher

[8] Smith, Krouse, and Atkinson

learns about the child's home background, home behavior and special problems, while the parent learns about the child's school progress and school behavior. Through the conference a teacher learns more about the child's home life and is better able to provide for his needs in school.

Question: HOW WILL THE CHILDREN KNOW WHAT CLASS THEY ARE IN?

While the children are in the "Primary School," their classes will be identified by the teachers' names.

The school will familiarize the children with the nongraded program and work to maintain their security and self-confidence. Each teacher will stress the following points in such orientation:

a. The nongraded program represents no change from the grade level into which they would have been placed. They will be in the "Primary School" and their classes will be identified by the teachers' names.
b. There will be no increase in the length of time any child will spend in the Old Bethpage School. The total length of the children's elementary school training will be the same number of years as before.

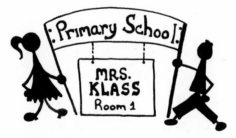

c. When the children finish the Primary School program, they will enter regular fourth grade classes.
d. There will be no change in activities, experiences, or curriculum.
e. The children will remain largely with children of their own age level.

Question: WHY DOES THE ADMINISTRATION AND STAFF OF THE OLD BETHPAGE SCHOOL ENDORSE THE NONGRADED PRIMARY?

The professional staff of the Old Bethpage School has welcomed and advocated the nongraded primary program because it "promotes and encourages the developmental and sequential offerings of experiences in terms of children's needs, and it eliminates the frustrations of grade textbooks and materials that all children must master at a particular time, avoids pushing all children to meet artificial end-of-year achievement scores, gets away from the demand that all youngsters get to a predetermined grade or year standard, and erases the need to specify which children can 'pass' and which children need to fail. The sole determinant of how long the child must spend in the primary unit is the child himself."[9]

Nongraded schools have found that children exhibit better mental health attitudes as a result of the decrease in pressure for performance. Children of average ability with leadership potential are given an opportunity to assume leadership roles heretofore denied them. Acceleration with its inherent loss of a full curriculum year, and retention with its inherent repetition of curriculum experiences are also both avoided in the nongraded school.

Approximately 25% of the elementary schools in the nation incorporate some elements of the nongraded plan. Many of their goals, e.g., regular revisions, flexible classroom grouping procedures, methods of reporting to parents, comprehensive techniques of pupil evaluation, etc., are already incorporated in our instructional program. Thus, the nongraded organization becomes a logical extension of our existing educational philosophy.

---

[9] Smith, Krouse, and Atkinson

(Reprint from building newsletter)

I. NEWS OF THE NONGRADED

Old Bethpage School   September 1964

In June Mrs. Glogau and Mr. Fessel had an opportunity to visit Public School 89, Queens. This school has been designated as the pilot school for the New York City exploration of the nongraded primary.

The program was set up with the collaboration of Dr. Robert Anderson of Harvard University, co-author of *The Nongraded Elementary School*. Mrs. Reba Mayer, the principal, was very gracious in providing a three-hour period during which they observed in each of the classrooms, conferred with the teachers, assistant principal, and principal, and were permitted to examine records of meetings, teachers' plan books, etc.

In Public School 89, Queens, children remain in the self-contained classroom for the entire school day, except for mathematics for which pupils move to a different class in accordance with their ability in this subject. The classes were organized on a heterogeneous basis and all contain interage groups. Kindergarten children were included in the nongraded organization.

Extensive discussion with the teachers brought out the following interesting attitudes:

1. The teachers felt that interage grouping was one of the prime strengths of the program.
2. The teachers indicated a preference for remaining with the same group of children throughout the nongraded program.
3. The degree of cooperative planning and interaction between the teachers increased as a result of the program.

Both Mrs. Glogau and Mr. Fessel felt that the visitation was a valuable one because of the insights they developed and the practical hints offered by Mrs. Mayer and the teachers involved in the program. Among these were the following:

1. It is important to begin the day with an integrating experience on a central theme to start everyone off together. Similarly, the school day is concluded in a similar manner with an evaluation discussion of the day's activities.
2. In the areas of social studies and science, unit topics of the

highest group are used to avoid redoing material. Units are cycled over a three-year span for future classes.

3. It is important to keep a record of reading levels of youngsters, both achievement and group functioning levels.
4. It is necessary to hold weekly meetings with the various groups of teachers.

There was a distinct air of exploration and on-going development in the school. Teachers and principal alike were conscious of the need to avoid crystallizing the pattern too soon.

They particularly noted two interesting outcomes reported by Mrs. Mayer:

1. Despite the fact that New York City public schools have traditionally avoided any formal reading instruction in kindergarten, those kindergarten-age children that are in the interage nongraded classes have informally picked-up reading skills by being in such a group. Thus, one-third to one-half of these children are now reading.
2. An improvement in scores achieved on end-of-year achievement tests has been found − − again, despite the fact that the standardized testing program has not received great emphasis in the building.

A final but significant point made by Mrs. Mayer related to the fact that changes in structure should never occur for their own sake, but rather, they must further the aim of individualization of instruction and development of better awareness and insight into pupil motivations and behavior.

Questions Parents Asks

1. *How do you place a child from another school?*

Each new entrant is administered an Informal Reading Inventory by the school's reading consultant at the time of registration. This is the same test that was used for placement of those pupils already in the school last June. Thus, the same criteria are used and new pupils enter a class containing children who achieve at the same levels. When the sending school has provided school records, these are also used in initial placement. New entrants, as well as other pupils, are discussed at weekly meetings. Should initial placement prove faulty, changes are made.

2. *Are the children moved individually or in groups?*

When possible, children move in groups. At times this is not possible and an individual is moved. In such cases, careful study of the child's adjustment to the new class is made. It is anticipated that any changes that are necessary at the end of the year, due to rezoning, will be made in terms of entire groups rather than individual children.

3. *How often do children move?*

In most cases, there will be no more than one movement in a school year. However, in certain unusual cases, where pupil adjustment is not favorable in the new class, an additional change may be required.

(Reprint from building newsletter.)

NEWS OF THE NONGRADED

Old Bethpage School   November 1964

Below is a summary of the Nongraded Progress Report #1 presented on the evening of October 27, 1964. We hope to devote subsequent issues to specific classroom activities, principles of the nongraded program, levels of achievement, reporting to parents, homework, individualized instruction etc.

Structure and Grouping of the Nongraded Primary (Mr. Fessel)

Mr. Fessel informed the parents that children had been placed in classes in a manner that would provide for three contiguous reading levels in each class. The grouping eliminates certain formerly accepted ideas of class grouping. It is important for parents to understand that: (1) the children are not graded in any way; (2) the teachers are not graded in any way; (3) attempts to attach labels to any teacher, class, or group can only lead to confusion. The principal defined a *grade* as a prescribed body of learning within a time limit. A *level*, on the other hand, has a prescribed body of learning without a rigid time limit. Mr. Fessel underscored the point that statistically there would be radically few gross changes in the time most children require to complete the primary school (i.e., the first three years of formal school). Only those youngsters who might have been accelerated in the past, under a graded program, will now complete the three—year program in two and only those youngsters who might have been retained in the past under a graded program will now complete the three-year program in four.

The Child and the Nongraded Primary (Miss Casey)

Our school psychologist spoke of pupil relationships and the ease with which most children adjusted to the nongraded program. She spoke of the positive values of interage grouping—indicating that a more natural grouping occurred with increased opportunities for social leadership.

Classroom Instruction and the Nongraded Program (Mrs. Edelman)

Mrs. Edelman, one of our classroom teachers, spoke of the ease with which her children adjusted to the wider range in ages. She described the manner in which the day is started with a center of interest activity of common interest to all children, then the subgrouping based upon pupil needs and interests. She displayed some of the materials and techniques used to differentiate instruction.

Reading and the Nongraded Program (Mrs. Warshavsky)

Our reading consultant described the manner in which children are evaluated for initial placement and subsequent change of class when necessary, indicating that a variety of formal and informal tests, teacher judgment, and evaluation by special personnel (nurse, —teacher, psychologist, reading consultant, speech therapist, administrators, etc.) are involved in the evaluation process.

The Special Teacher and the Nongraded Primary (Mrs. Hirshik)

Our librarian described the increasingly important role of the library as greater individualization takes place. The library becomes a resource center for all instructional activities. There is an increasing awareness of individual differences on the part of special teachers making for more individualized activities in these areas. Further there is an increasing use of the special teachers as consultants to the classroom teacher.

The Teacher and the Nongraded Primary (Mrs. Glogau)

Our Assistant Principal spoke of the disirable effects of the nongraded format in fostering changes in teaching methods and materials. To meet individual needs, teachers are using a variety of techniques and many additional types of materials and activities.

Question and Answer Period:

A period was set aside for questions at the close of the meeting. Below are listed some of the questions with a brief summary of the answers:

1. *Will a change in the budget affect the nongraded program?*

   The program was initiated and can be continued within normal budgetary provisions. Of course, additional funds would permit even greater gains—more differentiated materials, expansion of the library, etc.

2. *Will the children have the same teachers next year or will they change teachers?*

   The issue of teacher cycling is one that has not been resolved. While there are advantages to remaining with the same teacher in terms of avoiding a period at the beginning of the year in getting to know the children, it is obvious that personality clashes occur at times and a change is desirable, both for the teacher and the child.

3. *Will there be regrouping of children in June?*

   If our pupil population remains stable, there will be no need for major regrouping at the end of the year. Children will have been moved when necessary during the year and should begin in September where they left off in June. However, because some type of rezoning is anticipated, we expect to have to do some regrouping this year.

4. *How will the children adjust to a shift to a graded structure when the children reach the fourth grade?*

   Children should experience no difficulty in adjusting to the fourth grade. The vertical curriculum and planned grouping in existence in all schools enable children to begin instruction at the level where the teacher finds them and move them ahead as rapidly as the children can learn. The nongraded primary program also provides for this and, *in addition,* permits a large block of three years for pupils to complete required work.

5. *Why does my child still think he is in the second grade despite the fact that you are making all kinds of efforts toward concealing it?*

The graded school has had a full century to become established. It cannot be eradicated overnight. Books sometimes carry a grade level designation; parents continue to refer to grade levels; even teachers will on occasion refer to it. It will take several years before all such references are removed. About one-fifth of all schools in the country are now nongraded. Within twenty years almost all schools will be nongraded. Most leading educational authorities subscribe to the nongraded concept and feel that its extension is inevitable.

6. *How are the children from kindergarten evaluated for nongraded placement?*

We are using a combination of teacher judgment and the Metropolitan Readiness Test. This test has been used for many years with millions of children and has been found to be quite reliable. Where a question exists, a child is individually tested by the school psychologist.

7. *Will the children be retested and reevaluated at the end of the year?*

No further extensive testing program is anticipated. Children took a standardized achievement test in October. The results of this test are being used to check our prior findings and are also being used to diagnose areas of weakness so effective instruction can take place. When a particular problem occurs, the school psychologist and reading consultant will often test a particular child individually.

8. *If children have to move back to a lower level of work, will they not be more disturbed by such a move under the nongraded program than under a graded program?*

We believe not. First, we feel that we have done a more accurate job of placing pupils than ever before; the range of possibilities for placing children are greater. Where a difference arose between test results and teacher evaluation, the lower estimate was used for initial grouping in the conviction that it is less damaging to move a child ahead than back. When it becomes necessary to move a child back, he will move back by one level rather than a full year. The child will be given new material rather than repeat work already successfully completed. Last, it is less disturbing for a youngster to be moved back to a lower level than to remain on a level beyond his capabilities where he is constantly being exposed to failure.

J. EXCERPT FROM PLAINVIEW-OLD BETHPAGE SCHOOL NEWS

Graded? Un-Graded? Non-Graded?

The ungraded school is known by many names. When grade designations have been eliminated only in the primary grades, it is most often known as the Ungraded Primary School, or the Nongraded Primary School or, more simply, the Primary School. Otherwise, a school will be referred to as being a nongraded or ungraded school. In some instances, school officials will indicate that a school employs a Continous Progress Plan. In other instances, districts will indicate, by title, that ungrading has been employed only insofar as the reading program is concerned. Although grade numbers are not used to identify classes, there is a program of graded instruction in those areas other than reading. Thus we have *The Melrose Reading Program* or *The Van Dyke Level System of Reading* or some such similar title indicating that the reading program is "ungraded," and suggesting that other areas of instruction are not.

The *Dictionary of Education* defines the ungraded primary school as "a school that has a flexible system of grouping in which the children in the primary grades are grouped together regardless of age and in which extensive effort is made to adapt instruction to individual differences." Within the framework of that definition many schools have established themselves as being "ungraded"; each, however, has pursued the same goals in distinctively different fashions.

Advantages

Advantages sought through ungrading include: (1) improvement of achievement in reading; (2) improvement of achievement in other subject areas; (3) elimination or reduction of problems relating to promotion, retention, and acceleration; (4) the reduction of conflict between school goals and practices; (5) the lessening of unnecessary and undesirable pressures on the teaching staff; (6) the lessening of unnecessary and undesirable pressures on pupils; (7) the reduction of the less wholesome forms of competition among children; (8) greater administrative flexibility; and (9) the development of greater community understanding and support for school goals.

Let us briefly consider some of the basic arguments that very definitely favor the ungraded plan. A truly graded school calls for *grade* standards—realistic or not. It must annually deal with retention. Everlastingly concerned with the concept of "grade" and its artificialities, it produces an atmosphere most conducive to a striving toward false goals. Children are measured against the mythical average point and tend to measure each other in terms of that point. Teachers and children are expected to adjust to the program. If the program is ill-fitting, it appears to be a fault of the child, and efforts are made to promote a highly-prized conformity. The key point: *children are expected to adjust to the program.*

Ultimate Aim

A truly ungraded school has as its ultimate aim the tailoring of programs to each pupil. Children are measured in terms of their own real abilities. Teacher effort is geared toward bringing each child up to his potential. Age, years in school, lose significance as factors in program. The key point: *programs are developed to adjust to the child.*

Of course, it is possibly true that graded schools exist (not truly graded) that are less grade-conscious and more individualized than some ungraded schools (not truly ungraded). Thus, we can compare opposite extremes and "prove" that the graded schools are more effective at individualization than the ungraded—at the expense of logic.

The questions that must be asked repeatedly are: What is our basic belief? Do we believe that we adjust children to program or program to children? Are we using all our resources as fully as we can to attain the goals we have identified? Are there any aspects of our program which conflict in any degree with our goals?

Administrative Comfort

Stuart E. Dean, elementary school specialist for the U. S. Office of Education, describes the grading plan as "an almost perfect" arrangement for "neat, effective, and comfortable administration." He adds: "It has ignored the range of human differences as reflected in the normal curve. It is relatively oblivious to the extremely important factor of differences in learning rate. It is insensitive to specialized creative human talents and to human discrepancies. It is unmindful of the range of variability within the one child. It tends to overlook the child who may have some critically urgent and transitory needs ... It fails to realize that good teaching results from widening, rather than artificially narrowing the ability range within a class ... In short, the 'grade' is an arbitrary device through which the priority of the instructional program is sacrificed to administrative expediency. The essential purpose of the school is virtually renounced for the sake of efficient operation ... If we believe in, are committed to a doctrine of individual difference — the range of human variability — then our methods of organizing the educational program must operate in support of this conviction."

Whether we consider the graded plan the best arrangement for "neat, effective, and comfortable" administration will depend upon our goals. It must be the contention of those practicing administrators striving for a highly individualized program that the graded plan is a hindrance, a device which is ineffective and far from comfortable. The plan is best described after it is determined that it operates in support of or as a barrier to implementation of school philosophy and goals.

Dozens of communities throughout the United States have had variations of the ungraded school in operation for many years . . . and are proud of their successes. Our school district has considered the initiating of such a plan as another step in the direction of its expressed philosophy and goal. It is the writers' conviction that a carefully implemented ungraded school will, in fact, promote the advantages previously cited.[1]

---

[1] Frank R. Dufay and Murray Fessel, "Graded? Ungraded? Nongraded?" (Plainview—Old Bethpage District Newsletter, April 1964).

K. THE ART OF CONDUCTING PARENT-TEACHER CONFERENCES

General Principles:

I. Before the Conference

    A. Plan carefully

    B. Familiarize yourself with available information regarding parent and child.

    C. Arrange folder in chronological order. Have sufficient samples of child's work.

    D. Make notes of things you especially want to remember.

    E. Plan your schedule so you'll have a 20-minute conference and a 10-minute breather after each conference to jot down notes and assemble materials for the next set of parents.

    F. It's a good idea to schedule an easy, pleasant conference as a starter.

    G. Have the custodian place several chairs outside your room to accommodate early-arriving parents.

    H. Consider using the class mother as a hostess to greet parents outside the room.

    I. Give the school secretary a complete schedule of your conferences so they may be cancelled in the event of your absence.

    J. Interruptions are disturbing to parents as well as to you. Have a neat sign on your door: CONFERENCE IN SESSION. PLEASE DO NOT DISTURB.

    K. Make a list of those parents having two or more children in the school. Get together with the other teachers and plan on the date and time for conferences for those parents. Thus they can have conferences in succession and avoid repeated trips to school.

II. During the Conference

    A. Relax. Be a good host. Greet your guest and make him feel at ease.

    B. Be a good listener. Give close attention to what the par-

---

Lines IA-D, IIA-E, and IIIA-C are quoted from John L. Grindle and M. Genevieve Douglass, "Hints for More Effective Parent Conferences," *The Instructor*, November 1961, page 25. Lines IJ, IIF-Z, VA-F, and VIA-D are quoted from "Conference Time for Teachers and Parents", © NSPRA.

ent has to say. Let him do the talking at first. Listen for
ideas.

C. Find out how *he* feels about the child before you present
his school problem.

D. Convince the parent of your sincere desire for a need of
his help.

E. Accept anything the parent tells you without showing
surprise or disapproval.

F. Begin and end the conference with a positive comment
about the child.

G. It may be desirable to postpone plunging into the conference by walking about the classroom commenting on
some activity under way, materials, the view, perhaps
some irrelevant item. Express appreciation for the opportunity of having the parents come to work with you.

H. Don't let your desk be a barricade between you. Use two
or three chairs grouped together. The individual conference is a partnership, so don't let the presence of a desk
"break up" the partnership feeling.

I. Try not to take notes during the conference. Jot them
down immediately afterward. If you can't remember all
the points covered, jot them down as unobtrusively as
possible.

J. Hear criticism fully and get suggestions. Avoid arguments
and, when it is desirable to change a point of view, do
it diplomatically.

K. Try to put yourself in the place of the parent and try to
imagine what effect your remarks will have. Be truthful,
but remember that you are talking to a parent about his
most precious possession, his child. Combine truth with
tact.

L. Don't get bogged down in generalities.

M. It is usually possible to evaluate a pupil's progress without being critical. But be certain to be articulate about
what you are trying to explain.

N. When you offer suggestions to the parent, it's often desirable to offer alternative ones so that the parents may
make the decision as to which to use. Most parents really
don't want advice. They want support. But if they can
be led to making their own decisions, the advice will
more likely be accepted.

O. If the parent suggests a plan of action, accept it if at all possible, but leave no doubt as to the proper roles of the teacher and parents as far as conducting the business of the classroom is concerned.

P. If you have no suggestions for improving a bad trait, don't bring it up.

Q. Don't send the parent away loaded down with countless suggestions. Concentrate on one or two things on which you can work together to help the child. Similarly, don't confuse the parent by trying to show every piece of work his youngster has done in the past months. What you don't show at the conference, the parents can look over at home.

R. Don't press inquiries if the parent is obviously reluctant.

S. You may get an unflattering earful about "that" former teacher who taught the child. Here you will want to be sure that your attitude reflects only good of that teacher, and of other teachers and schools, too.

T. Don't let comments about other children enter the conversation. Don't compare brothers and sisters.

U. Don't suggest home activities that are really the responsibility of the school.

V. Don't attempt to resolve serious psychological problems of children. Refer them to the school psychologist.

W. Don't show the parents only the poorest or best work. Show the whole range. If possible, show how the work has improved or changed.

X. Be careful about terminology. Words such as "immature," "aggressive," "maladjustment," or "retarded" may have different meanings for the parent.

Y. Don't let the conference dribble off into inconsequentials past the point where nothing is accomplished. As a signal that the conference is over, stand up and escort the parent to the door. However, don't leave the impression that the conference is terminal. Make clear you welcome the chance to confer with them at any time. Suggest telephone follow-up, if necessary.

Z. The conference which began with encouraging news should end on a note of optimism. Summarize major areas discussed. Agree upon action needed. Clarify next steps.

III. After the Conference

    A. Review points the parent has mentioned.

    B. Evaluate the conference realistically and impartially.

    C. Put into operation at once any steps agreed upon in the conference. Get help or special services if needed.

IV. District Policy Regarding Information Provided to Parents

    A. Parents desiring information regarding progress reports, subject grades, I.Q. tests, achievement scores, medical records, psychological and psychiatric reports, selective guidance notes and the evaluation of pupils by educators must contact the building principal and fill out a form requesting such information.

    B. The principal will then contact the appropriate professional person to interpret this information to the parents and see that an appointment is set up mutually convenient to both.

    C. The appropriate people to interpret information to the parents are:

        1. Classroom Teacher: to interpret to parents information regarding progress reports, subject grades, achievement tests, and classroom (teacher-made) tests. ALL SUCH INFORMATION MAY BE PROVIDED THE PARENT DURING THE CONFERENCE.

        2. Psychologist: to interpret information to parents in regard to I.Q. tests, psychological and psychiatric reports. THIS INFORMATION IS NOT TO BE GIVEN BY THE TEACHER DURING CONFERENCES.

        3. Nurse: to interpret information to parents with regard to medical records.

    D. The above procedure will be followed so as to insure that the correct interpretation is given so as to be beneficial to the child.

V. Some Practical Guidelines

    A. *The other person will act as you act.* Talk loudly and he will talk loudly. Speak softly and he will speak softly. Be enthusiastic and he will react enthusiastically.

B. *First impressions are important.* If you want parents to believe that you are competent, friendly, and receptive, you must act that way. If you want the conversation to be informal and friendly, start it off that way. Think and talk positively. Don't ask "no" questions if you want "yes" answers.

C. *Listen in a sympathetic and understanding way.* Look at the person who is doing the talking, lean slightly toward him, appear interested, ask questions, don't interrupt with your views, ask him to tell you more, repeat some of the things he's said to prove you were listening. Preface some of your remarks with "as you were saying" or "as you pointed out." Remember that you invited the parent in to get as well as to give. You get by listening.

D. *No one ever wins an argument.* The idea is to make it possible for the other person to understand why you say what you say. Let him state his case fully before you start yours. Pause and reflect before answering his questions, to be certain you are carefully considering his side of the matter. Keep it impersonal and objective. Talk calmly but confidently.

E. *Be free with praise.* Before the conference begins, have several nice things to say about the pupil. The effect of a really sincere compliment can be electric.

F. *Make certain your presentation is consistent.* What you say in the conference should agree with what you write on the report card.

VI. Parents That Present Problems

A. *The Timid Parent*—Usually has a very high regard for teachers and is speechless before you. Considers education a one-way street and feels he's going the wrong way. Nothing sparks a reply. Suggestions:
   1. Offer several sincere compliments.
   2. Ask questions which can't be answered with a "yes" or "no."
   3. Be as friendly as possible without overdoing it.

B. *The Worried Parent*—Usually worried about a lot more than just his child. Figures, no matter what you say, his his youngster must be in some kind of trouble. Suggestions:
   1. If worry is expressed, recognize it and respect it.

2. If the child is doing satisfactorily, assure the parent of this immediately.
3. Assure the parent that few problems in child adjustment or learning are insoluble.
4. Plan a joint attack on the problem. This step usually relieves a worried person's mind.

C. *The Egotistical Parent*—Will probably come in smiling, self-confident. He's probably clever. Suggestions:
1. Don't deflate the balloon or you'll have a lifelong enemy. Remember, ego is a most precious possession.
2. Acknowledge his abilities.
3. Use the parent's abilities to the advantage of the child and possibly (as a resource person) of the entire class.

D. *The Critical Parent*—Comes in armed with "expert" opinions on how to teach children. Wants his child to have the three R's and nothing else. Has read all about this "progressive education" and wants none of it. Suggestions:
1. Don't argue; but try to inform by using both facts and an appeal to the emotions.
2. Talk about only those areas in which you are well equipped to speak.
3. Admit educators don't have all the answers. What profession does?

WHAT PARENTS ARE INTERESTED IN DISCUSSING

Omaha, Nebraska recently undertook a questionnaire to find out what parents would like to have covered in the parent-teacher conference. An example of responses show the areas of greatest interest.[1]

Question	Percent Answering Yes
1. Would you like to know what is typical for your child's age group so you can better understand him?	99%
2. Do you think the parent-teacher conference is worthwhile?	99%

[1] Department of Elementary School Principals, *Parents and the Schools*, 36th Yearbook (Washington, D.C., 1957) pp. 222-23.

3. Does it help you to have the teacher tell you what the child is the most interested in so that you can help him develop his interests at home? 96%

4. Are you notified long enough in advance of your conference so that you can plan what you would like to discuss with the teacher? 95%

5. Would you like to know more about testing, such as achievement, personality, and intelligence, showing how they are interpreted and scored? 95%

6. Would you like to discuss behavior problems with the teacher? 93%

7. Do you feel that 25 minutes is long enough? 91%

8. Would you like to discuss the individual differences in your child? 91%

9. Would you like to know how the teachers grade? 91%

10. Do you feel free to discuss with the teacher your hopes and aspirations for your child so that some of these ideas can be developed in his school education? 90%

11. Do you find it helpful for the teacher to go over your child's homework from the beginning of school up to the time of the conference? 89%

12. Do you get suggestions on how to help your child at home? 86%

13. Would you like to have a list of books that would help you to understand your child better? 83%

14. Do you as a parent take time to tell the teacher about the hobbies and home interests of your child? 82%

15. If your child is a gifted child or a rapid learner do you feel the conference helps you understand and plan for him? 76%

16. Do you think it would help the discussion to bring things that the child has made at home or to give an account of his activities? 72%

17. Would you like to discuss health problems with the teacher? 71%

18. Would you like an outline or plan of what will be discussed put on the back of the conference slip that is sent home, so that you can check them off as the conference takes place? 63%

19. Do you think it would help you to bring to the next conference a list of things you have done that were suggested at the first conference?   56%

20. Do you think the teacher would rather talk about your child's schoolwork than his conduct in school or on the playground?   55%

L. The Primary School Report

Pupil _____

Teacher _____

School _____

Principal _____

THE PRIMARY REPORT CARD

Dear Parents:

The purpose of this card is to give you information on your child's progress in school. While our concern is with academic matters, we are, in fact, aware of the need to consider all aspects of each child's development, including the physical, the social, and the psychological.

Although we expect to provide a reasonable amount of description through anecdotal-type reporting, we must acknowledge the greater effectiveness of the parent-teacher conference where parent and teacher may have the advantage of fuller exchanges of information. Therefore, we urge you to take full advantage of the scheduled conferences and to request additional conferences as needed.

In a nongraded primary school, which recognizes the infinite variety of growth patterns of children, our expectations for each child are based on *his* specific abilities and potential. Progress is determined by each child's ability and rate of learning — it is continuous.

YOUR CHILD'S PRIMARY SCHOOL YEARS ARE THE MOST IMPORTANT YEARS OF HIS SCHOOL LIFE. Your utmost cooperation is needed to insure the greatest degree of success.

SUPERINTENDENT OF SCHOOLS

CENTRAL SCHOOL DISTRICT #4
PLAINVIEW-OLD BETHPAGE

This report indicates the teacher's judgment of your child's growth in fundamental subject matter and skills. It is an individual report and takes into consideration the child's stage of development. The written comments are concerned with specific aspects. The circled letter indicates his development according to the following ratio scale:

E — Excellent Progress

S — Satisfactory Progress

M — More Progress Necessary

For your greater understanding, we have defined the various reading levels.

Level

ONE ....READINESS EXPERIENCES
TWO ....PRE-PRIMER — 1
THREE ....PRE-PRIMER — 2
FOUR ....PRE-PRIMER — 3
FIVE ....PRIMER (1¹)
SIX ....FIRST READER (1²)
SEVEN ....SECOND READER (2¹)
EIGHT ....SECOND READER (2²)
NINE ....THIRD READER (3¹)
TEN ....THIRD READER (3²)
ELEVEN ....FOURTH READER
TWELVE ....FIFTH READER

For your greater understanding, we have defined the various mathematics levels.

MATHEMATICS:

Level 1	Readiness
Level 2	Kgn. GCMP
Level 3	1/1 GCMP
Level 4	1/2 GCMP
Level 5	2/1 GCMP
Level 6	2/2 GCMP
Level 7	3/1 GCMP
Level 8	3/2 GCMP
Level 9	4/1 GCMP
Level 10	4/2 and Above GCMP

PERSONAL AND SOCIAL DEVELOPMENT

A check indicates your child's growth in the area of personal and social development according to the following rating scale:

S—Satisfactory   M—More improvement needed

	JANUARY		JUNE	
	S	M	S	M
SOCIAL HABITS				
Works independently				
Accepts responsibilities				
Cooperates				
Exerts good self-control				
Is considerate of others				
Respects school property				
Plays well with others				
Works well with others				
WORK HABITS				
Completes tasks				
Follows directions				
Listens attentively				
Uses books and materials carefully				
Works independently				
Works neatly				
HEALTH HABITS				
Cleanliness				
Posture				

COMMENTS _____

_____

_____

ATTENDANCE

Prompt and regular attendance is necessary for satisfactory development.

	JANUARY	JUNE
Days present		
Days Absent—Legal		
Days Absent—Illegal		
Times Tardy		

READING

JANUARY   **E**   **S**   **M**

Level_____

_____

_____

_____

_____

_____

_____

_____

_____

_____

_____

_____

JUNE   **E**   **S**   **M**

Level_____

_____

_____

_____

_____

_____

_____

_____

_____

_____

_____

_____

_____

_____

ARITHMETIC

JANUARY   E   S   M

JUNE   E   S   M

SOCIAL STUDIES

JANUARY   E   S   M

JUNE   E   S   M

SCIENCE

JANUARY   E   S   M

JUNE   E   S   M

A R T

JANUARY   E   S   M

_____

_____

JUNE   E   S   M

_____

_____

M U S I C

JANUARY   E   S   M

_____

_____

JUNE   E   S   M

_____

_____

PHYSICAL EDUCATION

JANUARY   E   S   M

_____

_____

JUNE   JANUARY

_____

_____

LANGUAGE ARTS

(includes written and oral language,
spelling and handwriting)

JANUARY   E   S   M

_____

_____

_____

_____

_____

_____

_____

_____

_____

_____

_____

_____

JUNE   E   S   M

_____

_____

_____

_____

_____

_____

_____

_____

_____

_____

_____

_____

PARENT'S COMMENTS

JANUARY

....
Parent's Signature

Your child _____

has been assigned to Room.. _____ for September 19__.

Date ....   Teacher ....

Old Bethpage School
January 11, 1965

M. INSTRUCTIONS FOR COMPLETING REPORT CARDS

In response to a number of requests for suggested guidelines in preparing report cards, I have prepared the attached list of *suggested* comments for consideration by the teacher. Teachers are free to use, or ignore, them as seen fit. If they are used, teachers are cautioned to *adapt* them to fit the teacher's analysis of the particular child being evaluated.

Teachers should keep the following items in mind regarding report cards:

1. The purpose of the report card is providing the parent with information about his child. In the absence of grade–level designations, this becomes increasingly important.

2. Teachers are requested to log the time it takes to prepare report cards. We hope, another year, to be able to shorten and simplify the clerical aspects of the job and your suggestions for the future are being sought.

3. The duplicate report card in the cumulative folders does not correspond to the report card that is provided the parent and is to be disregarded this year. Duplicate report cards for Old Bethpage and Parkway are being printed and should be available soon.

4. Teachers are again reminded that evaluation of each child is to be in terms of his ability. Comparisons with other children in the class are to be avoided.

5. The reading and mathematics levels at which each child is working must be recorded in the appropriate sections of the report card.

6. All children in the nongraded primary program are to be marked in all curricular areas shown with the circled E, S, or M. These marks will be supplied by the special teachers in the areas of art, music, and physical education.

7. Specialists should have the marks in the hands of the classroom teacher by *Monday, January 25th*. No written com-

ments are *required* in special areas, but may be included at the classroom teacher's discretion.

8. Checks must appear for *all* items listed in the category of "Personal and Social Development," under either "S" or "M." The Comment designation in this category is optional and may be left blank when no "M's" have been checked. Briefly describe reasons for "M's" in the Comments section.

9. Please cross out the designation "Days Absent—Illegal" and the word "Legal" on the line above that in the Attendance section. The legal—illegal designation is one we use for State reports only and leads to confusion when used in reporting to parents. Note that the days present, days absent, and times tardy should agree with your register of attendance cards.

10. Comments in the Language Arts area should refer to development in oral and written expression, handwriting, and spelling. In the lower primary, where formalized spelling is not taught, comments should refer to the child's progress using words from writing activities, and social studies and science units.

11. Teachers may wish to comment upon library skills and habits, as well as free reading activities in the Reading section of the report card.

READING

Comments can be made regarding the child's ability in terms of [1]

1. Correct pronunciation, careful enunciation.
2. Associating words with concrete objects or activities.
3. Developing appropriate auditory discrimination (identifying parts that rhyme, supplying the rhyming words, attention to sounds in the environment, identifying likenesses and differences in word beginnings and endings).
4. Developing visual discrimination (sensitiveness to likenesses and differences in configuration, detail, position, and arrangement).

---

[1] James F. Baker, *Elementary Evaluative Criteria* (Boston, Mass.: Boston University, School of Education, 1953), pp. 27-63. Comments in all curricular areas have been taken from one source, unless otherwise noted but are not direct quotations.

5. Developing visual memory (recall of objects, letters, and words).
6. Developing vocabulary in each of the content areas.
7. Reading widely to extend his vocabulary. Uses and enjoys books.
8. Developing word meaning skills (e.g., inferring meanings from context clues, recognizing synonyms and antonyms).
9. Developing a rapid recognition vocabulary.
10. Growing in the use of phonetic elements.
11. Success in recognition, transfer, and application of vowels, consonants, blends, and word parts.
12. Noting small words in larger words, recognizing words in their various forms, improving in syllabication.
13. Growing ability to recognize and/or use prefixes and suffixes, analyze compound words, recognize contractions and use derivatives.
14. Growing ability to use such dictionary skill exercises as alphabetizing, syllabication, pronunciation key.
15. Comprehending and interpreting meaning (e.g., recall details stated in the content, follow the sequence of a story, interpret picture stories).
16. Developing critical thinking (predicting outcomes, drawing conclusions, distinguishing fact from opinion).
17. Developing skill in locating information (e.g., using the table of contents, index, alphabetical arrangement, card files).
18. Increasing ability to use skimming techniques (looking for main ideas and words, locating information quickly).
19. Increasing ability to select and evaluate information (e.g., select words, sentences, stories in terms of a variety of specific purposes).
20. Developing the ability to organize what is read (e.g., find the main idea, find details to support facts, identify a sequence of events).
21. Using different methods of remembering what is read (e.g., making outline, selecting and underlining key words, writing brief summaries).
22. Developing skill in using information (e.g., follow directions of a specific type, classification, outlining, summarizing).
23. Developing rate of speed and power of comprehension.
24. Using leisure time for reading to a major extent (not from source).
25. Growth in listening skills.

26. Applying reading skills to other curricular areas (not from source).
27. Mastering the skills of word recognition.
28. Using reading as a tool for learning in other school subjects.
29. Showing an improvement in the study skills involving reading for gaining information, reading for details, solving problems, using references, collecting and remembering and reporting information.
30. Gaining knowledge about reading sources.
31. Increasing competence in oral reading.
32. Showing growth in understanding of word meanings.
33. Developing ability to interpret literature.
34. Showing discriminating abilities and interests in his selection of literature.
35. Indicating an interest in and appreciation for poetry.

MATHEMATICS

Comments can be made regarding the child's ability in terms of:

1. Counting and enumeration (e.g., forward and backward by one's, two's, five's, ten's, etc.).
2. Using numbers in the ordinal sense.
3. Identifying numbers through the hundreds level.
4. Writing numbers through the hundreds level.
5. Using numbers in various activities (e.g., scoring in games, taking attendance, ordering lunches, etc.).
6. Establishing ten as a basis of the number system.
7. Using measures (e.g., pint, quart, gallon).
8. Using number concepts for telling time and reading the calendar.
9. Mastering addition and subtraction facts through sums and minuends of ——.
10. Recognizing fractional parts of single objects and groups (e.g., halves, thirds, fourths).
11. Understanding simple place values through —— places.
12. Understanding zero as a place holder.
13. Adding and subtracting numbers through at least —— places with understanding.
14. Using addition and subtraction as processes in simple examples and one-step problems.
15. Understanding the principles involved in exchange in addition and subtraction.

16. Mastering the multiplication and division facts through ——.
17. Multiplying two and three place numbers by one place numbers with understanding.
18. Related even one figure division.
19. Computing with objects of value (e.g., play money, stamps, tokens).
20. Reading money values and making change.
21. Introducing distance, including inch, foot, yard, and use of each.
22. Introducing relationships in distance (e.g., twelve inches equal one foot, and three feet equal one yard).
23. Understanding the use of numbers in the cardinal and ordinal sense.
24. Estimating answers and checking computation.
25. Understanding of the basic number concepts.
26. Developing skill in using arithmetic fundamentals.
27. Having meaningful understandings and making meaningful applications.
28. Developing techniques of logical thinking in mathematical problem-solving situations.

SOCIAL STUDIES

Comments can be made regarding the child's ability in terms of:

1. Understanding and appreciating the need for individuals and groups to work cooperatively in the home, national, and world communities.
2. Understanding of the methods, uses, and importance of transportation and communication.
3. Understanding of the ways in which the physical environment contributes to and effects the way people live.
4. Understanding and appreciating technological improvements enabling people to overcome limitations imposed by nature.
5. Developing democratic attitudes and behavior in school.
6. Collecting and interpreting information, concerning social problems.
7. Drawing and testing conclusions concerning important problems.
8. Developing a sense of time relationship.
9. Developing a sense of place relationship.

10. Developing skill in map reading (e.g., understanding symbols, using key and scale, knowing the type of map to consult for one's purposes, using maps intelligently in connection with reading).
11. Developing skills in human relationships and group processes (e.g., making decisions, working cooperatively, planning cooperatively, group discussions, and group memberships).
12. Exhibiting an understanding of the structure and ideals of American democracy.
13. Exhibiting an understanding of the organization and his responsibilities regarding home, school, and community groups.
14. Exhibiting an understanding and appreciation of peoples of other lands and nations.
15. Exhibiting an understanding of the many and varied ways of making a living and the importance of the environment in the living process.
16. Exhibiting an understanding and appreciation of the contributions of the past to the presence.

SCIENCE

Comments can be made regarding the child's ability in terms of:

1. Developing knowledges and understandings concerning the scientific aspects of the child's immediate environment.
2. Developing scientific methods of thinking or investigation (e.g., defining problems, stating hypotheses, drawing conclusions).
3. Acquiring the general science concepts which are suitable to his maturity level.
4. Understanding of the contributions of science to daily living.
5. Using scientific techniques in solving problems in other areas (not from source).
6. Knowing and understanding science content covered (not from source).
7. Constructing and using simple scientific apparatus and equipment.
8. Developing elementary understandings concerning the composition of the earth and the earth-forming processes (rock formation, soil formation, the action of water).
9. Developing understandings concerning plant life (e.g., trees, flowers, fruit, vegetables).

10. Developing understandings concerning both wild and domesticated animal life (e.g., birds, fish, cattle).
11. Investigating elementary physical science phenomena (e.g., magnetism, light, sound, gravity, heat, chemical and physical change).
12. Developing understandings concerning the effect upon mankind of inventions, new processes, and products.
13. Exhibiting an understanding of elementary scientific principles.
14. Learning to use science equipment and materials effectively.
15. Demonstrating interest in the area of science.

ART

E—S—M must be circled. The art teacher will provide this evaluation. Additional comments can be made *at the discretion* of the classroom teacher. *Comments can be made in terms of criteria such as the following:*

1. To what extent do pupils show interest in arts and crafts?
2. To what extent are pupils developing effective arts and crafts skills and techniques?
3. To what degree do pupils demonstrate creative abilities with various media?
4. To what extent are manual skills and skills with tools being developed?
5. Are the children developing an understanding and appreciation of art as it applies functionally to the home, school, and community?

PHYSICAL EDUCATION

E—S—M must be circled. The physical education teacher will provide this evaluation. Additional comments can be made *at the discretion* of the classroom teacher. Comments can be made in terms of criteria such as the following:

1. To what extent is the pupil developing proficiency in fundamental knowledges and skills of a variety of games and activities?
2. To what extent is the child developing effective motor coordination and posture?
3. How effectively does this child participate in group physical education activities?

4. To what extent does the pupil exhibit an understanding of personal health problems?
5. To what extent does the pupil exhibit an understanding of personal safety problems?

MUSIC

E–S–M must be circled. The music teacher will provide this evaluation. Additional comments can be made *at the discretion* of the classroom teacher. Comments can be made in terms of criteria such as the following:

1. To what extent is the pupil developing effective singing skills?
2. To what extent is the pupil developing desirable music tastes?
3. To what extent is the pupil developing self-expression through music?

LANGUAGE ARTS

Written Language:

Comments can be made regarding the child's ability in terms of:

1. Participating in original or creative writing.
2. Writing a variety of letters (e.g., friendly letters, invitations, announcements, business letters).
3. Addressing envelopes and folding letters correctly.
4. Thinking clearly and expressing himself effectively.
5. Participating in writing poetry, plays.
6. Building an understanding of functional grammar.
7. Increasing ability to outline, take notes, and summarize.
8. Increasing ability to make book reports or review activities.
9. Increasing ability to write captions for pictures, label articles, and file materials.
10. Increasing ability in the skills of evaluation (self-evaluation, cooperative evaluation, and evaluation of work of other pupils).
11. Increasing ability to express his ideas clearly and interestingly (not from source).
12. Increasing ability to use correct forms (e.g., capitalization punctuation, and grammar) (not from source).

Oral Language and Speech:

Comments can be made regarding the child's ability in terms of:

1. Increasing ability to participate in group conversations and discussions.
2. Increasing ability to perform underlying processes of gathering organizing, and presenting ideas for speaking situations.
3. Increasing ability to participate in the evaluation and interpretation of materials presented by the teacher or other pupils.
4. Developing effective articulation and enunciation,. easy use of voice.
5. Increasing capability to speak before an audience.
6. Developing confidence in speaking before a group (not from source).
7. Expressing ideas clearly and interestingly (not from source).
8. Listening intelligently while others speak (not from source).

Spelling:

Comments can be made regarding the child's ability in terms of:

1. Increasing ability of the child to proofread all written work.
2. Using a few simple rules which apply to a large number of words.
3. Increasing ability to use syllabication as an aid to spelling.
4. Increasing ability to utilize dictionary skills.
5. Reviewing words previously learned.
6. Learning words that are within the reading ability of the child.
7. Maintaining an individual spelling list and lists of currently used words from content areas.
8. Illustrating word meanings and compiling picture dictionaries.
9. Articulating and pronouncing all words.
10. Correcting handwriting difficulties that handicap spelling.
11. Increasing ability to recognize correct and incorrect spelling.
12. Increasing ability to spell words needed for his writing.
13. Developing the habit of consulting the dictionary or some other source to verify spelling.
14. Learning spelling words easily, remembering spelling words, applying spelling words (not from source).

Handwriting:

Comments can be made regarding the child's ability in terms of:

1. Developing proficiency in the fundamentals of form in handwriting.
2. Developing legibility in his daily writing.
3. Developing speed in handwriting.
4. Effectively applying the techniques of good handwriting in other school subjects.
5. Increasing development of form, legibility, uniformity of slant, spacing, alignment, quality of line, speed.
6. Using good writing position for the sake of comfort and effective performance.
7. Writing with right (left) hand according to his natural tendency.
8. Participating in group discussions of common class errors.
9. Having begun the transition to cursive writing, being ready to begin the transition to cursive writing, not being ready at present for the transition to cursive writing (not from source).

Old Bethpage School

N. *THE PROBLEM OF HOMEWORK*[1]

Arguments Commonly Used in Support of Homework:

1. Homework keeps parents in touch with the school program and their child's progress, thus creating a closer bond between home and school.
2. It teaches a child to follow directions and helps him learn how to organize his time.
3. It teaches the child to accept responsibility and helps him develop self-reliance in his work; improves study skills and work habits.
4. Struggling with lessons is good discipline and a builder of character.
5. Homework provides constructive use of time which might otherwise be idly squandered; it keeps the child out of mischief after school.
6. It reinforces school learnings and gives needed drill on work taken up in class.
7. The amount of knowledge required by the curriculum simply cannot be imparted during school hours alone.

Arguments Commonly Given Against Homework:

1. After a six- or seven-hour school day, a child is tired, and it is too much to expect him to do homework. Not only is there too little time left for play but reading books for seven, eight, or more hours a day may lead to cramped lungs and eyestrain because children may be unable to obtain enough physical exercise.
2. The extra work load may reduce the interest and vigor with which the child faces the next day's work.
3. Homework is often work for the parents instead of the child, and parents frequently do it in a way not approved by the teacher. Thus, the parents just confuse the child.

---

[1] William D. Hedges, "Guidelines for Developing a Homework Policy" *The National Elementary Principal,* Volume XLIV, No. 2, November 1964. pp. 44-48. Copyright 1964, DESP, NEA. All rights reserved. (All items in this section from same source.)

4. Parents are seldom qualified to supervise home study. It is better for the children to do careful, guided study at school where their needs for special help or further information can be met.

5. Homes do not always provide suitable study conditions or facilities.

6. Other educationally valuable activities such as scout meetings, music lessons, church activities, club meetings, hobbies, recreational reading, educational TV programs, and play may be neglected.

7. Disagreeable tasks are too often assigned for homework instead of creative, interesting assignments.

8. The harmony of family life may be jeopardized, and in cases where the home offers cultural opportunities, its positive influence on the child's development may be reduced.

9. In some schools where homework has been abolished or severely limited, the sum total of achievement does not seem to have been affected.

What Parents Have a Right To Expect from Teachers:

1. Parents have a right to expect that teachers will be sure that the child understands the assignment. It should be definite and should always have been explained in class. Preferably, the child will have started it in class and under the guidance of the teacher to make sure he knows what to do. Too many assignments are vague.

2. Parents should be able to expect that teachers will *not* give homework for disciplinary reasons.

3. When homework is completed and turned in, parents should know that it will be carefully checked by the teacher. Otherwise, it should not be assigned.

4. Parents can properly expect that no homework will be given over weekends or holidays.

5. Parents can expect that assignments will not require use of books or other materials which are not available in the home.

6. Homework should be assigned only when it clearly serves a purpose. Students often don't know why they are to do this or read that. When assigned reading, for example, they need to be told whether they are to look for the main ideas in the material, learn specific facts, relate details to the main

idea, identify the author's pattern of thought, draw inferences and conclusions, etc. Thus, parents have a right to
expect that teachers will not make snap assignments but will
plan carefully in terms of the outcomes desired and the time
needed to do the work.

7. Parents have a right to expect that the homework will be
within the ability of the child. Otherwise, the child will be
forced to "borrow" his classmate's work; prevail upon Mom or
Dad to do it for him; worry and fret unduly over his being
unable to do it; or forget the whole matter with unpleasant
results for all.

8. Parents have a right to expect some homework when the
pupil has been absent or when he is not working up to ex-
pectancy and needs special remedial work.

What Teachers Have a Right To Expect from Parents:

1. Teachers have a right to expect that the parents will arrange
a quiet, comfortable place, well-lighted and with ample work
space, for the child to work.

2. If the assignment is reasonable, teachers have a right to expect the parents will cooperate by encouraging their child to
do it. It should be noted that what may seem to be an unrea-
sonable homework load may actually be the converse. A child
may have difficulty with homework because he lacks good
study habits.

3. Teachers have a right to expect the parents to refuse to carry
out the assignment for the child. This does not mean parents
shouldn't point out principles involved, help give illustrations,
and make suggestions. Parents should not nag their children
and put too much pressure on them. If they take over and
force, cajole, bribe, or punish, they may see to it that the
studying is done, but hardly in a way that suggests that learning can be an interesting occupation and certainly without
helping the child grow in his ability to assume responsibility.
It will help a good deal if the parent will take the initiative in
finding out what the school actually expects of the student.
This is sometimes widely at variance with what a child tells
his parents and may honestly believe.

4. Teachers also have a right to expect parents to take a broad
view of the values of various types of homework, since the
values differ under different circumstances and conditions.

Characteristics of Good Homework Assignments:

1. Homework should be carefully planned, with pupils motivated to complete the assignments: assignments that are definite, interesting, meaningful, and geared to individual abilities.
2. The teacher should take some responsibility for helping the child to form efficient study habits. How to study and learn is, unfortunately, not taught very well, if at all in most schools. Too many children waste too much of their study time because they have never learned how best to use it.
3. Most homework should be of an informal nature, supplementing formal preparation in the class and following the bent of the child: reading good fiction, poetry, history, popular magazines and newspapers, watching good TV programs, sesing excellent movies, etc.
4. The homework assignments should be made only after children understand the process and have had enough practice in class to do homework on the subject unaided.
5. Most homework assignments should be personalized, geared as far as possible to meet individual needs, and should be within the pupil's range of skill. This means that there should be very little or no regularly assigned drill-type homework for the entire class. Exercises that can be done mechanically encourage copying, while an assignment that calls for initiative and individual creative effort rules out copying and challenges the pupil to work effectively.
6. Most homework assignments should be of a type which can be better done away from school. This includes collecting information, sharing ideas with parents, and situations in which children are involved in something like creative writing or preparing reports.

O. SOCIAL STUDIES—UNIT OF STUDY

CENTRAL SCHOOL DISTRICT NO. 4
Old Bethpage School

* * * * COMMUNITY HELPERS * * * *
Experience Unit Title

Subject: *SOCIAL STUDIES*   Grade: *2nd Year primary*

Duration: 2 - 3 Weeks

Introduction of the Unit:

Walk in the neighborhood with instructions to remember every person seen. Follow-up discussion and evaluation, analysis of people seen, and the categories into which they fall.

I. *Objective — Expected Outcomes*

    A. Concepts

        We are dependent upon one another in many ways in our own community.

        People share and work together in our community to maintain efficient and happy group life.

        People should be governed only by their own consent. They should have the right to participate in the election of their own officials and the making of their laws.

        People's way of living depends on the location, surface, climate, and resources of the place in which they live.

        People depend on the work of others for many goods and services they cannot provide for themselves.

        The happenings of the past influence ways of living today.

        People have enriched their lives through religion, education, and the fine arts.

    B. Skills

        Increasing ability to —

        Reject solutions that do not work and try to find better ones.

Evaluate individual and group activities and make suggestions for improvement.

Request information from the right people.

Find details and explain pictures.

Obtain data from books.

Determine the best method of recording information.

Accept or reject ideas, suggestions, or opinions in terms of their value in achieving cooperatively established purposes.

Relate events in proper sequence.

Listen to others with attention and courtesy.

Use interview techniques.

Draw a simple map of the neighborhood.

Distinguish land forms on neighborhood walks.

II. *Content Elements of This Unit*

The local community in Plainview-Old Bethpage.

The economic, political, and social organization in Plainview-Old Bethpage as it relates to particular roles and responsibilities.

Specific roles: storekeepers, industrial employees, service (fire, police, roads, health, water, schools and religious institutions).

Specific responsibilities attached to these roles.

III. *Experiences and Activities To Achieve Objectives*

A. Activities to Get Information

Interviews

Library research

Field trips

Picture collections

Teacher lecture

Viewing of audio-visual materials (films, filmstrips, records)

Individualization

Advanced

Reading filmstrip titles in small groups

Locating books and other resource materials

Library research

Less Mature

Find unit pictures in books, magazines

Use observation to gain information

B. Activities To Use and Organize Ideas

1. Language activities
   Experience charts
   Writing reports
   Giving oral reports
   Making scrapbook with appropriate titles
   Making bulletin boards

   Individualization
   Advanced
   Writing report for group
   Proofread and correct reports of others
   Less Mature
   Develop titles for pictures
   Tell story with proper sequence of events

2. Reading: prose and poetry
   Rags, The Firehouse Dog—Morton
   The Fireman—Witty
   The Grocery Man—Wolf

   Individualization
   Advanced
   Reading of pertinent biographies

3. Arithmetic
   Community map—measuring distance

   Individualization
   Advanced
   Map scaling
   Profit motive
   Less Mature
   Record of class milk sales

4. Science
   The ecology of Plainview-Old Bethpage
   Conservation program
   Study of water and buoyancy

   Individualization
   Advanced
   Reports of the activities of the 4-H Club
   Reports on personal responsibility for conservation

5. Health and Safety
   Community need for people listed
   Visit to local county health station

   Individualization
   Advanced
   Role of the Red Cross in the community

6. Music   *Individualization*
   Sing a Song of Home Neigh-   Compose original songs
       borhood, and Community   about the community
   Songs of Safety — Frank   helpers
       Luther
   Building a City — Tom
       Glazer

7. Creative Activities   *Individualization*
   Arts and crafts
   Home-made movies dealing
       with individual commun-
       ity helpers
   Scrapbooks
   Puppetry — pantomime
   Three-dimensional objects
       for community map
   Drawings
   Creative Writing
   What I Want To Be When I
       Grow Up
   A Crisis in Plainview (fire,
       water shortage)
   Dramatics
   How to Put out Fires, Arrest   *Advanced*
       Robbers   Writing scripts

C. Summarizing Activities to Share Experiences and/or Culminating Activity
   Big hall bulletin board with hats (made or collected) indicative of every type of community helper studied; titled, "Do
   You Know Whom These Hats Belong To?" Legend: each hat
   belongs to one of our community helpers.

IV. *Materials and Bibliography*

   A. Materials Needed
      Newspapers and magazines depicting people at work.
      Arts and crafts materials for three-dimensional work, draw-
          ings, home movies, etc.

Toys depicting work of variety of community helpers.
Science materials for experiments on water buoyancy.

B. Teacher References — Books, Magazines

Biographies of famous personalities in the field of health and science.

Teachers' editions of all children's texts and references.

References in the Encyclopedia Britannica.

C. Pupil References

Chicago, Ill.:	*Visiting Our Neighbors* (Bobbs-Merrill).
Chicago, Ill.:	*How Doctors Help Us* (Benefic Press)—Meeker.
Chicago, Ill.:	*How Hospitals Help Us* (Benefic Press)—Meeker.
Chicago, Ill.:	*How Schools Help Us* (Benefic Press)—Meeker.
Chicago, Ill.:	*How Foods Are Preserved* (Benefic Press)—Meeker.
Chicago, Ill.:	*You Visit a Fire Station-Police Station* (Benefic Press)—Meshover.
Chicago, Ill.:	*You Visit a Dairy-Clothing Factory* (Benefic Press)—Meshover.
Chicago, Ill.:	*You Visit a Newspaper-Television Station* (Benefic Press)—Meshover.
Chicago, Ill.:	*You and the Neighborhood* (Benefic Press)—Samford, McCall, Gue, Cunningham.
Chicago, Ill.:	*Billy's Neighbors* (Follett)—Gross, Sorenson, Follet, McIntire et al.
Morristown, N. J.:	*Communities and Their Needs* (Silver Burdett)—Anderson, Phillips, Weaver, Stoddard, Coon, Dobler.

D. Audio-Visual Aids—Films, Records, Pictures

1. Records (New York: Educational Record Sales)
   Building a City—Tom Glazer
   Building a House
   Daddy Comes Home
   Health and Safety Through Music
   Health Can Be Fun
   How the Singing Water

Men Who Come to Our House
Sing a Song of Home, Neighborhood and Community
Songs of Safety—Frank Luther

2. Filmstrips

Indianapolis, Ind.	Purifying Drinking Water (Bobbs-Merrill)
Indianapolis, Ind.	Exploring Water Sources (Bobbs-Merrill)
Indianapolis, Ind.	The Doctor Examines You (Bobbs-Merrill)
New York, N. Y.	Community Helpers Series (McGraw-Hill)
	Community Services (William P. Gottlieb Co.)
Jamaica, N. Y.	Where Our Daddies Work (Eye-Gate House)
Jamaica, N. Y.	Our Neighborhood Stores (Eye-Gate House)
Jamaica, N. Y.	Some Neighborhood Helpers (Eye-Gate House)
Jamaica, N. Y.	Our Neighborhood Workers (Eye-Gate House)

V. *Evaluation and Criticism of This Unit*

A. Evidence of Pupil Growth (appraised by teacher)
Have there been changes in the children's behavior patterns?
Have the pupils improved in their capacity to accept constructive criticism?
Do the pupils participate more in class activities and discussions?

B. Teaching Performance (appraised by teacher)
Were my expected outgrowths attained through this unit?
Have the activities used aided the pupils in gaining skills?
Was the range of activities that were provided wide enough to challenge every child?
What in the unit was most real and interesting to the pupils?

C. Appraisal by Pupils
Did we enjoy this unit?
Did we finish our tasks?
How could we have done a better job?
Do we know where to go to find out about things?

P. A MULTIDISCIPLINARY APPROACH TO UNIT ON COMMUNITY HELPERS[1]

History

1. What were some of the early community services offered in this area?
2. How did people in this community obtain food, clothing, and housing?
3. What was the original name of the community?
4. What Indian tribe lived in this area before the coming of white settlers?
5. What examples of the early Indians and white settlers can be found in the community today?
6. When was the first fire department organized in the community?
7. When was the Plainview Water District first organized?
8. When was our first school district organized?

Geography

1. What major physical features does this community have?
2. In what part of the community is our school located?
3. What are some of the major buildings in our community?
4. By what communities is Plainview-Old Bethpage bounded?
5. How far is our community from New York City?
6. How can we describe the climate of our community?
7. What are some of the natural resources found in this community?
8. Why do we refer to different parts of the earth as hemispheres?
9. In what hemisphere, country, and state do we live?
10. Why does the globe show the Equator, the Tropic of Cancer and the Tropic of Capricorn? What do these imaginary lines on the earth mean to us?
11. Why do so many people usually decide to live together in the same community?

Materials in this section come from the source indicated below as well as original materials:

[1] *Social Studies K-3: An Experimental Outline* (Albany, N.Y.: The New York State Education Department, 1965).

Political Science

1. What are some of the rights and freedoms we enjoy as Americans?
2. Why must we respect the rights and freedoms of others?
3. What is meant by private property?
4. Why must the property of others be respected?
5. What are some of the rules, laws, and regulations which have grown up over the years to insure the common good?
6. Why must we, all of us, live within these laws?
7. Why do we elect our local officials?
8. Why are there different forms of local government?
9. Who are some of the local officials who are appointed by elected officers?
10. Why do local governments, rather than private businesses, supply such services as police and fire protection, roads and streets?
11. Why must people pay taxes to local governments?
12. Who are the people who run our school district? Which ones are elected, which appointed?
13. Why do our school board members serve our schools without pay?
14. Where does the money come from that pays for our schools?
15. Why does the State contribute money to our school district?

Sociology

1. Why do people seem to prefer to live in community groups? Have they always done so?
2. What are the limits of the community in which you live?
3. Do you and your parents participate in the life of more than one community? What makes this possible?
4. Why have many people come to our country to live?
5. What is meant by ethnic group?
6. How many ethnic groups are represented in your class, your school, and your community?
7. Why must people of all ethnic groups be given equal freedom and opportunity?
8. How many churches are there in our community?
9. What religious faiths are represented?
10. What are some of the services that churches perform?
11. Why do churches do charitable work?

12. Why do some churches operate schools?
13. Why do people form service clubs?
14. What are some of the community services which these clubs perform?
15. Why do we need organizations which provide recreational programs and facilities?
16. Why do people organize cultural groups such as orchestras and theater associations?
17. What can children learn through participation in scouting programs?

Economics

1. Why do almost all communities have many service industries?
2. What are some of the service industries in Plainview-Old Bethpage?
3. What manufacturing industries does our community have? What do they make and where do the raw materials come from?
4. What are some of the different jobs that men and women have in manufacturing plants? Why do they have many different jobs?
5. Why do we need basic industries?
6. Why must businesses and industries make a profit?
7. Why do businessmen keep their costs as low as possible?
8. Why do businesses charge as low a price as they can for goods and services?
9. Why do people "shop around" when they want to buy something?
10. Why do we need highways, railroads, and airways?
11. Could our community survive without transportation links to other communities, particularly New York City?
12. How did people communicate before the days of the telephone and telegraph?
13. Why does our national government maintain a mail service?
14. Why do the local, state, and national governments build and maintain roads?
15. Why do people need jobs?
16. Why must local business and industry be operating at a profit in order to maintain jobs?
17. What is consumer demand?

18. Why must consumer demand be high to maintain good times?
19. How do communities depend upon one another for goods and services?
20. How is the prosperity of one community linked to the prosperity of other communities?

Psychology

1. In what ways do community helpers cooperate with us?
2. How do our community helpers work together to help us?
3. In what ways do these people help their own families?

Anthropology

1. Do people elsewhere in the world have the same types of community services as we do? Why?
2. How many children have parents who are community helpers? Do they perform their services in our community or in another community?

Philosophy

1. How many ways are there to find answers?
2. Is there a correct answer?

Q. SOCIAL STUDIES CURRICULUM—SUGGESTED UNITS OF STUDY

KINDERGARTEN

The Family—The role of its members.
The Family—Its role in the economy.
The Family—Comparison with a family in another culture.
The School Environment—The contribution of education.
Map and Globe Skills—The classroom and school.
Holidays—Patriotism and our American Heritage.

First PRIMARY YEAR

The Family—Comparison with family of yesteryear (American).
The School—Comparison with schools of yesteryear (American agrarians).
The Neighborhood—Community resources which service us.
Agrarian Community Today—Types of farms.
Map and Globe Skills—The neighborhood and its geographic features.
Holidays—Patriotism and our American Heritage.

Second PRIMARY YEAR

The Local Community—either Plainview—Old Bethpage, Nassau County, Township of Oyster Bay, or Long Island.
The Economy—Industries.
Political Science—Community Services, who provides, who pays.
Transportation—connection with larger community.
Communication—connection with larger community.
Service Organizations—service groups, religious groups etc.
Comparison with other community in U. S. (urban, or rural).
Map and Globe Skills—Community and its connection to outside world, larger geographic terms (river, mountain, etc.).
Holidays—Patriotism and our American Heritage.

Third PRIMARY YEAR

Biographical and historical approach to study of greatness of our country.
Discoverers and Explorers; examples: Columbus, Hudson, La Salle et. al.

Colonial and Revolutionary leaders; examples; Smith, Williams, Franklin, Adtms et. al.

National Leaders; examples: Washington, Jefferson, Madison, Hamilton et. al.

American Freedom Leaders; example: Paine, Marshall, Lincoln, Tubman, Adams, Washington, Riis, King et. al.

Industrial and Scientific Leaders; examples: Whitney, McCormick, Edison, Bell, Carver, Salk, Ford, Rockefeller, Carnegie et. al.

Arts Leaders; example: Thoreau, Longfellow, Poe, Lewis, Hughes, Foster, McDowell, Gershwin, Handy, Andersen, Homer, Whistler et. al.

Immigration—the basis of our country's population.

Contributions of Sub Cultures—Negro, Indian, Puerto Rican, Irish et. al.

Map and Globe Skills—routes of explorers, etc., origin of immigrants etc.

World and Globe Emphasis.

Patriotic and American Citizenship and Traditions—Holidays, etc.

INDEX

INDEX